Golden®

SCIENCE

Study Material

CURIOSITY

Based on New NCERT Textbook

CLASS VI

Multi Colour EDITION

- Interesting Mind Map
- Points to Remember/Keywords
- NCERT Intext Questions *(Solved)*
- NCERT Let us Enhance our Learning Exercises *(Solved)*
- Exam Oriented Questions with Answers
- Objective Type Questions with Answers
- Activities with Answers
- NCERT Exemplar Important Problems (*Solved*)
- Multiple Choice Questions
- Exercises for Practice
- Golden® Sample Papers

By

S GUPTA

&

NEW AGE Editorial Board

Committed to Educate the Nation

NEW AGE

Publishing Globally

IN INDIA

NEW AGE INTERNATIONAL (P) LIMITED, PUBLISHERS

LONDON • NEW DELHI

Bengaluru • Chennai • Cochin • Guwahati

Hyderabad • Kolkata • Mumbai

Visit us at www.newagegolden.com

Published by New Age International (P) Ltd., Publishers
New Edition

GLOBAL OFFICES

- **New Delhi** **NEW AGE INTERNATIONAL (P) LIMITED, PUBLISHERS**
7/30 A, Daryaganj, New Delhi-110002, (INDIA), **Tel.:** (011) 23253472, 23253771, **Mob.:** 9315905300
E-mail: contactus@newagepublishers.com • Visit us at www.newagepublishers.com

- **London** **NEW AGE INTERNATIONAL (UK) LTD.**
27 Old Gloucester Street, London, WC1N 3AX, UK
E-mail: info@newacademicscience.co.uk • Visit us at www.newacademicscience.co.uk

BRANCHES

- **Bengaluru** 167, 1st Floor, 11th Cross, Mulkatamma Temple Road,Near Rajiv Gandhi Sports Complex, Vittal Nagar Bengaluru – 560026, **Tel.:** (080) 26756823, **Mob.:** 9315905288, **E-mail:** bangalore@newagepublishers.com
- **Chennai** 26, Damodaran Street, T. Nagar, Chennai-600 017, **Tel.:** (044) 24353401, **Mob.:** 9315905309 **E-mail:** chennai@newagepublishers.com
- **Cochin** CC-39/1016, Carrier Station Road, Ernakulam South, Cochin-682 016 **Tel.:** (0484) 4051304, **Mob.:** 9315905289, **E-mail:** cochin@newagepublishers.com
- **Guwahati** Hemsen Complex, Mohd. Shah Road, Paltan Bazar, Near Starline Hotel Guwahati-781 008, **Tel.:** (0361) 2513881, **Mob.:** 9315905296, **E-mail:** guwahati@newagepublishers.com
- **Hyderabad** 105, 1st Floor, Madhiray Kaveri Tower, 3-2-19, Azam Jahi Road, Near Kumar Theater Nimboliadda Kachiguda, Hyderabad-500 027, **Tel.:** (040) 24652456, **Mob.:** 9315905326 **E-mail:** hyderabad@newagepublishers.com
- **Kolkata** RDB Chambers (Formerly Lotus Cinema) 106A, 1st Floor, S N Banerjee Road Kolkata-700 014, **Tel.:** (033) 22273773, **Mob.:** 9315905319, **E-mail:** kolkata@newagepublishers.com
- **Mumbai** 142C, Victor House, Ground Floor, N.M. Joshi Marg, Lower Parel, Mumbai-400 013 **Tel.:** (022) 24927869, 24915415, **Mob.:** 9315905282, **E-mail:** mumbai@newagepublishers.com
- **New Delhi** 22, Golden House, Daryaganj, New Delhi-110 002, **Tel.:** (011) 23262368, 23262370 **Mob.:** 9315905300, **E-mail:** sales@newagepublishers.com

C-26-02-15372

Printed in India at Goyal Offset Works (P) Ltd., Sonipat, Haryana.
Typeset at In-house, Delhi.

NEW AGE INTERNATIONAL (P) LIMITED, PUBLISHERS
7/30 A, Daryaganj, New Delhi-110002
Visit us at **www.newagegolden.com**
(CIN: U74899DL1966PTC004618)

PREFACE

We are pleased to announce the publication of the revised and updated edition of Golden® **Science** for Class VI, aligned with the latest NCERT textbook (CUROSITY) as per new National Education Policy (NEP) 2020 and National Curriculum Framework for School Education (NCF-SE) 2023. This edition has been meticulously crafted to ensure seamless alignment with the current academic requirements.

Special Features:

- Interesting Mind Map
- Points to Remember
- Keywords
- NCERT Intext Questions (*Solved*)
- NCERT Let us Enhance our Learning Exercises (*Solved*)
- Exam Oriented Questions with Answers
- Objective Type Questions with Answers
  - Match the Columns
  - Fill in the Blanks
  - True or False
  - Multiple Choice Type Questions
- Activities with Answers
- NCERT Exemplar Important Problems (*Solved*)
- Exercise for Practice
- Two Golden® Sample Papers

Video Animation: Each chapter is accompanied by a video animation, accessible by scanning the QR code provided at the back cover page of the book. This feature helps students better connect with the content and creates interest in their understanding of each chapter.

We value the feedback and suggestions from educators and students, which have been instrumental in refining this edition. Their insights will continue to guide us in future updates.

We are confident that this book will serve as an indispensable resource in your academic journey, enabling you to achieve excellence in Science. We strive to provide a comprehensive learning experience and support your academic success.

AUTHORS

CONTENTS

The Wonderful World of Science

1 Science

- It's a way of thinking to understand and uncover the wonders of the world.

2 Science is a big adventure

- It inspires us to ask questions, explore the world and try to understand the working of things.

3 Science is a giant and unending jigsaw puzzle

- A discovery leads to new knowledge. New knowledge leads to new questions and new discovery. That is, discovery is an unending journey.

4 Scientific method

- It helps us to find out the cause of an event.

1 The Wonderful World of Science

I. POINTS TO REMEMBER

- The most wonderful thing about science is that it is everywhere.
- **Science** is a fascinating subject that helps us understand the world around us. It involves asking questions like: How a flower knows when to bloom? or why the stars shine? It helps in exploring the mysteries of the universe. From studying tiny grains of sand to massive mountains, there is always something new to discover.
- By studying Science, we think and observe. This helps us to unravel many unsolved questions.
- Science is like a giant puzzle, and every new discovery adds a piece to that puzzle. The best part is that there is no limit to what can be discovered, as each new piece of knowledge leads to more questions and more things to find out.

Fig. A mountainous region

- In this journey through the world of Science, we will explore a wide range of topics, from the environment and different cuisines to the properties of water and the mysteries of the universe. By observing, asking questions, thinking about their probable answers and accordingly conducting experiments, and analyzing results, we can discover new things and solve many daily problems.
- **Science** is not just about memorizing facts and figures; it is about following a step-by-step process to find answers to infinite questions.

Fig. A Coastal region

- The planet Earth is our home. It is the only planet that supports life. It has an environment and we must protect our environment for future generations.

- A seed grow into a plant, a caterpillar changes into a beautiful insect. All living things, plants, animals and humans eat food to grow.
- By learning science, we can develop our capabilities for finding solutions to many problems.
- Anyone who follows the **scientific method** is working like a **scientist**, whether they are cooking food, fixing a bicycle, or solving an electrical problem. By being curious, observant, and willing to ask questions, we can all become better scientists and discover more about the world around us.

Fig. A variety of cooked food

Fig. Bicycle repair

- Science is rarely done alone, as scientists often work together in teams to solve complex problems.
- The world is full of things we do not know. To explore those things we must work together.
- As we embark on this journey of exploration and discovery, remember to keep asking questions, keep exploring, and never stop wondering about the mysteries of the universe. Enjoy your scientific journey and enjoy the exploration. And remember, this is just the beginning of your journey into the exciting world of Science.

II. KEYWORDS

1. **Science:** It is a way of thinking, observing and doing things to understand the world we live in and to uncover the secrets of the universe.
2. **Earth:** It is the only planet that supports life of humans, plants and animals.
3. **Scientific Method:** First, we observe something which we find interesting or we do not understand. This makes us wonder and perhaps think of a question about it. Then, we guess a possible answer to that question. We test this guess through experiments or more observations. Then we try to analyse the results to see if it actually answered our question.
4. **Scientists:** They are people who follow the scientific method to solve problems or to discover new things. Science is rarely done alone. Scientists across the world work together, often in large teams.

III. NCERT INTEXT QUESTIONS

Q. 1. ***What is Science?*** ***(Page 1)***

Ans. Science is a way of thinking, observing and doing things to understand the world we live in and to uncover the secrets of the universe.

Q. 2. ***What will we explore with the help of this book?*** ***(Page 3)***

Ans. In this book we will explore and understand the beautiful world we live in and the natural phenomenon we witness.

Q. 3. ***How can we try to find answers to our questions on our own?*** ***(Page 5)***

Ans. We can find answers on our own by using scientific inquiry. Our observations and our experimentation helps us to find the answer.

Q. 4. ***After all, to be a wise person, you must be a "whys" person!*** ***(Page 8)***

Ans. A curious mind is a wise mind. A person who asks questions displays critical and analytical mind, which shows wisdom. Hence a **"whys"** person is said to be wise.

IV. EXAM ORIENTED QUESTIONS

Very Short Answer Type Questions

Q. 1. ***What makes Earth unique?***

Ans. Earth is unique as it is the only known planet supporting life with diverse ecosystems and species that live across different regions.

Q. 2. ***What do you understand by the term curiosity?***

Ans. Curiosity is when we ask questions, explore the world and try to understand how things work.

Q. 3. ***Describe scientific discovery.***

Ans. Scientific discovery is like solving a continuous puzzle where each new finding adds another piece, expanding our understanding of the world.

Q. 4. ***Give examples that illustrate the broad scope of science.***

Ans. These are studying nature, weather, vastness of the outer space, phenomena like diversity in food, exploring new places etc.

Q. 5. ***Describe the process of growth in plants and animals.***

Ans. Science is about observing transformations of seeds to plants and caterpillars to butterflies, sparking curiosity about their growth mechanisms.

Q. 6. ***What do you think is the role of water?***

Ans. Water is essential for life. We enjoy drinking cool water in summer. Water when cooled becomes ice by freezing. It changes into steam when boiled by evaporation. Water cycle plays a very important role in our life.

Q. 7. ***What analogy is used to describe Science?***

Ans. Science is like a jigsaw puzzle where each discovery adds a piece, continuously reshaping and expanding our knowledge.

Q. 8. ***How does the passage relate everyday problem-solving to science?***

Ans. Everyday problem-solving, like fixing a pen or other household issues, by the scientific method of observation, guess, and testing.

Q. 9. ***What message about learning Science do you gather from the chapter?***

Ans. We are encouraged about **curiosity, observation,** and **questioning** as fundamental to learning Science, which involves continuous exploration and discovery.

Short Answer Type Questions

Q. 1. ***What is the purpose of science?***

Ans. The purpose of science is to understand the world we live in by observing, asking questions, and conducting experiments to uncover the secrets of the universe.

Q. 2. ***How does Science help us understand the world?***

Ans. Science helps us understand the world by providing a systematic way of thinking and exploring. It allows us to ask questions, conduct experiments, and analyze results to gain knowledge about natural phenomena and how things work.

Q. 3. ***How are curiosity and science related?***

Ans. Curiosity is when we ask questions, explore the world and try to understand how things work. Science is a way of thinking, observing and doing things to understand the world we live in and to unravel the mysteries of the universe.

Q. 4. ***Give an example of applying the scientific method in daily life.***

Ans. The application of the scientific method in daily life is to find the answer. For example, Why a light bulb isn't working? We observe the problem (the bulb doesn't light up), form a guess (the bulb might be burnt out), test the guess (replace the bulb with a new one), and analyze the results (if the new bulb lights up, our guess was correct).

Q. 5. ***Describe the process of scientific inquiry.***

Ans. Scientific inquiry involves several steps: **observing** something interesting, **asking a question** about it **formulating** a guess (a possible answer), testing it through experiments or further observations, analyzing the results, and drawing conclusions based on evidence.

Q. 6. ***What is the scope of scientific exploration?***

Ans. The scope of scientific exploration is very vast. It ranges from studying our planet Earth and its ecosystems to exploring the depths of oceans, the vastness of outer space, and everything in between—such as materials, living organisms, and natural phenomena.

Q. 7. ***How do everyday activities connect to scientific thinking?***

Ans. Everyday activities often involve problem-solving and decision-making processes that use the scientific method. Whether it's fixing a broken item or cooking, we make observations, form guesses, and test them to find solutions.

Q. 8. ***What makes the study of science enjoyable?***

Ans. The study of science is enjoyable because it encourages curiosity, discovery and understanding. It involves exploring fascinating questions, conducting experiments, and uncovering how things work, which can be both exciting and rewarding.

Q. 9. ***What is the advice you learnt as young learners about learning Science?***

Ans. As young learners, the advice about learning Science is to be **curious, observe keenly, ask questions** (especially "why" and "how"), and explore the world around us. It encourages us to embrace challenges and see learning as a continuous journey of discovery.

Q. 10. ***Describe the collaborative nature of scientific work.***

Ans. Scientific work is often collaborative, with scientists from around the world working together in teams. They share ideas, data, and findings, which accelerates the pace of discovery and helps in comprehensive understanding of complex problems and phenomena.

Long Answer Type Questions

Q. 1. ***Do you think curiosity plays a crucial role in the study of science? If yes, give reason to substantiate your answer.***

Ans. Curiosity is the driving force behind scientific inquiry. It motivates us to ask questions and seek answers, leading to new discoveries and a deeper understanding of the world. Without curiosity, the journey of scientific exploration would not be so beautiful and useful. It is the curiosity that increases our interest in studying various phenomena and helps us in finding explanations for the mysteries of the universe.

Q. 2. ***Why is Science described as a big adventure?***

Ans. Science is described as a big adventure because it involves exploring the unknown, asking questions, and making discoveries. The study of Science is an adventurous journey where we continuously uncover new pieces of knowledge, much like solving a giant jigsaw puzzle. Each discovery leads to more questions and further exploration, making the process exciting and never-ending.

Q. 3. ***How does Science help us understand natural phenomena like the blooming of a flower or the shining of stars?***

Ans. Science helps us understand natural phenomena by providing explanations based on observation, experimentation, and analysis. Through scientific inquiry, we learn about the processes and mechanisms. We know that the stars have their own light which they emit. The stars consist mostly of gases and there are nuclear fusions taking place that result in emission of lot of heat and light. Likewise environment (Sun) plays a very important role in flowering.

Q. 4. ***Why is the Earth considered a special planet?***

Ans. The Earth is considered special because it is the only known planet that supports life. A large variety of plants and animals is found in different regions of the Earth. The Earth has an environment and we must protect it.

Q. 5. ***What are some of the daily life situations mentioned in the passage where Science can be applied?***

Ans. The passage provides examples of daily life situations where Science is applied, such as finding out why a pen stops writing, or determining why dal spills out of a cooker, or identifying the source of a flat bicycle tyre, or an electrician trying to find why a light bulb is not working. These examples illustrate how the scientific method is used in solving daily problems. It demonstrates that Science is not confined to laboratories but is an integral part of our daily lives.

Q. 6. ***Explain the scientific method using the example of a pen that stops writing.***

Ans. When a pen stops writing, the scientific method involves observing the problem, asking why it happened, guessing possible reasons and testing these guesses. For example, we may guess that the ink is finished and check the refill. If the ink is not finished, another guess might be that the ink had dried up. This step-by-step process of guessing and testing is an example of the scientific method.

Q. 7. ***How can studying Science help in solving bigger problems and mysteries of the universe?***

Ans. Studying Science helps us with the skills to solve larger and more complex problems by increasing our ability to observe, analyze, and do experiment. It encourages critical thinking and systematic problem-solving, which are essential for solving global issues, such as environmental problems, medical advancements, and technological innovations. Science provides us the tools and techniques needed to explore and understand complex phenomena and find effective solutions.

Q. 8. ***Why is teamwork important in scientific discovery?***

Ans. Teamwork is important in scientific discovery because it allows the pooling of knowledge, resources, and skills. Scientists often work in large teams to solve complex problems, share diverse ideas, and collaborate on experiments. The scientific progress is often a collective effort, and working together increases the chances of making significant discoveries. Scientific learning is quite enjoyable and productive.

Q. 9. ***Describe the role of observation and experimentation in the scientific method.***

Ans. Observation and experimentation are fundamental components of the scientific method. Observation involves carefully noting and recording phenomena, while experimentation tests guesses made through controlled and repeated procedures.

Q. 10. ***Why could we say that Science is everywhere around us?***

Ans. Science is everywhere. It has applications in our daily life, from cooking and repairing bicycles to understanding natural phenomena and exploring outer space. Science helps explain the behaviour of water, the growth of plants, and the materials used in everyday objects. This type of presence of Science is important in understanding and improving our world.

Q. 11. ***What steps should we follow to find answers to scientific questions?***

Ans. To find scientific answers, we should follow these steps: observe an interesting phenomenon, ask questions about it, formulate a guess (a possible answer), test it through experiments or further observations, and analyze the results to see if they support the guess. This systematic approach helps in drawing accurate conclusions and building our scientific knowledge.

V. OBJECTIVE TYPE QUESTIONS

Multiple Choice Questions (MCQs)

Choose the correct option in the following questions:

1. *What is the primary goal of science?*
   (a) To memorize facts and figures
   (b) To understand the world we live in and uncover the secrets of the universe
   (c) To perform experiments without any purpose
   (d) To follow instructions without questioning
2. *What is the most important trait needed to explore and understand the world through science?*
   (a) Memorization
   (b) Discipline
   (c) Curiosity
   (d) Obedience
3. *Science is compared to which of the following?*
   (a) A complex equation
   (b) A big adventure
   (c) A boring task
   (d) A straightforward activity
4. *What is one of the most fascinating aspect of science?*
   (a) It is limited to laboratories.
   (b) It only involves studying large objects.
   (c) It is like a giant and unending jigsaw puzzle.
   (d) It has a fixed amount of knowledge to discover.
5. *How are scientific studies conducted?*
   (a) Alone
   (b) In large teams
   (c) By memorizing facts
   (d) Without asking questions

ANSWERS

Multiple Choice Questions (MCQs)

1. (b) 2. (c) 3. (b) 4. (c) 5. (b)

VI. EXERCISE FOR PRACTICE

1. Which method do scientists use to find reliable answers and solve problems?
2. What is necessary for a seed to grow into a plant besides water and sunlight?
3. What drives scientific discoveries?
4. At what temperature does water boil?
5. Write the purpose of science.
6. Explain the process of scientific curiosity.
7. Give three examples of applying the scientific method in daily life.

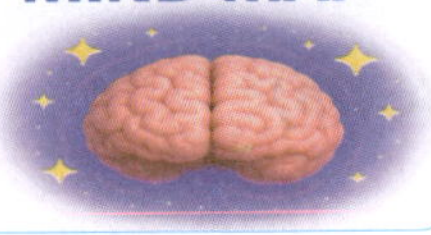

INTERESTING MIND MAP

Diversity in the Living World

1 Diversity in Plants and Animals Around Us

- Biodiversity is an important feature of the living world.

3 Plants and Animals in Different Surroundings

- Desert, mountains, ocean, forest and plains are the habitats of plants and animals. Plants and animals of these surroundings differ from each other in their features. E.g. camel of Rajasthan differs from camel of Ladakh.

2 How to group Plants and animals?

- We can group them on the basis of their similarities and differences.

2b How to group animals?

- They're grouped on the basis of their movement, shape, size, structure, colour, and other features.

2a How to group plants?

- **On the basis of their height and nature of stem.**

  Tree: Tall plant with hard, thick, brown, and woody stem.

  Shrub: Plant with many hard, thin and brown stems which branch very close to the ground.

  Herb: A small plant with soft and green stems.

  Climber: Plant needing support to climb and grow.

  Creeper: Plant that grows while creeping along the ground.

- **On the basis of the veins on their leaves having reticulate venation and parallel venation.**

  Veins: The thin lines on the leaves of the plants.

  Venation: The pattern of veins on the leaf.

  Reticulate Venation: A net-like pattern of veins on both sides of a thick middle vein.

  Parallel venation: Parallel veins form parallel venation.

- **On the basis of roots which can be taproot or fibrous roots.**

  Taproot: The one main root from which many small side roots arise.

  Fibrous Root: A bunch of similar-sized thin roots that arise from the base of the stem.

2

Diversity in the Living World

I. POINTS TO REMEMBER

- **Biodiversity:** The variety of plants and animals found in a particular region contributes to the biodiversity of that region. Each member in the biodiversity of a region has a different role to play. For example, plants provide food and shelter to animals and some birds and animals help in spreading seeds after eating fruits.
- **Grouping:** Grouping makes it easier to understand and study plants and animals on the basis of their similarities and differences.
- **Animals:** Animals are grouped on the basis of features like what they eat, where they live, how they move, etc.
- **Herbs, shrubs and trees:** Plants are usually grouped into herbs, shrubs and trees on the basis of their heights, types of stem and branches:

  (*a*) **Herbs:** Plants with green and tender stems are called **herbs**. They are usually short and sometimes do not have branches. *For example:* **Grasses, Mint.**

  (*b*) **Shrubs:** Some plants have branches arising from the base of the stem. The stem is hard but not very thick. They are called **shrubs**. *For example:* **Hibiscus**, **Rose.**

  (*c*) **Trees:** Some plants are very tall and have hard and thick stem. They have branches arising from upper part of the stem. They are called **trees**. *For example:* **Mango**, **Neem**, **Banyan.**

  (*d*) **Climbers:** Some plants have weak stems. They need support to climb and grow. They are called **climbers**. *For example:* **Grapevine**, **Money plant**, **Beans**.

  (*e*) **Creepers:** Some plants with weak stems creep along the ground. They are called **creepers**. *For example:* **Pumpkin**, **Watermelon.**

(*a*) Herbs (*b*) Shrubs (*c*) Tree (*d*) Climber (*e*) Creeper

Fig. Different types of Plants

- Plants can also be grouped as dicotyledons (dicots) and monocotyledons (monocots) based on the number of cotyledons in their seeds.
- **There is a relation between the type of leaf venation, type of root and number of cotyledons in the seed of the same plant.**
- **Monocot plants:** Monocot plants have one cotyledon in the seed, parallel venation and a fibrous root system.

  For example: **Grass, wheat, rice, maize, garlic, coconut.**
- **Dicot plants:** Dicot plants have two cotyledons in the seed, reticulate venation and a taproot system.

  For example: **Mustard plant**, **chickpea**, **radish** and **carrot.**

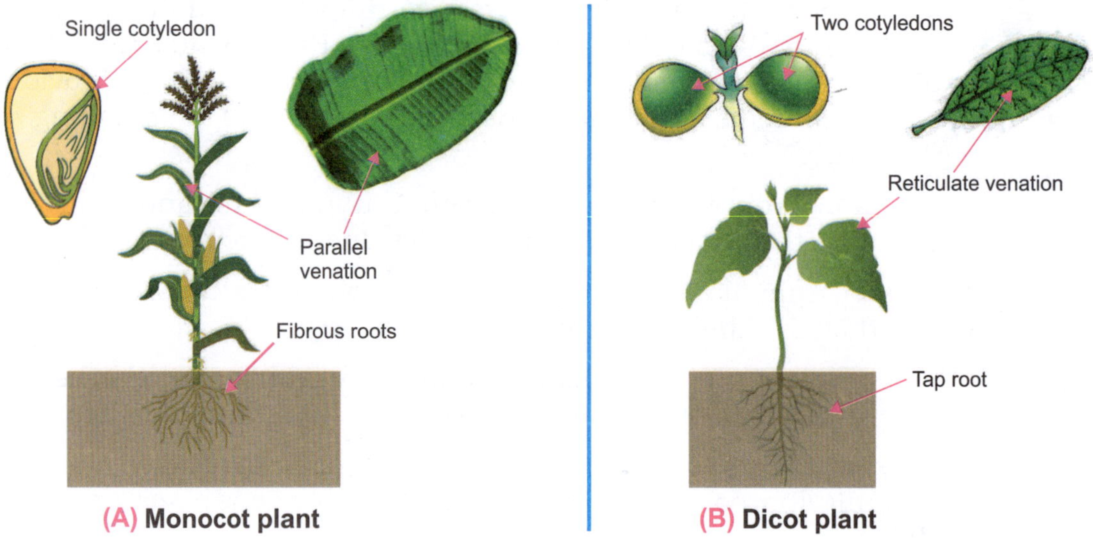

Fig.

- **Venation:** Thin lines on the leaves of plants are called **veins**. The arrangement of veins on the leaves is called **venation**.
- **Reticulate venation:** Net-like pattern of veins on both sides of thick middle vein is called **reticulate venation.**
  For example: **Hibiscus (Shoe-flower)**, **Sunflower.**
- **Parallel venation:** Veins run parallel in **parallel venation**.
  For example: **Grasses**, **Wheat**, **Banana**.
- **Taproot:** Roots consist of one main root and small side roots arising from it. Main root is called **taproot**.
  For example: **Mustard**, **Hibiscus**, **Chickpea.**
- **Fibrous roots:** Roots appear as a bunch of similar-sized thin roots arising from the base of the stem are called **fibrous roots**.
  For example: **Grasses**.
- **Movement in animals:** All animals (living things) show movement using different body parts.

For example: cat, dog, cattle, goat, etc. walk and jump with their legs. Birds fly using their wings and walk with their two legs. Insects like housefly, mosquitoes, cockroach, etc. fly using their wings and walk with their legs. Ants move with their legs. Fish swim in water using their fins. Humans walk, run and jump by their two legs.

- We can group animals based on their movement and other features like shape, size, structure, colour, etc.
- **Habitat:** The place where plants and animals live is known as their habitat. It provides them food, water, air, shelter and other needs for their survival.
- **Aquatic habitat**
  - (*i*) When organisms live in water, this place of living is known as aquatic habitat.
  - (*ii*) Ponds, lakes, rivers, oceans, etc., are examples of aquatic habitat.
  - (*iii*) Water is a medium in aquatic habitat.

    For example: Fish, Whale, Dolphin.

- **Terrestrial habitat**
  - (*i*) When organisms live on land, this place of living is known as terrestrial habitat.
  - (*ii*) Forests, deserts, orchards, tea gardens and mountains are the examples of terrestrial habitat.
  - (*iii*) Air is the medium in terrestrial habitat.

    For example: Goat, Cow, etc.
- Several kinds of plants and animals share the same habitat.
- Frog is an **amphibian** as it lives in water as well as on land.
- **Adaptations:** The specific features that enable plants and animals to survive in a particular habitat are called adaptations.
- **Plants and animals:** Plants and animals found in different regions are different from each other. In hot deserts **days are very hot** and **nights are cold.** In these areas plants and animals are adapted to tolerate and survive in such conditions. **Cactus** plants growing in desert have fleshy stems to store water. **Camels** in hot deserts have long legs with wide hooves so that they can walk easily in the sand. (c.f. **Camels** found in cold deserts have shorter legs so that they can move easily in mountain regions.)

- Camels in hot deserts have one hump and those found in cold deserts have two humps. They use food stored in their humps during hot and cold conditions respectively.
- Mountain regions have extreme cold conditions with frequent rains and snowfall. Pine plants growing in mountains are cone shaped with slopping branches. Snow slides off easily from such plants.
- **Rhododendron:** Plants growing in the Shola forests of Nilgiris have shorter height and smaller leaves and they differ from those growing in Sikkim where plants are comparatively taller.
- **Components of a habitat**

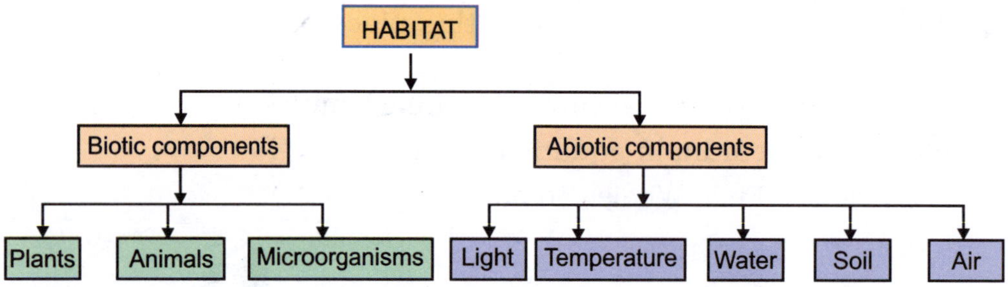

- Damage to the habitats of plants and animals result in loss of their homes, food and other resources, thereby loss of biodiversity.

II. KEYWORDS

1. **Adaptation:** The change in specific features and habits which enable a plant or an animal to live in a particular habitat is called adaptation.
2. **Amphibians:** Some animals can live in water as well as on land. These are called amphibians.
3. **Aquatic:** When organisms live in water, their place of living is known as aquatic habitat.
4. **Biodiversity:** It is the variety and variability of living organisms on the earth.
5. **Cotyledon:** Cotyledon refers to the significant part of the embryo found within the seed which stores food.
6. **Dicot Plants:** Dicot plants like Hibiscus have reticulate venation and a taproot system.
7. **Fibrous Root:** Roots in which many thin branches come out from the base of the stem are called fibrous roots.
8. **Habitat:** The place where an organism survives, flourishes and reproduces is called its habitat.
9. **Herbs:** Plants with green and tender stem are called herbs.
10. **Monocot Plants:** Monocot plants like grasses have parallel venation and a fibrous root system.
11. **Parallel Venation:** In the leaves of grass, veins are parallel to one another. This is called parallel venation.

12. **Reticulate Venation:** When veins and veinlets form a net like design on both sides of midrib, the venation is called reticulate venation.

13. **Sacred Groves:** Sacred groves are tracts of forest which are preserved by the local community.

14. **Shrubs:** Some plants have branches arising from the base of the stem to have bushy appearance. The stem is hard but not very thick. They are called shrubs.

15. **Taproot:** The root system in which a single root arises from the base of the stem, with side branches is called a taproot system.

16. **Terrestrial:** Terrestrial habitats are ones that are found on land.

17. **Tree:** Tall plants with hard, thick and woody stem are called trees.

18. **Venation:** The pattern of veins (thin lines) on the leaf is called venation.

III. LET US ENHANCE OUR LEARNING *(Pages 31–33)*

Q.1. ***Here are two types of seeds. What differences do you find among the roots and leaf venation of their plants?***

(a) Wheat

(b) Kidney beans

Ans. Differences between wheat and kidney beans:

	Features	Wheat (Monocot)	Kidney Beans (Dicots)
(i)	Root system	Fibrous root system	Taproot system
(ii)	Root characteristics	Dense network of thin roots	Central thick taproot with lateral branches
(iii)	Leaf venation	Parallel venation	Reticulate venation
(iv)	Leaf venation characteristics	Veins run parallel along the length of the leaf.	Network of branching veins with a prominent midrib.

Q. 2. ***Names of some animals are given below. Group them based on their habitats. Write the names of aquatic animals in the area marked 'A' and terrestrial animals in the area marked 'B'. Enter the names of animals living in both habitats in part 'C'.***

Horse, Dolphin, Frog, Sheep, Crocodile, Squirrel, Whale, Earthworm, Pigeon, Tortoise

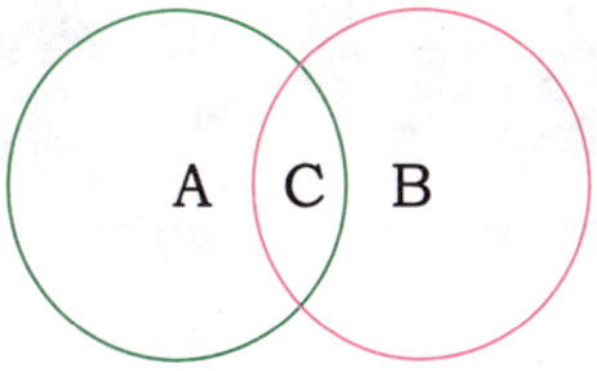

Ans.

(A) Aquatic animals:

(*i*) Dolphin (*ii*) Whale

(B) Terrestrial animals:

(*i*) Horse (*ii*) Sheep
(*iii*) Squirrel (*iv*) Earthworm
(*v*) Pigeon

(C) Both A and B (Amphibians)

(*i*) Frog (*ii*) Crocodile
(*iii*) Tortoise

Q. 3. ***Manu's mother maintains a kitchen garden. One day, she was digging out radish from the soil. She told Manu that radish is a kind of root. Examine a radish and write what type of root it is. What type of venation would you observe in the leaves of radish plant?***

Ans. Radish is a type of root known as a taproot. Main root is called taproot and from it many side roots arise. Tap root goes deep into the soil. Radish tap root is modified to store food and so it becomes swollen.

Leaf Venation: The leaves of radish plant exhibit reticulate venation, which is typical of dicotyledonous plants. This venation pattern consists of a prominent central vein called midrib with smaller veins branching out, forming a network.

Q. 4. ***Look at the image of a mountain goat and a goat found in the plains. Point out the similarities and differences between them. What are the reasons for these differences?***

(a) Mountain Goat

(a) Goat found in the plains

Ans. Similarities:

(1) Both are goats and belong to the same family.

(2) **Herbivore diet:** Both are herbivores. That is they eat plants including roots, stems, leaves etc.

(3) Both walk, run or jump with the help of their four legs.

Differences:

S. No.	Mountain Goat	Goat found in the Plains
1.	It has thick, long fur to protect from cold temperatures of mountains.	It has shorter hair (fur) suited for warmer climates.
2.	Generally it is stockier and more muscular, adapted for climbing rocky terrains.	It is of leaner build and suitable for flat, open areas.
3.	It has specialised hooves with a rough texture for better grip on rocky surfaces.	It's hooves are more suited for walking on flat, grassy lands.

Q. 5. ***Group the following animals into two groups based on any feature other than those discussed in the chapter— cow, cockroach, pigeon, bat, tortoise, whale, fish, grasshopper, lizard.***

Ans.

(*i*) Flying Animals:

(*a*) Pigeon (*b*) Bat
(*c*) Cockroach
(*d*) Grasshopper

(*ii*) Non-flying Animals:

(*a*) Cow (*b*) Tortoise
(*c*) Whale (*d*) Fish
(*e*) Lizard

Q. 6. ***As the population grows and people want more comfortable lives, forests are being cut down to meet various needs. How can this affect our surroundings? How do you think we can address this challenge?***

Ans. **Impact of Deforestation:**

(1) Loss of Biodiversity

(2) Changes in Climate

(3) Soil Erosion

(4) Water Cycle Disruption

(5) Poor Air Quality.

Addressing the Challenge

(*i*) ***Protected Areas:*** Establishing more national parks and wildlife sanctuaries to protect existing forests and animals.

(*ii*) ***Community Involvement:*** Engaging local communities in forest conservation efforts.

We should plant more trees near our surroundings.

(*iii*) ***Legislation:*** Implementing and enforcing laws that prevent illegal poaching and deforestation.

Q. 7. ***Analyse the flowchart. What can be examples of 'A' and 'B'?***

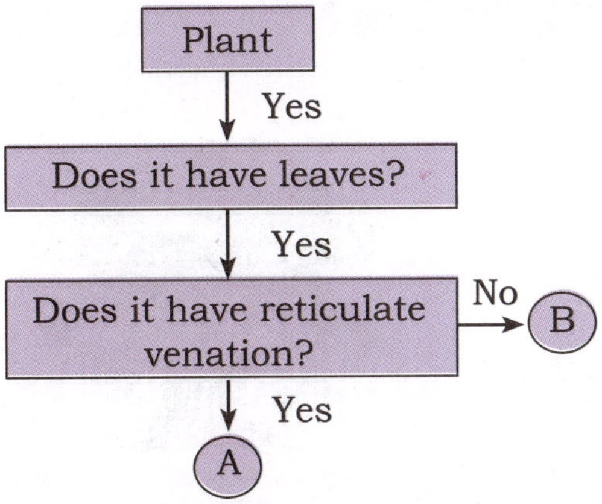

Ans. **Examples of 'A':** These are plants that have reticulate venation in their leaves.

Examples: Mango, Hibiscus, Rose, Chickpea (*Chana*), Mustard.

Examples of 'B': These are plants that do not have reticulate venation (*i.e.*, they have parallel venation).

Examples: Wheat, Maize, Grass.

Q. 8. ***Raj argues with his friend Sanjay that "Gudhal (hibiscus) plant is a shrub". What questions can Sanjay ask for clarification?***

Ans. 1. What is the nature of its stem?

2. What is the height of the *Gudhal* (hibiscus) plant?

3. Is the stem of the *Gudhal* plant soft green or woody?

Q. 9. ***Based on the information in the table, find out examples of these plants for each group.***

Group	Type of seed	Type of root	Examples
A	Dicot	Taproot	
B	Monocot	Fibrous roots	

(*a*) What other similarity do plants of group A have?

(*b*) What other similarity do plants of group B have?

Ans. Examples for group A and B.

1. Rose, mango, radish, carrot and hibiscus

2. Grass, wheat, onions, maize and rice etc.

(*a*) **Similarity of Plants in Group A:** Plants in Group A (dicots) typically have leaves with reticulate venation.

(*b*) **Similarity of Plants in Group B:** Plants in Group B (monocots) generally have leaves with parallel venation.

Q. 10. ***Observe the labelled part of a duck in the picture given below. What differences do you observe in the feet of the duck compared to the other birds? Which activity would the duck be able to perform using this part?***

(a) Duck (b) Pigeon

Ans. Differences in the Feet

(*a*) Duck has webbed feet

(*b*) Pigeon does not have webbed feet. It has regular bird feet with separate toes.

Activities the Duck Can Perform with Webbed Feet

- ***Swimming:*** The webbed feet help the duck to paddle through water efficiently.
- ***Walking on Muddy or Wet Surfaces:*** Webbed feet provide stability and prevent the duck from sinking in mud.
- The webbed feet of duck are specially adapted for swimming, allowing it to move smoothly in water.

IV. EXAM ORIENTED QUESTIONS

Q. 1. ***What are herbs?***

Ans. The small plants with **soft/tender**, **green**, small stem are called herbs. Herbs do not attain height more than 1.5 metres. Their stems are not woody. A herb may or may not have branches, e.g., tomato, mint, paddy, etc.

Q. 2. ***With the help of diagrams, tabulate the differences between a shrub and a tree, based on the properties of the stem.***

Ans.

Shrub	Tree
1. More branches arise from the base of stem.	1. The branches arise from the stem.
2. The stem is hard and thin.	2. The stem is hard, thick and woody.
 Fig. Shrub	 Fig. Tree

Q. 3. ***Look carefully at the plants shown in Fig. and identify their type. Are they herbs, shrubs or trees? Are they similar in shape? Which category has the biggest plants and which has the smallest?***

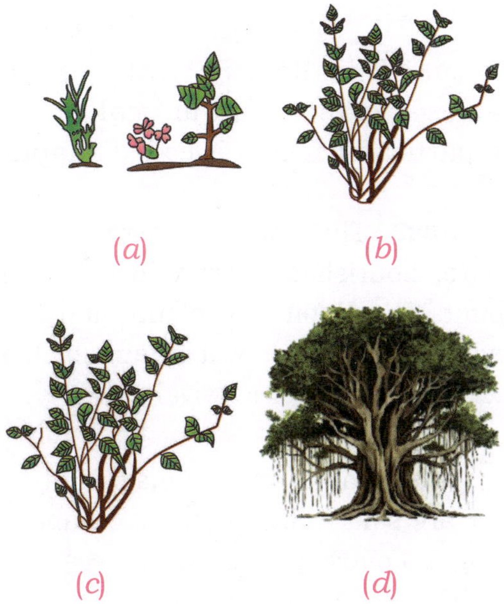

Fig. Different types of plants

Ans. Close look of these plants make it clear that these plants are not of the same type.

Plants (*a*) and (*b*) are small and have soft and thin stem. These are called **herbs.**

Plant (*c*) has many branches arising from the base and its stem is thin but hard. It is a **shrub.**

Plant (*d*) is tall. Its stem is thick, hard and woody, it is a **tree.**

Q. 4. ***From the members of the various groups given below, find the odd one out.***

(*a*) Coriander (dhania), mint (pudina), jamun, grass.

(*b*) Rose, mehndi, guava, morepankh.

Ans. (*a*) **Jamun** (Jamun is a tree while others are herbs).

(*b*) **Guava** (Guava is a tree while others are shrubs).

Q. 5. ***You are shown three branches of a rose in Fig. (a), (b) and (c) (below). Which one will help you best to recognize the plant?***

Fig. Rose: (*a*) A leafless branch, (*b*) A branch with leaves, and (*c*) A branch with leaves and flowers

Ans. (*c*) A branch with leaves and flowers.

Q. 6. ***What are climbers and creepers? Give some examples.***

Ans. In some plants like grape vines, money plant, beans, pumpkin plants, etc., the stem is so weak that it cannot hold it straight. They either stand up with some support or they just spread on the ground. The plants which climb up are called **climbers**. For example grapevine, money plant. The ones which spread on the ground are called **creepers**. For example pumpkin plants.

Q. 7. ***Read the function of parts of a plant given below:***

(*a*) fixes plant to the soil

(*b*) prepares starch

(*c*) takes part in reproduction

(*d*) supports branches and bears flowers

In the diagram given in Fig. write the names of the parts whose functions you have just read, at the appropriate space. (*NCERT Exemplar*)

Ans.

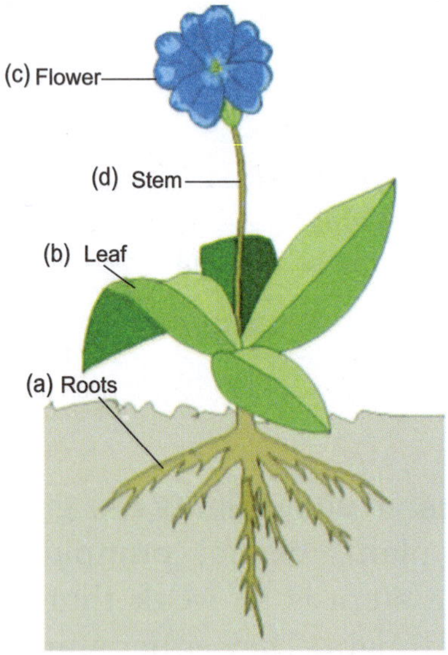

(*a*) Fixes plant to the soil – root.

(*b*) Prepares starch – leaf.

(*c*) Takes part in reproduction – flower.

(*d*) Supports branches and bears flowers – stem.

Q. 8. *Why do animals move from one place to other?*

Ans. Animals move from one place to other:

(*i*) To obtain their food and shelter.

(*ii*) To protect themselves from enemies and unfavourable climate.

Q. 9. *Name the organs of locomotion of:*

(*a*) Man (*b*) Bird (*c*) Fish.

Ans. (*a*) Man – Two Legs

(*b*) Bird – Wings + legs

(*c*) Fish – Fins.

Q. 10. *What is adaptation?*

Ans. The specific features, which enables a plant or an animal to survive in a particular region is called adaptation.

Q. 11. *What is habitat?*

Ans. The place where organisms survive, flourish and reproduce is called a habitat. The Habitat of plants and animals provides them food, water, air shelter and other needs for their survival.

Q. 12. *What are aquatic habitats?*

Ans. Plants and animals that live in water are said to live in aquatic habitat. *For example*: Ponds, rivers, lakes, oceans etc.

Q. 13. *What are terrestrial habitats? Give examples.*

Ans. The plants and animals that live on land are said to live in terrestrial habitats. For example, forests, grasslands, deserts, coastal and mountain region.

Q. 14. *What are biotic components?*

Ans. The living things such as plants and animals in a habitat are its biotic components.

Q. 15. *Explain abiotic components.*

Ans. Various non-living things such as rocks, soil, air and water in a habitat constitute its abiotic components.

Q.16. *Classify the following habitats into terrestrial and aquatic types.*

Grassland, Pond, Ocean, Rice field

(*NCERT Exemplar*)

Ans. Terrestrial habitats–Grassland, Rice field

Aquatic habitats – Pond, Ocean

Q. 17. ***Write the adaptation in aquatic plants due to which*** *(NCERT Exemplar)*

(*a*) submerged leaves can bend in the flowing water.

(*b*) leaves can float on the surface of water.

Ans. (*a*) Leaves are narrow and ribbon like. *For example*: **Potamogeton, Hydrilla**.

(*b*) Stems/stalks of leaves are long, hollow and light. *For example:* **Lotus.**

Q. 18. ***Mention one adaptation present in the following animals:*** *(NCERT Exemplar)*

(*a*) In camels to keep their bodies away from the heat of sand.

(*b*) In frogs to enable them to swim.

(*c*) In dolphins and whales to breathe in air when they swim near the surface of water.

Ans. (*a*) **Long legs** (*b*) **Webbed feet** (*c*) Blow holes (nostrils)

Q. 19. ***Some desert plants have very small leaves whereas some others have only spines. How does this benefit the plants?*** *(NCERT Exemplar)*

Ans. Some desert plants have very small leaves whereas some others have only spines. These are adaptations of desert plants to survive in extreme dry conditions. As a result of these modifications the surface of lamina is reduced which reduces water loss by transpiration.

Q. 20. ***What are the specific features present in a deer that helps it to detect the presence of predators like lion?*** *(NCERT Exemplar)*

Ans. The specific features present in a deer that helps it to detect the presence of predators like lion are:

(*a*) Long ears to hear movement of predators.

(*b*) Eyes on the sides of its head which allow it to look in all directions.

V. OBJECTIVE TYPE QUESTIONS

1. *Match the following items given in Column A with that in Column B:*

Column A		Column B	
(*a*)	Creeper	(*i*)	Absorption of mineral and water.
(*b*)	Herb	(*ii*)	Manufacture food.
(*c*)	Shrub	(*iii*)	Transport food, water and mineral.
(*d*)	Tree	(*iv*)	Reproduction.
(*e*)	Root	(*v*)	Need support to stand up.
(*f*)	Stem	(*vi*)	Hard and thick stem.
(*g*)	Leaf	(*vii*)	Green and tender stem.
(*h*)	Flower	(*viii*)	Hard but thin stem.

2. *State whether the statements given below are True or False:*

(*i*) Herbs are usually soft and green.

(*ii*) In shrubs, branches arise from the base of the stem.

(*iii*) In trees, branches arise from the upper part of stem.

(*iv*) Stem absorbs water and minerals from the soil.

(*v*) Roots hold the plant firmly in the soil.

(*vi*) Leaves manufacture the food in presence of sunlight by the process of transpiration.

(*vii*) Plants having leaves with reticulate venation have fibrous roots.

(*viii*) All plants have colourful flowers.

Multiple Choice Questions (MCQs)

Choose the correct option in the following questions:

1. *Which is an example of a shrub?*
   (*a*) Spinach (*b*) Mango tree
   (*c*) Tomato plant (*d*) Lemon
2. *Which of the following type of plants has thick, hard and woody stem?*
   (*a*) Tree (*b*) Shrub
   (*c*) Herb (*d*) All of these
3. *Parallel venation is not found in*
   (*a*) sugarcane (*b*) peepal
   (*c*) maize (*d*) wheat
4. *Which one of the following is a function of leaves?*
   (*a*) Photosynthesis
   (*b*) Transpiration
   (*c*) Both (*a*) and (*b*)
   (*d*) Support fruits
5. *Leaf venation and type of root is correctly paired in*
   (*a*) parallel venation, fibrous roots
   (*b*) parallel venation, taproot
   (*c*) no relation exists in leaf venation and type of roots
   (*d*) reticulate venation, fibrous roots
6. *Which of the following combination of features would you observe in grass?* *(NCERT Exemplar)*
   (*a*) Parallel venation and fibrous root
   (*b*) Parallel venation and tap root
   (*c*) Reticulate venation and fibrous root
   (*d*) Reticulate venation and tap root
7. *Which of the following cannot be called a habitat?* *(NCERT Exemplar)*
   (*a*) A desert with camels.
   (*b*) A pond with fishes.
   (*c*) A jungle with wild animals.
   (*d*) Cultivated land with grazing cattle.
8. *Given below are features of plants*
   (*i*) *They lose a lot of water through transpiration.*
   (*ii*) *Their leaves are always broad and flat.*
   (*iii*) *They lose very little water through transpiration.*
   (*iv*) *Their roots grow very deep into the soil.*

   Which of the combination of above features are typical of desert plants? *(NCERT Exemplar)*
   (*a*) (*i*) *and* (*ii*) (*b*) (*ii*) *and* (*iv*)
   (*c*) (*ii*) *and* (*iii*) (*d*) (*iii*) *and* (*iv*)
9. *Boojho comes across an animal having a stream-lined and slippery body. What is the habitat of the animal?* *(NCERT Exemplar)*
   (*a*) Water (*b*) Desert
   (*c*) Grassland (*d*) Mountain
10. *Which of the following are characteristics of living beings?* *(NCERT Exemplar)*
    (*i*) *Respiration*
    (*ii*) *Reproduction*
    (*iii*) *Adaptation*
    (*iv*) *Excretion*

    Choose the correct answer from the options below:
    (*a*) (*i*), (*ii*) *and* (*iv*) *only*
    (*b*) (*i*) *and* (*ii*) *only*
    (*c*) (*ii*) *and* (*iv*) *only*
    (*d*) (*i*), (*ii*), (*iii*) *and* (*iv*)

ANSWERS

1.

Column A		Column B	
(*a*)	Creeper	(*v*)	Need support to stand up.
(*b*)	Herb	(*vii*)	Green and tender stem.
(*c*)	Shrub	(*viii*)	Hard but thin stem.
(*d*)	Tree	(*vi*)	Hard and thick stem.
(*e*)	Root	(*i*)	Absorption of mineral and water.
(*f*)	Stem	(*iii*)	Transport food, water and mineral.
(*g*)	Leaf	(*ii*)	Manufacture food.
(*h*)	Flower	(*iv*)	Reproduction.

2. True or False:

(*i*) True (*ii*) True (*iii*) True (*iv*) False (*v*) True
(*vi*) False (*vii*) False (*viii*) False

Multiple Choice Questions (MCQs)

1. (*d*) **2.** (*a*) **3.** (*b*) **4.** (*c*) **5.** (*a*) **6.** (*a*) **7.** (*d*) **8.** (*d*) **9.** (*a*) **10.** (*d*)

VI. EXERCISE FOR PRACTICE

1. What is the difference between a shrub and a tree?
2. Classify the following into herbs, shrubs and trees:

   Wheat, Henna, Coconut, Paddy, Carrot, Lemon.
3. Define habitat.
4. What is stem? Give different functions of the stem in a plant.
5. Name some animals that live in water.
6. What do you mean by aquatic habitats?
7. Define adaptation.
8. What is meant by terrestrial habitat? Give two examples.
9. What are the adaptive features in desert plants?
10. How are camels adapted to live in desert?
11. Which biotic component can trap solar energy and how?
12. How do animals like rats, snakes and lizards adapt themselves to live in desert?
13. What protects the animals that live in very cold conditions?
14. What makes it possible for fish to live in water?

1 What Do We Eat?

- A variety of food as per seasons and time.

1a Food in different regions

- Food crops, taste preferences, culture and tradition influence the choice of food.

1b How have cooking practices changed over time?

- Due to technological development, improved transportation and better communication.

2 What are the Components of Food?

- Carbohydrates, fats, proteins, vitamins, minerals, roughage, and water.

3 How to Test Different Components of Food?

- Simple tests can help to detect the presence of starch, fat and protein.

INTERESTING MIND MAP

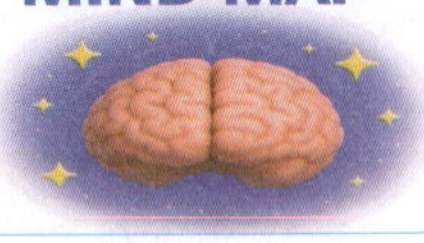

Mindful Eating: A Path to a Healthy Body

3a Test for Starch

- Change of colour of food into blue-black on putting 2-3 drops of iodine solution shows presence of starch.

3b Test for Fats

- Leaving of an oily patch on the paper wrapped around the food shows the presence of fat.

3c Test for Proteins

- Violet colour in the test tube due to addition of 2-3 teaspoons of water, 2 drops of copper sulphate solution and 10 drops of caustic soda solution to the food shows presence of proteins.

4 Balanced Diet

- A diet containing all essential nutrients, roughage and water in the right amount.

5 Millets: Nutrition-rich Cereals

- *Jowar, bajra, ragi* and *sanwa*—the highly nutritious grains are millets.

6 Food Miles: From Farm to Our Plate

- Food miles is the entire distance a food travels from the farmland to our plate.

3

Mindful Eating: A Path to a Healthy Body

I. POINTS TO REMEMBER

- **Food:** All of us eat food everyday. Food is the primary source of energy for all living organisms in the world. Food plays an important role in the development of living organisms.
- The food consumed varies according to the region (like hilly areas or coastal areas), culture and traditions, age (like babies or children or old people), and physical conditions (ill-health, sportsman, etc.)
- India is an **agricultural country** with diverse soil and climate types. Different crops are grown in different regions depending on the soil types and climatic conditions. **Traditional food of any state is usually based on the crops grown in that state.** So in different regions of India, the choice of food varies depending on the cultivation of food crops, taste preferences, culture and traditions.
- **Cooking:** **Cooking practices are called culinary practices.** There is a significant difference between traditional and modern culinary practices. Culinary practices have changed over time due to development of technology, improvement in transportation and better communication in modern times.
- **Various food components:** Food contains different types of nutrients such as **carbohydrates, proteins**, **fats**, **vitamins**, **minerals**, **dietary fibres**, and **water**.

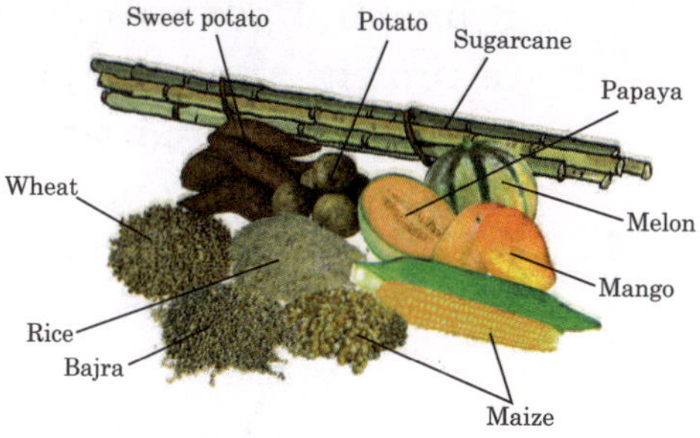

Fig. Carbohydrates

- **Energy-giving foods:** **Carbohydrates** and **fats** are the main sources of energy for our body and together they are known as **energy-giving foods.**
- **Sources of Carbohydrates:** Sources of **carbohydrates** are cereals (like wheat, rice, maize), potato, sweet potato, banana, pineapple, mango.
- **Sources of Fats:** Sources of **fats**, which are obtained from plants are groundnuts, walnuts, coconut, almonds, pumpkin seeds and sunflower seeds. Butter and ghee are obtained from animals. Fat is a source of stored energy.

Fig. Fats

- **Body building foods:** Proteins are essential for growth and repair of body. Hence they are called **body building foods.** Milk products and pulses are good sources of proteins. Excellent plant sources of proteins are pulses, nuts, beans and peas. Animal sources of protein are milk, paneer, egg, fish and meat. Growing children and sportspersons must have right amount of proteins in their diet.

Fig. Proteins

- **Protective foods:** Vitamins and minerals protect us from infections and are called **protective foods.**

Fig. Vitamins and Minerals

- **Deficiency diseases:** Vitamins and minerals protect our body from various diseases and deficiency of these result in **deficiency diseases.**

- **Nutrients:** Food components that provide energy, support growth, help in growth and repair of our body and protect our body from diseases, and maintain different body functions are called **nutrients**.

- **Roughage or Dietary fibres:** Fruits and vegetables are rich in dietary fibres or roughage. They do not provide nutrients to our body but are essential components of our food.

- Water is also very essential part of our diet. It helps the body absorb nutrients from food.

- **Balanced Diet:** A balanced diet provides all necessary nutrients in the right quantities, along with sufficient fibre and water.

Fig. Balanced Diet

- **Junk foods** are unhealthy as they contain high levels of sugar and fats but little protein, minerals, vitamins, and dietary fibres.
- **Millets:** Millets like jowar, bajra, ragi, etc. have very high nutritional value, hence are known as nutri-cereals.
- **Food miles:** Distance travelled by a food item from farm to plate is called food miles. We must aim to minimize food miles.
- We should avoid wasting food rather respect food and the effort put by our farmers.

II. KEYWORDS

1. **Carbohydrates:** Carbohydrates provide energy to our body.
2. **Culinary practices:** Cooking practices are called culinary practices.
3. **Deficiency diseases:** Diseases that occur due to lack of nutrients over a long period are called deficiency diseases.
4. **Fats:** Fats also provide energy to our body. Fat is a source of stored energy.
5. **Food components:** The food we eat consists of carbohydrates, fats, proteins, vitamins, water, minerals and fibres.
6. **Food miles:** Food miles is the distance food travels from the location where it is produced or made until it reaches the consumer.
7. **Iodized salt:** The salt which is mixed with required proportions of the element iodine is known as the iodized salt.
8. **Millets:** Millets are small-sized grains which have remarkable nutritive value.
9. **Minerals:** Minerals like calcium, iron etc. are needed by our body in small amounts.
10. **Nutrients:** Components of food that are required by our body for growth, energy and to stay healthy are called nutrients.
11. **Proteins:** Proteins are required for growth and repair of our body.
12. **Rickets:** Disease caused by lack of Vitamin D in food.
13. **Roughage:** Dietary fibres are known as roughage. It is mainly provided by plant products in our foods.
14. **Scurvy:** Disease caused by lack of Vitamin C in food.
15. **Vitamins:** Vitamins help in protecting our body against diseases.

III. LET US ENHANCE OUR LEARNING *(Pages 56–58)*

Q. 1. *Pick the odd one out and give reasons:*

(*i*) *Jowar, Bajra,* Ragi, Chana

(*ii*) Kidney beans, Green gram, Soya bean, Rice

Ans.

(*i*) The odd one out is "Chana". *Jowar, Bajra,* and Ragi are different types of millet crops, whereas Chana refers to chickpeas, which is a pulse crop.

(*ii*) The odd one out is "Rice." Kidney beans, green gram, and Soya bean are protein sources while rice is a carbohydrate.

Q. 2. *Discuss traditional versus modern culinary practices in India.*

Ans. **Traditional Practices**

(*i*) Cooking was mostly done on chulhas (traditional stoves).

(*ii*) Grinding was done manually using tools like sil-batta (stone grinder).

(*iii*) Emphasis on using fresh, locally grown ingredients.

Modern Practices

(*i*) Use of modern gas stoves and electric appliances like grinders and mixers.

(*ii*) Availability and use of pre-packaged and processed foods.

(*iii*) Influence of global cuisines and fusion cooking.

Reasons for Change

(*i*) Technological advancements.

(*ii*) Time constraints and lifestyle changes.

(*iii*) Improved transportation and availability of a variety of ingredients.

Q. 3. *A teacher says that good food may act as medicine. Ravi is curious about this statement and has some questions for his teacher. List at least two questions that he can ask.*

Ans. 1. "How does good food act like medicine for our bodies?"

2. "Give examples of foods that are considered 'medicine'."

Q. 4. *Not all delicious foods are necessarily healthy, while not all nutritious foods are always enjoyable. Share your thoughts along with a few examples.*

Ans. Delicious food is not always healthy: Like, burgers, pizzas, chats, potato chips etc. are very tasty but not nutritious. These foods contain refined flour (Maida), spices and a lot of oil which is not good for health.

On the other hand, nutritious food may not always be delicious to eat, for example, boiled vegetables, pulses, leafy vegetables etc., which are not always tasty but are very good for health. These foods contain important nutrients (proteins, vitamins, minerals etc.) which help us to keep our body strong and healthy.

Q. 5. *Medu does not eat vegetables but enjoys biscuits, noodles and white bread. He often has stomach ache and constipation. What changes should he make in his diet to get rid of these problems? Explain your answer.*

Ans. Medu should include whole grains, whole pulses, fresh fruits and vegetables in his diet to get rid of his stomach ache and constipation. These food items contain roughage (dietary fibre) which is lacking in Medu's diet.

Medu should avoid eating biscuits, noodles and white bread as they are made up of refined flour (Maida) which does not contain any roughage or fibre. Roughage prevents constipation.

Q. 6. *Reshma had trouble seeing things in dim light. The doctor tested her eyesight and prescribed a particular vitamin supplement. He also advised her to include a few food items in her diet.*

(*i*) Which deficiency disease is she suffering from?

(*ii*) Which food component may be lacking in her diet?

(*iii*) Suggest some food items that she should include in her diet to overcome this problem (any four).

Ans.

(*i*) Reshma is suffering from night blindness which results in difficulty of seeing things in dim light.

(*ii*) Deficiency of vitamin A causes night blindness. Hence vitamin A might be lacking in her diet.

(*iii*) In her diet, Reshma can include food items such as carrot, spinach, papaya, milk, green leafy, vegetables, mango, fish oil, etc. which are rich in vitamin A.

Q. 7. ***You are provided the following:***

(*i*) *Canned fruit juice*

(*ii*) *Fresh fruit juice*

(*iii*) *Fresh fruit*

Which one would you prefer and why?

Ans. I would prefer fresh fruit over canned fruit juice and fresh fruit juice because fresh fruits provide more nutrients, dietary fibre, compared to fresh fruit and canned fruit juice. Canned fruit juices often have added sugars to enhance flavour and extend shelf life.

Q. 8. ***Gourav got a fracture in his leg. His doctor aligned the bones and put on a plaster. The doctor also gave him calcium tablets.***

On the second visit, the doctor gave him Vitamin D syrup along with calcium tablets. Refer to Fig. 3.5 (*See textbook Page 44*) and answer the following questions:

(*i*) Why did the doctor give calcium tablets to Gourav?

(*ii*) On the second visit, why did the doctor give Vitamin D syrup along with calcium tablets?

(*iii*) What question arises in your mind about the choices made by the doctor in giving the medicines?

Ans. (*i*) The doctor gave calcium tablets to Gourav because calcium plays a crucial role in bone health. When a bone is fractured, calcium is essential for the process of bone healing.

(*ii*) The doctor gave Vitamin D syrup along with calcium tablets on the second visit to Gourav because Vitamin D helps in calcium absorption.

(*iii*) One question that arises about the choices made by the doctor in giving the medicines is:

"How long does Gourav need to continue taking the calcium tablets and Vitamin D syrup?"

Q. 9. ***Sugar is an example of carbohydrates. Sugar is tested with iodine solution but it does not change to blue-black colour.***

What can be a possible reason?

Ans. The reason why sugar does not change to a blue-black colour when tested with iodine solution is because iodine solution gives blue black colour with starch, not with simple sugars. Iodine solution is used to test the presence of starch in a substance. When iodine is added in starch, it forms a blue-black colour. Therefore, when sugar is tested with iodine solution, there will be no colour change observed because sugars do not produce the blue-black colour.

Q. 10. ***What do you think of Raman's statement, "All starches are carbohydrates but not all carbohydrates are starches." Describe the design of an activity to test your answer.***

Ans. Raman's statement, "All starches are carbohydrates but not all carbohydrates are starches," is correct. **Carbohydrates are a broad category which include sugars, starches, and fibres.** Starches are a type of carbohydrate that consists of long chains of glucose molecules bonded together while, carbohydrates also include simpler sugars like glucose, fructose, and sucrose, as well as complex carbohydrates such as cellulose (fibre).

To design an activity to test this statement, following experiment is conducted:

Activity: To test different types of Carbohydrates

Requirements

- Iodine solution (potassium iodide solution with iodine dissolved in water)

Different food samples like

- Starch sources (Potato, rice, bread)
- Sugar sources (Sugar crystals (sucrose), honey, fruits (like banana)
- Fibre source (Raw vegetable)

Procedure

- Prepare small samples of each food item on separate containers.
- Label each container according to the food sample (e.g., 1: Potato, 2: Sugar crystals).
- Add a small amount of iodine solution on each sample. Be careful not to mix the samples.

Observations

- Observe and record colour changes.

Results

- **Starch sources (e.g., potato, rice, bread):** Iodine solution turns starch into blue-black colour.
- **Sugar sources (e.g., sugar crystals, honey, fruits):** Sugar samples will not change colour with iodine solution; they remain unchanged.
- **Fibre source (e.g., raw vegetable):** Fibre does not react with iodine solution and no change in colour occurs.

Conclusion

- Starches (potato, rice, bread) show blue-black colour change with iodine solution, indicating the presence of starch.
- Sugars (sucrose, honey, fruits) do not show colour change with iodine solution. They do not have starches.
- Fibre (raw vegetable) does not react with iodine solution, indicating that it is not a starch.

Explanation

This activity demonstrates that while all starches are carbohydrates (as they react with iodine solution), not all carbohydrates (such as sugars and fibre) react in the same way with iodine. Therefore, Raman's statement is confirmed through this simple experiment, showing that starches are a type of carbohydrates with their characteristic reaction with iodine solution.

Q. 11. ***While using iodine in the laboratory, a few drops of iodine fell on Mishti's socks and a few fell on her teacher's saree.***

The drops of iodine on the saree turned blue-black while the colour on the socks did not change. What can be a possible reason? *(NCERT Exemplar)*

Ans. Iodine solution turned blue-black because the saree worn by Mishti's teacher must have contained starch and starch turns blue-black with iodine solution. Saree must be made of cotton, which has starch. Mishti's socks would have been free from starch that's why her socks did not change colour.

Q. 12. ***Why are millets considered a healthy choice of food? Can eating just millets suffice for the nutritional requirements of the body? Discuss.***

Ans. Millets are considered a healthy choice of food because of their numerous health benefits. They are good sources of vitamins, minerals like iron and calcium, and dietary fibres as well. That is the reason they are also called **nutri-cereals**. Yes, eating just millets can suffice for the nutritional requirements of the body as they are nutri-cereals and also contribute to a balance diet.

Q. 13. ***You are given a sample of a solution. How would you check the possibility of it being an iodine solution?***

Ans. To check if the sample of solution is iodine solution, following test is performed—

Starch Test (Iodine Test):

- Add a few drops of the solution to a small amount of starch solution. Iodine forms a deep blue-black colour with starch. If the solution contains iodine, the colour changes to blue-black. It indicates the presence of iodine.

IV. EXAM ORIENTED QUESTIONS

3.1 WHAT DO WE EAT?

Q. 1. ***What is food?***

Ans. Food is the basic requirement for all living organisms. It provides energy for carrying out all the daily activities.

Q. 2. ***Mention which of the following culinary practices are traditional and which are modern***

(*a*) Modern chulha (*b*) Sil-batta
(*c*) Electrical grinder
(*d*) Modern gas stove

Ans.

(*a*) Modern chulha: Traditional culinary practice
(*b*) Sil-batta (stone grinder): Traditional culinary practice
(*c*) Electrical grinder: Modern culinary practice
(*d*) Modern gas stove: Modern culinary practice

Q. 3. ***Explain the importance of food for living organisms.***

Ans. Food is important for living organisms as it

- provides energy to do various activities.
- helps in growth.
- helps to repair and replace damaged parts of the body.
- protects us from diseases.

Q. 4. ***What are culinary practices?***

Ans. Cooking practices are known as culinary practices.

Q. 5. ***Why is there diversity in food in different states of India?***

Ans. There is diversity in food in different states of India because of diversity in soil, climate, culture, traditions, ethnic groups and occupations.

Q. 6. ***What are the significant differences between traditional and modern culinary practices?***

Ans. Earlier, most cooking was done using a chulha. Nowadays, we cook using a modern gas stove. Earlier, most grinding was done manually using a sil-batta. These days, we use an electrical grinder for easy grinding.

Q. 7. ***Do you think that all living beings need the same kind of food?***

Ans. No, all living beings do not need same kind of food.

Q. 8. ***Write factors due to which culinary practices have changed over time.***

Ans. Culinary practices have changed overtime due to

- technological development
- improved transportation and
- better communication.

Q. 9. ***Compare your food habits with food habits of your friend who lives in Tamil Nadu.***

Ans. My food habits: Chapati, pulses, lassi, rice, vegetables, mustard oil. Food habits of my friend: Idli, dosa, sambhar, vada, rasam, upma and coconut oil, etc.

3.2 WHAT ARE THE COMPONENTS OF FOOD?

Q. 1. ***Name the major nutrients in our food.***

Ans. The major nutrients in our food are Carbohydrates, Proteins, Fats, Vitamins, Minerals and dietary fibres.

Q. 2. ***Name the food materials which contain fat.***

Ans. The food materials which contain fat are of two types

(*i*) **Animal fats:** Ghee, butter

(*ii*) **Plant fats:** Nuts like groundnuts, coconut, walnut, almond, sunflower seeds, pumpkin seeds, mustard seeds.

Q. 3. ***What are nutrients?***

Ans. The components of food that are necessary for growth and development of our body are called nutrients.

Q. 4. ***What is nutrition?***

Ans. The process of taking nutrients from our food for the growth and development of body and to obtain energy is known as nutrition.

Q. 5. ***Name two nutrients which protect the body from diseases.***

Ans. The two nutrients which protect the body from diseases are vitamins and minerals.

Q. 6. ***Why do you think a marathon runner drinks glucose water during and after a race?***

Ans. Glucose provides instant energy. Glucose is an example of a carbohydrate. Carbohydrates are one of the primary sources of energy in our diet.

Q. 7. ***What is dietary fibre?***

Ans. Dietary fibres are the plant derived food that cannot be completely broken down by the human digestive system. For example- vegetables, fruits, whole grain oats etc.

Q. 8. ***Name the food rich in proteins.***

Ans. The food rich in proteins are pulses, beans, peas, nuts, chicken, fish, milk, cheese etc.

Q. 9. ***Why should we eat cooked food?***

Ans. We should eat cooked food because by cooking harmful bacteria (germs) are killed. Cooked food can be easily digested and absorbed by our body. Cooking also improves the taste of food.

Q. 10. ***Define deficiency diseases.***

Ans. A disease caused by the lack of an element in the diet like vitamin or mineral is known as a deficiency disease. For example- scurvy, rickets etc.

Q. 11. ***What are the symptoms of carbohydrate deficiency?***

Ans. The symptoms of deficiency of carbohydrates are feeling tired and less energetic.

Q. 12. ***What is dehydration?***

Ans. Dehydration is the condition when our body loses more fluid than we consume. Basically, excess loss of water from the body leads to dehydration.

Q. 13. ***Why should a meal have different food items?***

Ans. A meal should have different food items because our body needs different kinds of nutrients for proper growth and development.

Q. 14. ***Which type of food is called body-building food?***

Ans. The food containing proteins is called body-building food.

Q. 15. ***People who eat sea-food do not suffer from Goitre. Explain.***

Ans. Sea-food is a rich source of Iodine and Goitre is a deficiency disease caused due to lack of Iodine.

Q. 16. ***Write the functions of water in our body.***

Ans. Water helps our body to absorb nutrients from the food. It also helps in removing the waste from the body in the form of urine and sweat.

Q. 17. ***What is goitre?***

Ans. Swelling at the front of the neck is a symptom of a disease called goitre, which is caused by the deficiency of iodine.

Q. 18. ***Name any 2 vitamins, their sources and deficiency diseases caused by them.***

Ans.

- **Vitamin A:** It is important for normal vision, healthy skin, growth and a healthy immune system. The deficiency of vitamin A can cause night blindness, poor vision. Foods rich in vitamin A are papaya, carrot, milk, mango, etc.
- **Vitamin C:** It is needed by the body to fight diseases. Deficiency of vitamin C can cause scurvy, a disease that is characterized by bleeding gums, and slow healing of wounds. Foods rich in vitamin C are amla, guava, Citrus fruits, chillies etc.

Q. 19. ***Which of the following food items does not provide any nutrient?*** (*NCERT Exemplar*)

Milk, Water, Orange juice, Tomato soup.

Ans. Water does not provide any nutrient.

Q. 20. ***Which mineral keeps our bones and teeth healthy ? Give sources of this mineral.***

Ans. Calcium keeps our bones and teeth healthy. Sources of calcium are milk or soya milk, curd, cheese, paneer.

Q. 21. ***Which vitamin helps our body in the absorption of calcium for making bones and teeth healthy? Name the disease caused by its deficiency. What are the sources of this vitamin ?***

Ans. Vitamin D helps our body absorb calcium for bone and teeth health. Vitamin D causes **Rickets**. Sources to obtain vitamin D are exposure to sunlight, milk, butter, fish and eggs.

3.3 HOW TO TEST DIFFERENT COMPONENTS OF FOOD?

Q. 1. ***How will you test for starch in a food sample?***

Ans.

- Take a small quantity of food samples.
- Then add 2-3 drops of iodine solution to it.
- The appearance of a blue-black colour indicates that the food sample contains starch.

Q. 2. ***What happens when two or more drops of iodine solution fall on starchy substance?***

Ans. The colour of the substance becomes blue-black.

Q. 3. ***If any food item gives blue-black colour with iodine then which nutrient is present in the food?***

Ans. Starch.

Q. 4. ***How can you test presence of proteins in a given food item?***

Ans. Take a small quantity of the food item. If the sample is solid, grind it. Put some part of this in a clean test tube, add 10 drops of water to it and shake the test tube. Now, with the help of a dropper, add two drops of solution of copper sulphate and 10 drops of solution of caustic soda to the test tube. Shake well and place the test tube in test tube stand for a few minutes. Observe colour of the contents of test tube. If colour of the contents turns violet, the food item contains protein.

Food + water + copper sulphate + caustic soda → violet colour → protein rich food.

Q. 5. ***Write test for detecting, presence of fat.***

Ans. Take small quantity of the food item. Rub it on a piece of white paper. Observe carefully, you will find that the piece of white paper shows an oily patch on it which indicates that the food item contains fat.

3.4 BALANCED DIET

Q. 1. *What is a balanced diet? Write the components of balanced diet.*

Ans. A diet which provides the right proportion of all the nutrients that our body needs along with roughage and water is called balanced diet. The various components of balanced diet are carbohydrates, fats, proteins, vitamins, minerals, roughage and water.

Q. 2. *What is junk food?*

Ans. Some foods have more calories due to high sugar and fat content. They contain very low amounts of proteins, minerals, vitamins, and dietary fibres. These foods are called junk foods. For example : Pizza, burger, chips and cold drinks etc.

Q. 3. *What are the health risks of consuming junk food?*

Ans. Junk food is full of calories, unhealthy fats, sugars, and sodium. It lacks essential nutrients. Regular consumption of junk food can lead to weight gain, increased risk of heart disease, diabetes, and other health problems.

Q. 4. *Are nutritional requirements the same for all humans ?*

Ans. No, nutritional requirements are not the same for everyone. It depends on age, gender, physical activity, health status and life style of humans.

3.5 MILLETS: NUTRITION-RICH CEREALS

Q. 1. *What are millets?*

Ans. Millets are small-sized grains. They are widely grown around the world and are known for their nutritional benefits.

Q. 2. *What are the nutritional benefits of millets? Why they are called nutri-cereals?*

Ans. Millets are good sources of vitamins, minerals like iron and calcium, and dietary fibres as well. That is the reason they are also called nutri-cereals.

Q. 3. *Name four millets. Is it easy to cultivate them?*

Ans. Four common millets are jowar, bajra, ragi and sanwa. These are native crops of India. These can be easily cultivated in different climatic conditions.

3.6 FOOD MILES: FROM FARM TO OUR PLATE

Q. 1. *What are food miles?*

Ans. Food miles refer to the distance food travels from where it is grown or produced to where it is consumed.

Q. 2. *How do food miles affect the environment?*

Ans. Food miles contribute to carbon emissions and pollution from transportation vehicles, impacting air quality and contributing to climate change.

Q. 3. *What are the ways to reduce food miles?*

Ans. Buying locally grown or produced food, supporting farmers' markets, and choosing seasonal produce are the ways to reduce food miles.

Q. 4. *Give an example of a food item with high food miles and one with low food miles.*

Ans. 1. High food miles example: Fresh strawberries imported from another continent.

2. Low food miles example: Apples or grapes grown in a nearby orchard and sold at a local farmers' market.

Q. 5. *Give examples of foods that are typically imported from other countries.*

Ans. These are tropical fruits like bananas or mangoes, coffee, tea, and certain spices.

Q. 6. *With the help of a flowchart, show various contributors involved when we eat a chapati.*

Ans.

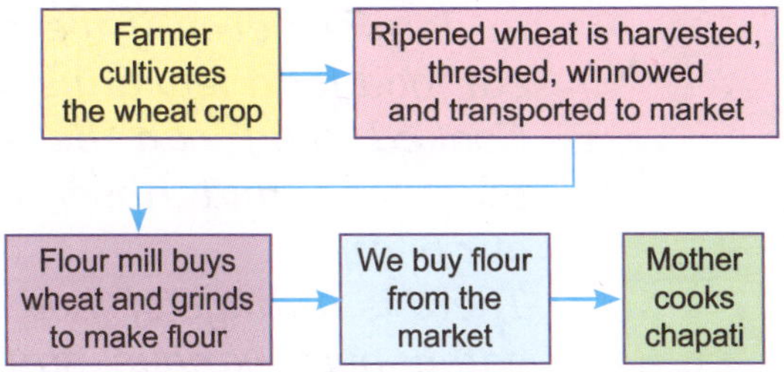

Flowchart

Q. 7. *Make flowchart for the preparation of honey.*

Ans.

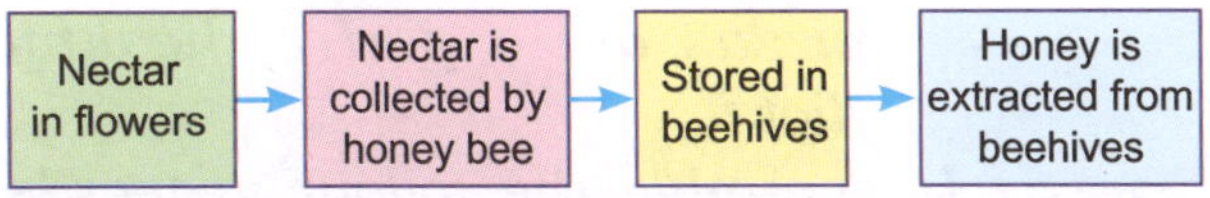

Q. 8. *Make flowchart for the preparation of ghee.*

Ans.

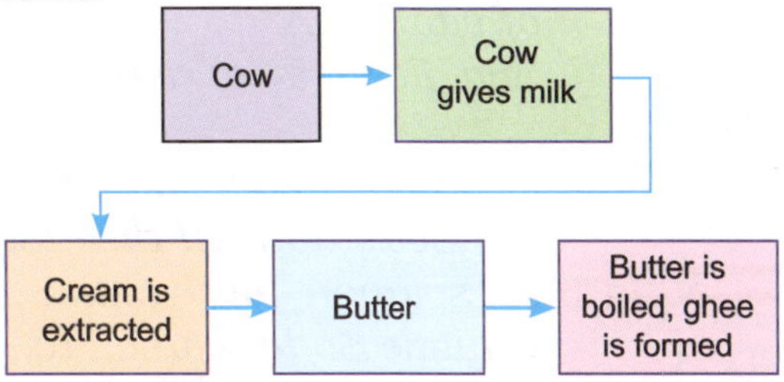

Q. 9. *Why reducing food miles is important?*

Ans. Reducing food miles is important because it

- helps to cut down the cost and pollution during transport.
- helps support local farmers.
- keeps our food more fresh and healthy.

V. OBJECTIVE TYPE QUESTIONS

1. *Match the following items given in Column A with that in Column B:*

Column A (Vitamin)	Column B (Disease)
(*a*) *Vitamin A*	(*i*) *Goitre*
(*b*) *Vitamin B_1*	(*ii*) *Scurvy*
(*c*) *Vitamin C*	(*iii*) *Rickets*
(*d*) *Vitamin D*	(*iv*) *Beri Beri*
(*e*) *Calcium*	(*v*) *Anaemia*
(*f*) *Iron*	(*vi*) *Bone and tooth decay*
(*g*) *Iodine*	(*vii*) *Loss of vision*

2. *Fill in the blanks with appropriate words:*

(*a*) *................ is caused by the deficiency of Vitamin D.*

(*b*) *Deficiency of................ causes a disease known as Beriberi.*

(*c*) *Deficiency of Vitamin C causes a disease known as ....*

(*d*) *Night blindness is caused due to deficiency of .... in our food.*

(*e*) *Egg yolk is rich in .... and egg albumin is rich in ....*

(*f*) *Deficiency diseases can be prevented by taking a ....*

(*g*) *Eating too many fat-rich foods may lead to a condition called ....*

(*h*) *The component of food that does not provide any nutrient to our body and yet is essential in our food is ....*

(*i*) *The vitamin that gets easily destroyed by heating during cooking is ....*

(j) *Spinach is a good source of the mineral ....*

(k) *............. (fruit) is a rich source of vitamin A.*

(l) *Sea Food is a rich source of ....*

(m) *............ helps in protecting our body against diseases.*

(n) *A solution of .... and Caustic Soda is used to detect the presence of proteins.*

(o) *Food containing .... are often called the body building foods.*

(p) *.......... keeps our skin healthy.*

(q) *........... is essential for forming haemoglobin in the blood.*

(r) *Wounds take longer time to heal when we have deficiency of ....*

(s) *............. for the body should contain a variety of food items.*

3. *Give one word answer:*

(a) The nutrients which mainly give energy to our body.

(b) The nutrients that are needed for the growth of our body.

(c) A vitamin required for maintaining good eyesight.

(d) A mineral that is required for keeping our bones healthy.

(e) Nails and hair are made up of

(f) Component of food that protects us from diseases.

4. *State whether the statements given below are True or False:*

(i) *By eating rice alone, we can fulfill the nutritional requirements of our body.*

(ii) *Deficiency diseases can be prevented by eating a balanced diet.*

(iii) *Balanced diet for the body should contain a variety of food items.*

(iv) *Meat alone is sufficient to provide all nutrients to the body.*

(v) *Different people have different choices of food.*

(vi) *If a person does not get food he feels weak and is likely to fall ill.*

(vii) *There is no effect on our ability to do work even if we do not eat food for a few days.*

(viii) *Cooked food can be easily consumed and absorbed by our body.*

(ix) *There is a range of food items eaten over various states of India.*

(x) *For every item that we eat there are a number of persons who have contributed.*

(xi) *Food items like burgers and pizzas are a part of healthy diet.*

5. *Unscramble the following words related to components of food and write them in the space provided:*

(a) Reinpot ____________

(b) menliars ____________

(c) tivanmi ____________

(d) bocatradhyers ____________

(e) nitesturn ____________

(f) tfa ____________

Multiple Choice Questions (MCQs)

Choose the correct option in the following questions

1. *Which of the following is a primary source of energy for the body?*

(a) Proteins (b) Fats

(c) Carbohydrates

(d) Vitamins

2. *Which region of India is known for dishes like dosa and idli?*

(a) Punjab (b) West Bengal

(c) Maharashtra (d) Tamil Nadu

3. *Which of the following foods is rich in proteins?*

(a) Apples (b) Spinach

(c) Milk (d) Rice

4. *What does "food miles" refer to?*
   (*a*) Distance travelled by food from farm to plate
   (*b*) Nutritional value of food
   (*c*) Number of meals consumed in a day
   (*d*) Amount of food waste
5. *Which cooking advancement is NOT part of modern methods?*
   (*a*) Gas stoves
   (*b*) Electric grinders
   (*c*) Sil-battas
   (*d*) Microwave ovens
6. *Which vitamin is crucial for the absorption of calcium?*
   (*a*) A (*b*) B
   (*c*) C (*d*) D
7. *Which of the following is a rich source of dietary fibres?*
   (*a*) Milk (*b*) Butter
   (*c*) Brown rice (*d*) Chicken
8. *Which region of India is known for the dish "vada pav"?*
   (*a*) Punjab
   (*b*) Tamil Nadu
   (*c*) West Bengal
   (*d*) Maharashtra
9. *What are millets known for?*
   (*a*) Being a source of fats
   (*b*) Being easy to cultivate and highly nutritious
   (*c*) Being a type of fruit
   (*d*) Being a source of vitamins only
10. *Which of the following is used to test the presence of starch in food?* (*NCERT Exemplar*)
   (*a*) Iodine solution
   (*b*) Copper sulphate
   (*c*) Caustic soda
   (*d*) Litmus paper
11. *Which one of the following food items does not provide dietary fibre?* (*NCERT Exemplar*)
   (*a*) Whole grains
   (*b*) Whole pulses
   (*c*) Fruits and vegetables
   (*d*) Milk
12. *Which of the following sources of protein is different from others?* (*NCERT Exemplar*)
   (*a*) Peas (*b*) Gram
   (*c*) Soybeans
   (*d*) Cottage cheese (paneer)
13. *Which of the following nutrients is not present in milk?* (*NCERT Exemplar*)
   (*a*) Protein (*b*) Vitamin C
   (*c*) Calcium (*d*) Vitamin D
14. *Read the food items given below:* (*NCERT Exemplar*)
   (*i*) Wheat (*ii*) Ghee
   (*iii*) Iodised salt
   (*iv*) Spinach (palak)
   Which of the above food items are "energy-giving foods"?
   (*a*) (*i*) and (*iv*)
   (*b*) (*ii*) and (*iv*)
   (*c*) (*i*) and (*ii*)
   (*d*) (*iii*) and (*iv*)
15. *Read the following statements about diseases.* (*NCERT Exemplar*)
   (*i*) They are caused by germs.
   (*ii*) They are caused due to a lack of nutrients in our diet.
   (*iii*) They can be passed on to another person through contact.
   (*iv*) They can be prevented by taking a balanced diet.

Which pair of statements best describes a deficiency disease?

(*a*) (*i*) and (*ii*)

(*b*) (*ii*) and (*iii*)

(*c*) (*ii*) and (*iv*)

(*d*) (*i*) and (*iii*)

16. *Given below are the steps to test the presence of proteins in a food item:*

(*i*) Take a small quantity of the food item in a test tube, add 10 drops of water to it and shake it.

(*ii*) Make a paste or powder of food to be tested.

(*iii*) Add 10 drops of caustic soda solution to the test tube and shake well.

(*iv*) Add 2 drops of copper sulphate solution to it.

Which of the following is the correct sequence of the steps?

(*a*) (*i*), (*ii*), (*iv*), (*iii*)

(*b*) (*ii*), (*i*), (*iv*), (*iii*)

(*c*) (*ii*), (*i*), (*iii*), (*iv*)

(*d*) (*iv*), (*ii*), (*i*), (*iii*)

ANSWERS

1.

Column A	Column B
(*a*) *Vitamin A*	(*vii*) Loss of vision
(*b*) *Vitamin B_1*	(*iv*) Beri Beri
(*c*) *Vitamin C*	(*ii*) Scurvy
(*d*) *Vitamin D*	(*iii*) Rickets
(*e*) *Calcium*	(*vi*) Bone and tooth decay
(*f*) *Iron*	(*v*) Anaemia
(*g*) *Iodine*	(*i*) Goitre

2. Fill in the blanks:

(*a*) Rickets (*b*) Vitamin B_1 (*c*) Scurvy (*d*) Vitamin A

(*e*) Fat, protein (*f*) Balanced diet (*g*) Obesity (*h*) Roughage

(*i*) Vitamin C (*j*) Iron (*k*) Papaya (*l*) Iodine

(*m*) Vitamins (*n*) Copper sulphate (*o*) Proteins (*p*) Vitamin A

(*q*) Iron (*r*) Vitamin C (*s*) Balanced diet

3. (*a*) Carbohydrates (*b*) Proteins (*c*) Vitamin A (*d*) Calcium
   (*e*) Protein (*f*) Vitamins
4. True or False:
   (*i*) False (*ii*) True (*iii*) True (*iv*) False (*v*) True
   (*vi*) True (*vii*) False (*viii*) True (*ix*) True (*x*) True
   (*xi*) False
5. (*a*) Protein (*b*) Minerals (*c*) Vitamin (*d*) Carbohydrates
   (*e*) Nutrients (*f*) Fat

Multiple Choice Questions (MCQs)

1. (*c*) 2. (*d*) 3. (*c*) 4. (*a*) 5. (*c*) 6. (*d*) 7. (*c*) 8. (*d*) 9. (*b*) 10. (*a*)
11. (*d*) 12. (*d*) 13. (*b*) 14. (*c*) 15. (*c*) 16. (*b*)

VI. EXERCISE FOR PRACTICE

1. 'Water does not provide nutrients, yet it is an important component of food.' Explain?
2. Name two plant food items which provide proteins.
3. Name two sources of proteins provided by animals.
4. List various types of nutrients and write the functions of each.
5. Write two sources of Vitamin C.
6. Explain in detail carbohydrates studied by you.
7. Which disease will you suffer from, if you eat a lot of fat?
8. Which nutrient is required the most by a growing child and why?
9. Name two foods, each rich in:
   (*a*) Fats (*b*) Starch
   (*c*) Dietary fibre (*d*) Protein
10. Why is fibre important in your diet? Name two sources of dietary fibre.
11. What are vitamins and minerals? Why are they important for your body? Provide an example of a vitamin and a mineral and explain their functions.
12. Why is it important to have a balanced diet? Give examples of foods from different food groups that contribute to a balanced diet.
13. Explain the different food groups.
14. What are energy giving foods? Give two examples of energy giving food.
15. Write the name of any two sources of vitamins B and C.
16. What is the function of roughage in our body?
17. What is the function of fats in our body?
18. Name two food items in which vitamin A is found.
19. Give two benefits of cooking food.
20. Write the main symptoms of vitamin C deficiency (or scurvy).
21. Name the disease caused by the deficiency of proteins in the diet of children.

INTERESTING MIND MAP

Exploring Magnets

1 Magnetic and Non-magnetic Materials

- A magnet attracts **magnetic** materials. E.g. Iron.
- A magnet does not attract **non-magnetic** materials. E.g. Wood.

2 Poles of Magnet

- A magnet has a north pole and a south pole. A magnet with only one pole does not exist.

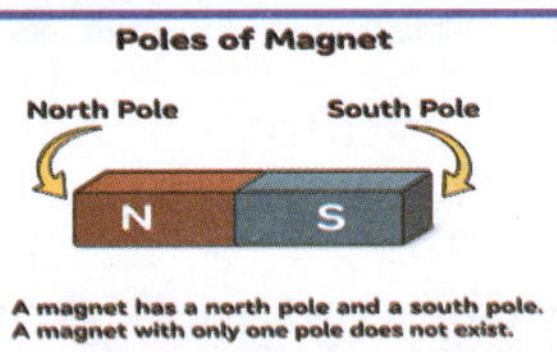

3 Finding Directions

- Resting of a freely suspended magnet in the North-South direction (its north pole points to north direction and its south pole points to south direction) helps to find direction.

4 Attraction and Repulsion between Magnets

- Similar poles of two magnets repel. E.g. North pole and North pole or South pole and South pole of two different magnets repel each other.
- **Different poles attract** each other. E.g. North pole and South pole of two different magnets attract each other.

5 Fun with Magnets

- A magnet can take out a paper clip fallen in a glass of water without touching it.

4

Exploring Magnets

I. POINTS TO REMEMBER

1. **Magnet:** Magnets are rocks or metals that create an invisible field (magnetic field) around themselves. Magnets attract or get attracted towards magnetic materials.
2. **Uses of a magnet:** A magnet is used at many places. For example, refrigerator's door, some pencil boxes, many toys, magnetic stickers, soap stand, pin stand.

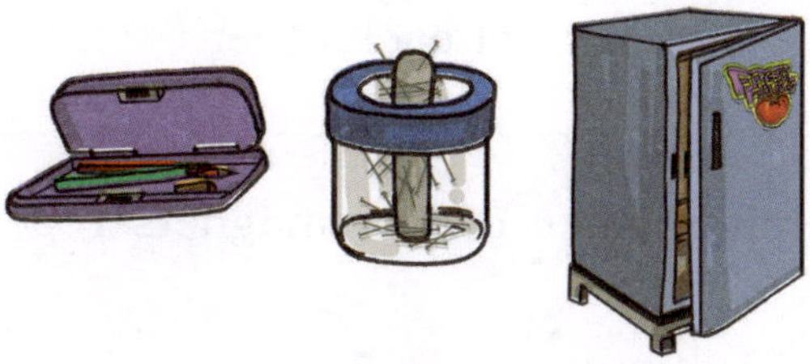

Fig. Uses of magnet

3. **Shapes of magnets:** Magnets are made in different shapes; Bar magnet, U-shaped (horseshoe) magnet, cylindrical magnet, disc magnet, ring magnet or spherical magnet.

Fig. Shapes of magnets

4. **Magnetic materials:** The materials which get attracted towards the magnet are known as magnetic materials, *e.g.*, iron, nickel, cobalt.
5. **Non-magnetic materials:** The materials which are not attracted towards the magnet are known as non-magnetic materials, *e.g.*, leather, plastic, cloth, paper.
6. **Magnetic poles:** All magnets have two poles: a north pole and a south pole. Magnetic poles always exist in pairs. If a bar magnet is broken into two, each piece will have a north and south pole.
7. Magnetic attraction is maximum near the ends of the magnet. These ends are called **magnetic poles.**

Fig. Magnetic poles

8. A freely suspended magnet will always come to rest in North-South direction.

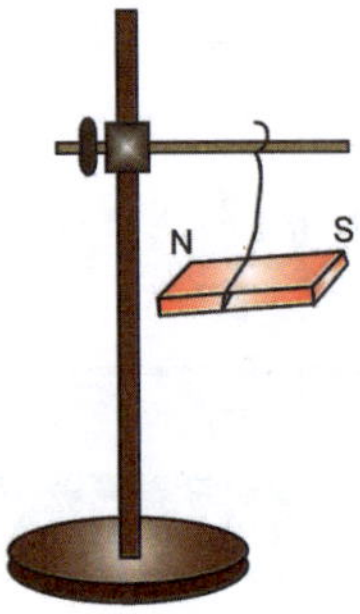

Fig. A freely suspended magnet

9. The end of the magnet that points towards the North direction is called **North-seeking pole** or **North pole** of the magnet. The other end points towards the South direction and is called **South-seeking pole** or **South pole** of the magnet.

10. **Lodestone:** **Naturally occurring magnets** called lodestones were discovered in ancient times. These were also used by sailors in olden days for finding directions.

11. **Compass:** This device is made of a small glass case containing a magnetised needle pivoted on a nail. The needle can rotate freely. Its needle always rests in north-south direction. Normally the north-pole of the needle is painted red or some other indication is given to identify north and south-poles. Using this device, north and south directions can be identified.

Fig. Magnetic compass

12. **Attraction between two poles:** Opposite poles of two magnets attract each other.

13. **Repulsion between two poles:** Similar poles of two magnets repel each other.

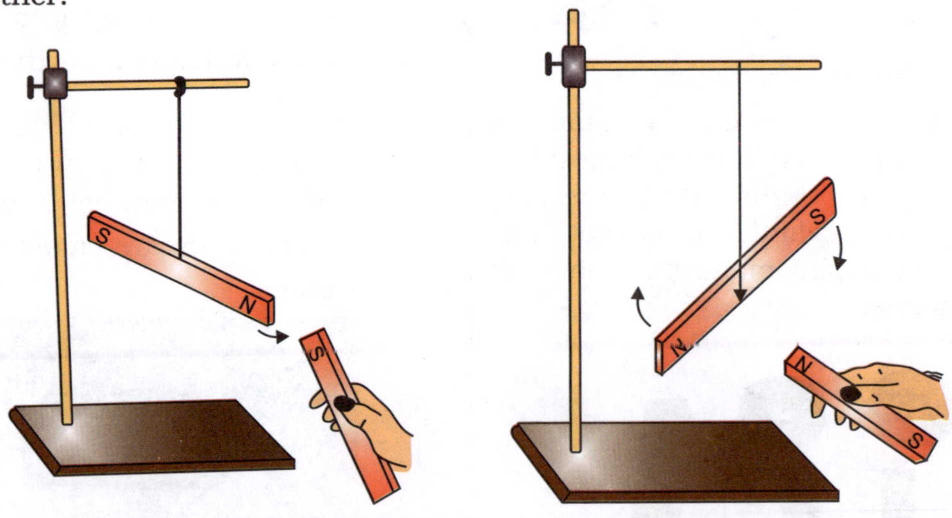

(*a*) Unlike poles attract each other (*b*) Like poles repel each other

Fig. Attraction and repulsion between two poles

14. Magnets lose their magnetic properties when they are heated, hammered or dropped.

Fig. Magnets lose their property on heating, hammering and dropping

15. We can magnetise an iron needle. Same (one) pole of a magnet when moved over the needle along its length repeatedly (in the same direction) 30–40 times, magnetises the needle.

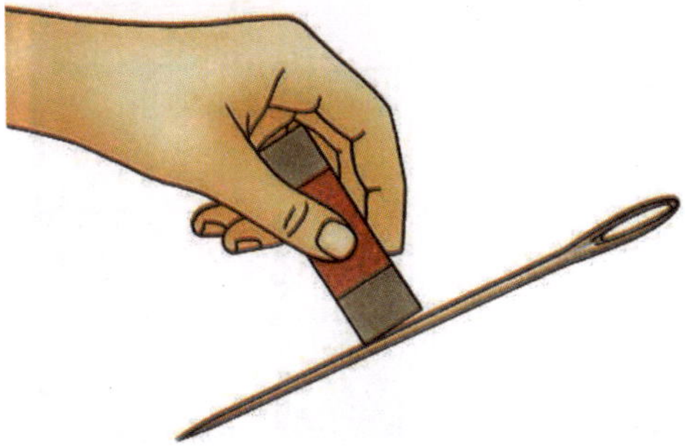

Fig. Making an iron needle a magnet

16. To keep them safe, bar magnets should be kept in pairs with their unlike poles on the same side. They must be separated by a piece of wood while two pieces of soft iron should be placed across their ends. For U-shaped (horseshoe) magnet, one should keep a piece of iron across the poles.

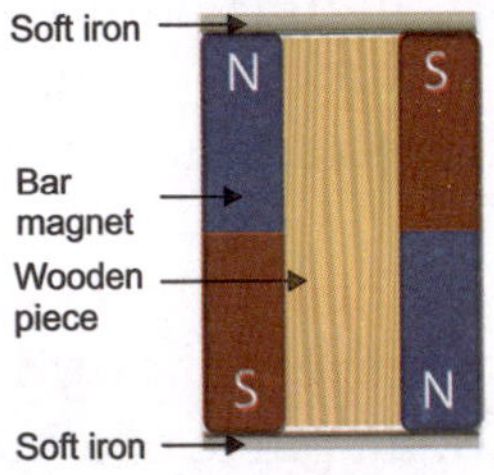

Fig. Store your magnets safely

II. KEYWORDS

1. **Attraction:** When two or more things tend to come closer. e.g. the north pole of a magnet is attracted to the south pole of another magnet.
2. **Bar magnet:** A magnet that is in the shape of a rectangular bar.
3. **Magnetic compass:** Device with a freely moving magnetic needle, used for finding directions.
4. **Magnetic materials:** Materials attracted by magnets and which can be used to make magnets.
5. **Non-magnetic materials:** Materials not attracted by magnets.
6. **North pole of a magnet:** A pole of a magnet also called north-seeking pole that points towards north direction when the freely suspended magnet comes to rest.

7. **Repulsion:** When two or more things tend to move away from each other e.g. the north pole of a magnet is repelled by the north pole of another magnet.

8. **Ring magnet:** Any round magnet that has a central hole.

9. **South pole of a magnet:** A pole of a magnet also called south-seeking pole that points towards south direction when the freely suspended magnet comes to rest.

10. **U-shaped magnet:** Any magnet that has a U shape.

III. NCERT INTEXT QUESTIONS

Q. 1. *Do magnets stick to objects made of certain materials only?*

(Page 62)

Ans. Yes, magnets attract certain materials. The materials which get attracted towards a magnet are called magnetic materials e.g. iron, nickel, cobalt etc. The materials which are not attracted towards a magnet are called non-magnetic materials. In their natural states, metals such as aluminium, brass, copper, gold, lead and silver do not attract magnets.

Q. 2. *Do all parts of a magnet attract magnetic materials equally?* *(Page 64)*

Ans. No, all parts of a magnet do not have equal magnetic strength. In a bar magnet, the magnetic field around the poles is stronger than the middle part, where the magnetic field is weaker. Also in case of U-shaped (horseshoe) magnet, the magnetic strength is higher near the poles.

Q. 3. *Can we find a magnet with a single pole?* *(Page 65)*

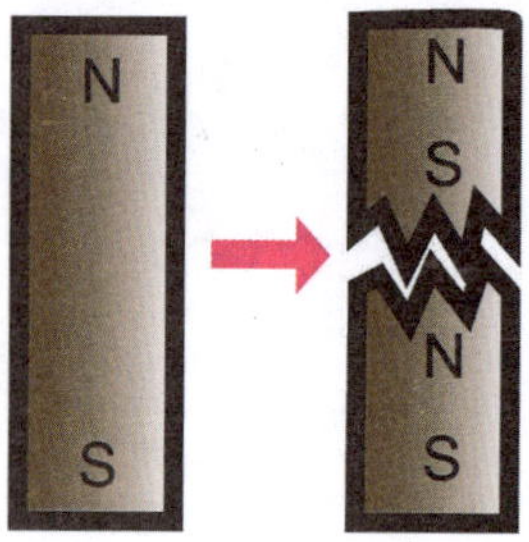

Ans. No, all magnets always have two poles namely north and south. If a magnet is broken into smaller pieces, North and South poles always exist in pairs even in the smallest piece of a magnet. A single North pole or a South pole cannot exist.

IV. LET US ENHANCE OUR LEARNING *(PAGES 74–76)*

Q. 1. *Fill in the blanks*

(*i*) Unlike poles of two magnets ________ each other, whereas like poles ______ each other.

(*ii*) The materials that are attracted towards a magnet are called ______________.

(*iii*) The needle of a magnetic compass rests along the _______ direction.

(*iv*) A magnet always has ________ poles.

Ans. (*i*) attract, repel
(*ii*) magnetic materials
(*iii*) north-south
(*iv*) two

Q. 2. ***State whether the following statements are True (T) or False (F).***

(*i*) A magnet can be broken into pieces to obtain a single pole. [ ]

(*ii*) Similar poles of a magnet repel each other. [ ]

(*iii*) Iron filings mostly stick in the middle of a bar magnet when it is brought near them. [ ]

(*iv*) A freely suspended bar magnet always aligns with the north-south direction. [ ]

Ans. (*i*) F (*ii*) T (*iii*) F (*iv*) T

Q. 3. ***Column I shows different positions in which one pole of a magnet is placed near that of the other. Column II indicates the resulting action between them for each situation. Fill in the blanks.***

Column I	Column II
N – N	....
N – ...	Attraction
S – N	....
... – S	Repulsion

Ans.

Column I	Column II
N – N	Repulsion
N – S	Attraction
S – N	Attraction
S – S	Repulsion

Q. 4. ***Atharv performed an experiment in which he took a bar magnet and rolled it over a heap of steel U-clips (Fig.)***

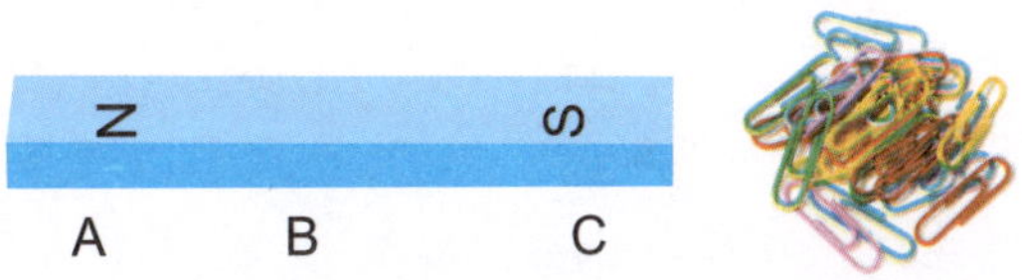

Fig. Bar magnet and heap of steel U-clips

According to you, which of the options given in Table is likely to be his observation?

Table: Number of pins attracted by the magnet at its various positions

	Position A	Position B	Position C
(i)	10	2	10
(ii)	10	10	2
(iii)	2	10	10
(iv)	10	10	10

Ans. The strength of the magnetic field of a magnet is maximum at its poles (positions A and C in the figure). Therefore, more U-clips will be attracted to A and C positions compared to position B.

Hence option (*i*) is correct.

Q. 5. ***Reshma bought three identical metal bars from the market. Out of these bars, two were magnets and one was just a piece of iron. How will she identify which two amongst the three could be magnets (without using any other material)?***

Ans. If one pole of a magnet is brought near another magnet it will either attract or repel the other magnet. But if it is brought near a bar of a magnetic material (not a magnet), it will only attract the bar and not repel.

Step 1: Reshma has to bring one end of the first bar near one end of the second bar. In case, the two bars repel each other, both first and second bars are magnets and third bar is not a magnet.

In case the bars attract each other then:

Step 2: She has to bring the other end of the first bar close to the **same end** of the second bar. In case of repulsion the first and the second bars are confirmed to be magnets.

In case the two bars again attract each other then:

CHAPTER-4

Step 3: She has to repeat the activity in step 1 and step 2 using first and the third bar. In case repulsion is observed in step 1 or in step 2, first and third bars are confirmed to be magnets and second bar is not a magnet.

In case attraction is observed in these two steps again then second bar and third bar are confirmed to be magnets and first bar is not a magnet.

The result can be checked again using second and third bar in step 1 and step 2. Bars will repel each other in either step 1 or in step 2.

Q. 6. ***You are given a magnet which does not have the poles marked. How can you find its poles with the help of another magnet which has its poles marked?***

Ans. To find the poles of an unmarked magnet, bring one end of the marked magnet near one end of the unmarked magnet. If they attract, the unmarked magnet's end is the opposite pole (i.e., if the marked North pole attracts, then the unmarked end is South pole). If they repel, then the poles are similar.

Q. 7. ***A bar magnet has no markings to indicate its poles. How would you find out near which end its North pole is located without using another?***

Ans. When a bar magnet is suspended freely, it always rests in north-south direction. The end pointing towards north is called north-seeking end or the north-pole and the end pointing towards south is called south-seeking end or the south pole of the magnet.

Q. 8. ***If the earth is itself a magnet, can you guess the poles of earth's magnet by looking at the direction of the magnetic compass?***

Ans. Yes, we can guess the poles of Earth's magnet by looking at the direction of the magnetic compass. The north-seeking end of the compass needle points towards the geographic North Pole of the Earth.

Q. 9. ***While a mechanic was repairing a gadget using a screw driver, the steel screws kept falling down. Suggest a way to solve the problem of the mechanic on the basis of what you have learnt in this chapter.***

Ans. The mechanic needs to magnetise his screw driver which will not just lift the screw but hold it in place while he works.

To magnetise a screw driver he needs a magnet. He is advised to, "place the screw driver on a wooden table. Then keep one end (pole) of the magnet at one end of the metallic part of the screw driver. Move the magnet along the length of the metallic part of screw driver. Lift it and bring the same pole of magnet to the same end of screw driver he began, and repeat moving it over the length of the screw driver. On repeating this process about 30 times the screw driver will get magnetised".

Q. 10. ***Two ring magnets X and Y are arranged as shown in Fig. (on next page). It is observed that the magnet X does not move down further. What could be the possible reason? Suggest a way to bring the magnet X in contact with magnet Y, without pushing either of the magnets.***

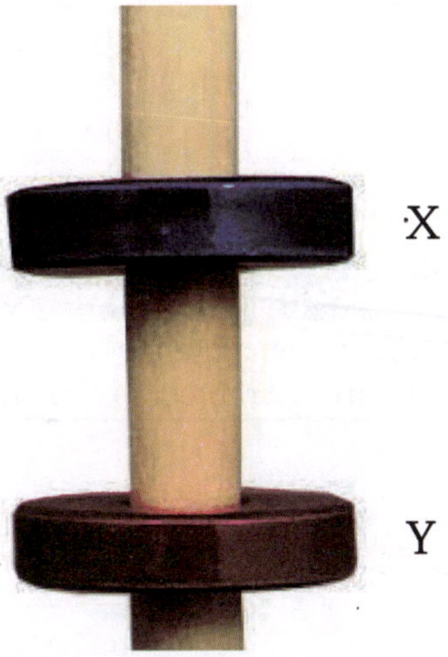

Fig. Two ring magnets

Ans. Magnet X must be floating because the like poles are facing each other (like poles repel each other). If we change the direction of the magnet X by rotating it, the unlike poles will face each other and the magnets will come closer.

Q. 11. ***Three magnets are arranged on a table in the form of the shape shown in Fig. (below). What is the polarity, N or S, at the ends 1, 2, 3, 4 and 6 of the magnets? Polarity of one end (5) is given for you.***

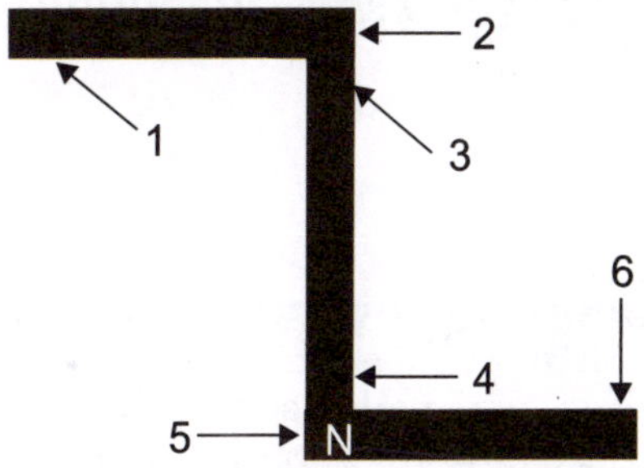

Fig. Three bar magnets

Ans.

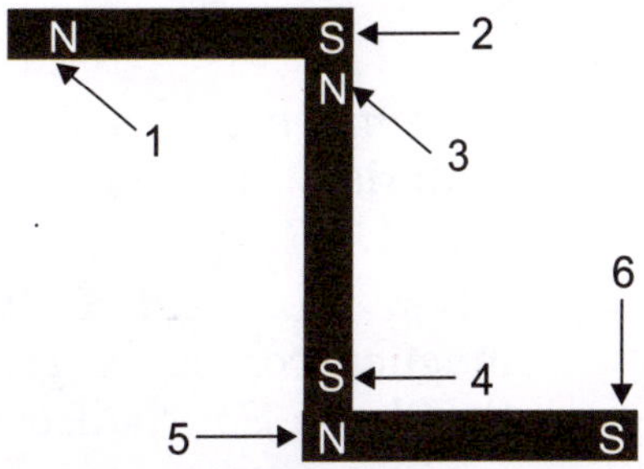

Point	Polarity
1	N
2	S
3	N
4	S
6	S

V. EXAM ORIENTED QUESTIONS

4.1. MAGNETIC AND NON-MAGNETIC MATERIALS

Very Short Answer Type Questions

Q. 1. ***What are magnetic materials (substances)?***

Ans. Materials which get attracted by the magnet are called magnetic materials (substances).

Q. 2. ***What are non-magnetic substances?***

Ans. Substances which are not attracted by magnet are called non-magnetic substances.

Q. 3. ***Write the names of some non-magnetic substances.***

Ans. Rubber, Cotton, Plastic, Wood, Cloth, etc.

Q. 4. ***Name the first magnet.***

Ans. Lodestone.

Q. 5. ***What is lodestone?***

Ans. Lodestone is a stone that has the properties of attracting magnetic materials. It is also called a Natural Magnet.

Short Answer Type Questions

Q. 1. ***Make a list of given substances into two groups—*** *magnetic* ***and*** *non-magnetic.*

Key, Wood, Glass, Pin, Chalk, Pencil, Nail, Cup of tea, Book, Rubber, Needle, Fork.

Ans.

Magnetic substances	Non-magnetic substances
Key, pin, nail, needle, fork (because all these are attracted to the magnet)	Wood, glass, chalk, pencil, cup of tea, book, rubber. (none of these are attracted to the magnet)

Q. 2. ***What are the properties of a magnet?***

Ans.

(*i*) A magnet attracts all magnetic materials like iron, nickel cobalt.

(*ii*) When suspended freely, a magnet comes to rest along the North-South direction.

(*iii*) A magnet always has two poles North pole and South pole.

(*iv*) Strength of magnetic field is maximum at the poles and minimum at the center.

Q. 3. ***What are soft and hard magnetic materials?***

Ans. Soft iron is called soft magnetic material because it loses its magnetism easily. Soft iron is used in making electromagnets.

Steel is called a 'hard' magnetic material because it does not lose its magnetism so easily. It is used to make permanent magnets.

Q. 4. ***How will you test that 'tea dust' is not adulterated with iron powder?*** *(NCERT Exemplar)*

Ans. We will test that 'tea dust' is not adulterated with iron powder by using magnet. If it has iron powder, iron powder will stick onto the magnet.

Long Answer Type Questions

Q. 1. ***Four identical iron bars were dipped in a heap of iron filings one by one. Fig. shows the amount of iron filings sticking to each of them.*** *(NCERT Exemplar)*

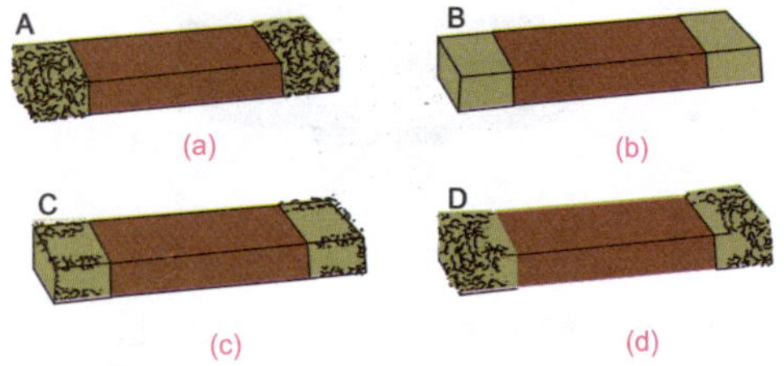

(a) *Which of the iron bar is likely to be the strongest magnet?*

(b) *Which of the iron bars is not a magnet? Justify your answer.*

Ans.

(*a*) Iron bar 'A' is the strongest magnet because maximum iron filings stick to its poles.

(*b*) Iron bar B is not a magnet because there are no iron filings sticking to it.

Q. 2. ***Suggest an arrangement to store a U shaped magnet. How is this different from storing a pair of bar magnets?*** *(NCERT Exemplar)*

Ans. U shaped magnet –One metal plate is placed across the two poles of the U shaped magnet.

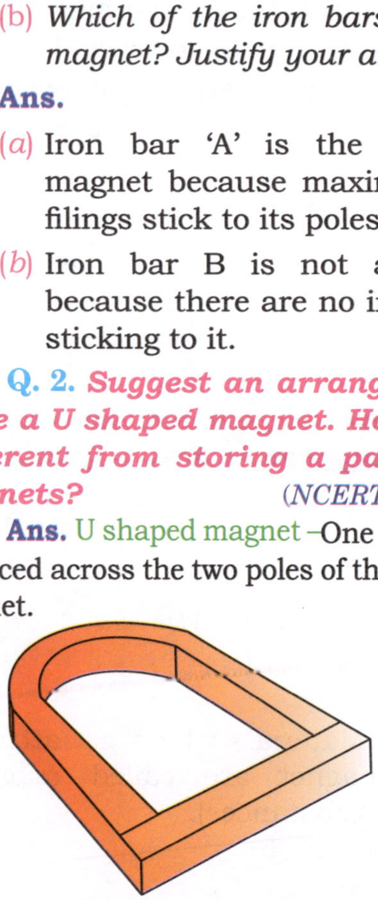

Bar magnet – Use two metal plates and one wooden block, arrange them as shown in the figure.

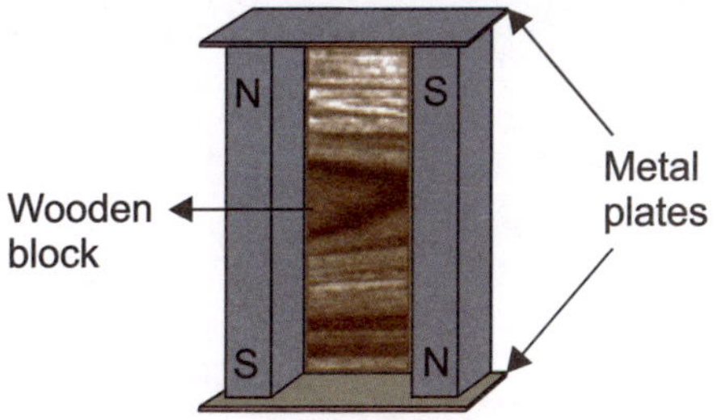

4.2. POLES OF MAGNET

Very Short Answer Type Questions

Q. 1. *Fill in the blanks:*

(i) *When a suspended magnet comes to rest, one pole always points towards the ....*

(ii) *And the other pole always points towards the ....*

Ans. (*i*) North (*ii*) South

Q. 2. *How many poles are there in a magnet?*

Ans. There are two poles in a magnet, North-pole and South-pole.

Q. 3. *To which part of the magnet do the most of the iron filings (or pins) stick?*

Ans. Most of the iron filings (or pins) stick to the poles, *i.e.,* North and South poles. At the poles of magnet, magnetic effect is the maximum.

Q. 4. *To which part of the magnet do none or only a few iron filings (or pins) stick?*

Ans. Minimum number of iron filings stick to the middle part of the magnet. Magnet has its magnetic effect least in this part (middle part).

Q. 5. *Are both poles of a magnet similar?*

Ans. No, the two poles of a magnet are not similar (alike). The pole that points towards the north is called north-pole while the pole pointing always towards the south is called south-pole.

Q. 6. *Which is the north-pole of a bar magnet?*

Ans. When a bar magnet is suspended free to rotate, it comes to rest in North-South direction. The end of the bar magnet that faces geographic North is the North-seeking pole or the North pole.

Q. 7. *Which is the south-pole of a bar magnet?*

Ans. When a bar magnet is suspended free to rotate, it comes to rest in North-South direction. The end of the bar magnet that faces geographic South direction is the South-seeking pole or South pole.

Short Answer Type Questions

Q. 1. *Why does a freely suspended magnet always rest in the north-south direction ?*

Ans. Our earth is a huge magnet that has two poles North pole in North direction and South pole in South direction. A freely suspended magnet always comes to rest, in the North-South direction due to magnetic effect of the Earth. It is a convention to name the pole of the magnet that faces geographic North, as North pole of the magnet. The pole of the magnet that faces geographic South is called South pole.

Q. 2. *Can we isolate north-pole or south-pole?*

Ans. No, we cannot isolate north-pole of a magnet from its south-pole or *vice versa.* If you break a bar magnet into two halves, you will not get a single north or south pole but two magnets each with its north and south-poles.

Q. 3. *What happens when a pole of a bar magnet say its north-pole is marked with a chalk and suspended freely? What do you observe on rotating the bar magnet?*

Ans. The marked pole comes to rest in north direction. On rotating, it again comes to rest in north direction.

Long Answer Type Questions

Q. 1. *Do magnetic poles exist separately like charges? Explain.*

Ans. Magnetic poles do not exist separately like positive and negative charges. This means that it is not possible to isolate a north pole of a magnet from its south pole by cutting the magnet from the middle. Whenever a bar magnet is cut into two halves, we get two new magnets, each with its north and south poles. This will continue indefinitely even if extremely small pieces of bar magnets are obtained. Thus magnetic poles always exist in pairs.

Q. 2. *Where are the poles of a ring magnet? How will you find this?*

Ans. Ring magnets are flat circular magnets with hole in the center. Ring magnets can be magnetised:

(*i*) **Axially:** The two magnetic poles are on the top and bottom of the flat circular surfaces.

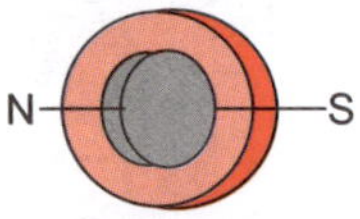

(*ii*) **Radially:** The poles extend to an inner circle and an outer circle.

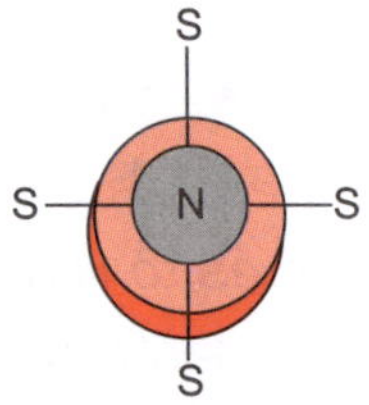

Fig. Ring Magnet

(*iii*) **Laterally:** The two poles extend on lateral sides of the ring magnet.

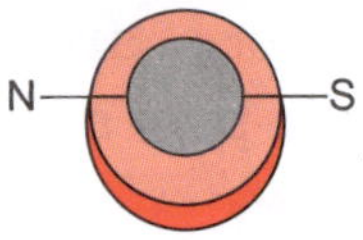

Q. 3. *Mark the north-poles of two bar magnets and bring the poles of the magnets near each other, and note down your observations in table.*

Ans.

Poles, facing one another	They are called	We observe
North-South	Opposite poles	Attraction
North-North	Similar poles	Repulsion
South-South	Similar poles	Repulsion
South-North	Opposite poles	Attraction

Q. 4. *What will happen to the magnet when we cut it into two pieces?*

Ans. When we cut a bar magnet into two pieces, both these pieces act as magnets and we get two magnets (Fig.).

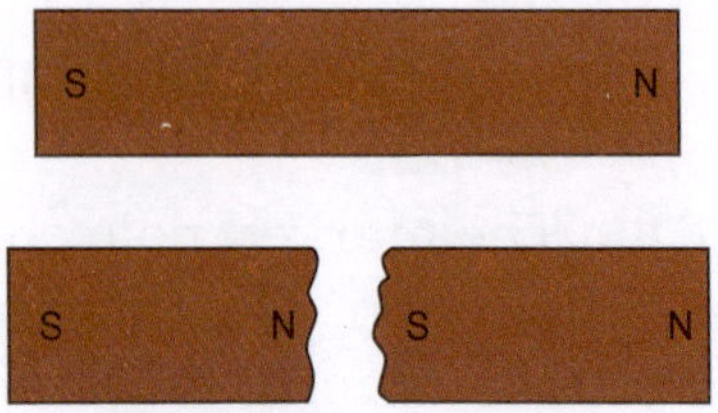

Fig. Magnet

Q. 5 (*i*) *A toy car has a bar magnet laid hidden inside its body along its length. Using another magnet how will you find out which pole of the magnet is facing the front of the car?*

(*ii*) *You are provided with two identical metal bars. One out of the two is a magnet. Suggest two ways to identify the magnet.* (*NCERT Exemplar*)

Ans.

(*i*) If the front of the toy car gets attracted to the north pole of the given magnet then it is the south pole of the bar magnet hidden inside the car. On the other hand, if it repels, then it has a north pole in front.

(*ii*) Two ways to identify the magnet are:

1. By suspending the metal bars
2. By attracting iron filings.

4.3. FINDING DIRECTIONS

Very Short Answer Type Questions

Q. 1. *In which direction does freely suspended magnet rest?*

Ans. A freely suspended magnet always points in the north-south direction.

Q. 2. *How do the shipmen find the direction even when north pointing pole star is not visible?*

Ans. Shipmen during navigation can find the direction with the help of magnetic needle.

Short Answer Type Questions

Q. 1. *Why is compass needle kept in a closed glass vessel?*

Ans. Compass needle is a small and thin magnet used to find the directions. If it is kept in open, it may deflect in any direction due to pressure exerted by air. So to know right direction, it is kept covered by glass covering.

Q. 2. *Does the compass needle point in different directions?*

Ans. The compass needle has a magnetic needle closed in a glass covering. The needle is mounted on a pin on which it can rotate freely. Its red marked end always indicates towards the north direction. It always rests in north-south directions. We use it to find out the direction.

Q. 3. *Hang a bar magnet with a thread on a stand and rotate the base of stand. What will happen?*

Ans. The direction of bar magnet is not changed as we rotate the stand. It is because a freely suspended magnet comes to rest in particular direction, *i.e.*, north-south directions.

Long Answer Type Questions

Q. 1. Fig. shows a magnetic compass. *What will happen to the position of its needle if you bring a bar magnet near it? Draw a diagram to show the effect on the needle on bringing the bar magnet near it. Also draw the diagram to show the effect when the other end of the bar magnet is brought near it.*

(*NCERT Exemplar*)

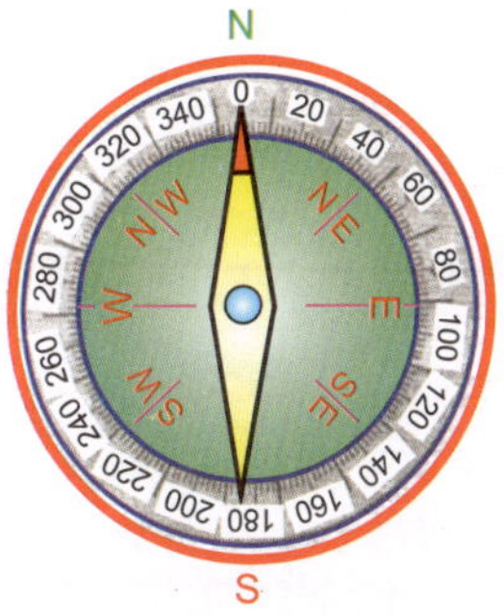

Fig.

Ans. The magnetic needle of the compass will get deflected.

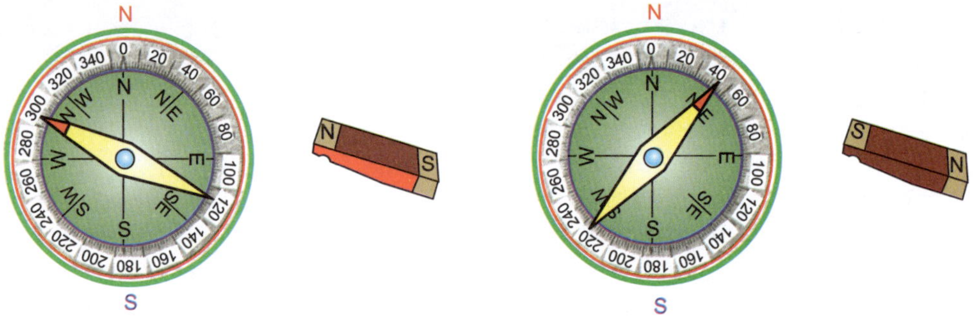

4.4. ATTRACTION AND REPULSION BETWEEN MAGNETS

Very Short Answer Type Questions

Q. 1. ***What happens when similar poles of two magnets come close to each other?***

Ans. They repel each other.

Q. 2. ***When do two magnets attract each other?***

Ans. Two magnets attract each other when their unlike (opposite) poles come close to each other.

Q. 3. ***What do you mean by magnetic field?***

Ans. The region around the magnet where its magnetic influence can be felt is called the magnetic field of the magnet.

Short Answer Type Questions

Q. 1. ***Boojho kept a magnet close to an ordinary iron bar. He observed that the iron bar attracts a pin as shown in Fig.*** *(NCERT Exemplar)*

Fig.

What inference could he draw from this observation? Explain.

Ans. The inference he could draw from this observation is that the magnetic properties are induced into the iron bar and it acts like a magnet.

Q. 2. ***A bar magnet is cut into two pieces A and B, from the middle, as shown in Fig.*** *(NCERT Exemplar)*

Fig.

Will the two pieces act as individual magnets? Mark the poles of these two pieces. Suggest an activity to verify your answer.

Ans. Yes, by the test of repulsion.

Long Answer Type Questions

Q. 1. *How can you show that unlike poles attract each other while like poles repel each other?*

Ans. Suspend a magnet on a stand with the help of a string. Now it rests in N-S directions. Take another magnet which has been marked N-S on it and bring N-pole of this magnet near the N-pole of the suspended magnet. You will find that the suspended magnet rotates and moves away showing that like poles repel each other. The same can be observed by bringing south-pole of one magnet near south-pole of suspended magnet.

It can be repeated by bringing south-pole near a north-pole and north-pole near south-pole of suspended magnet. You will find that unlike poles attract each other.

Q. 2. *Bhawana witnessed an interesting game at the fair. A duck was floating in a tub. When a plate containing some grains of rice was brought close to the duck, the duck moved towards the plate. But, when a plate containing some pebbles was brought close to the duck, it moved away from the plate. Explain how this could have been possible.*

Ans. A bar magnet is fixed under the toy duck. The front side of the duck has the pole that is known to the person playing the game. The plates containing grains of rice and pebbles also have magnets fixed under them. When a plate containing rice is brought near the front end of the duck, the pole of the magnet under the plate is selected opposite to the pole of the magnet under the duck. The duck is attracted towards the plate.

When the plate containing pebbles is brought close to the duck, the pole similar to the pole of the magnet under the front of the duck is brought near. The duck is repelled and moves away.

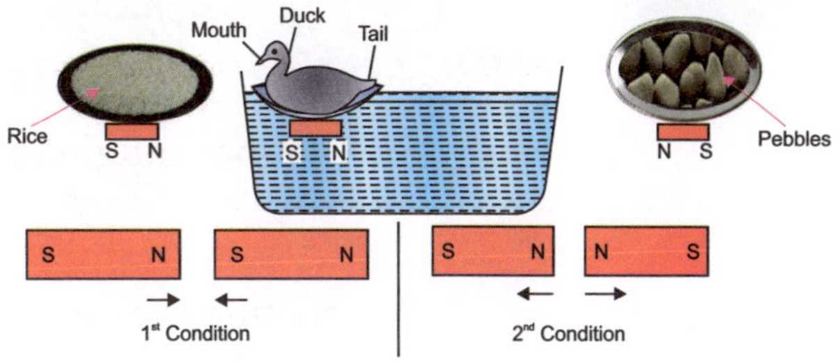

Fig. Magnet based game

4.5. FUN WITH MAGNETS

Very Short Answer Type Questions

Q. 1. *Why should we not heat or hammer a magnet?*

Ans. By heating or hammering, a magnet may loose its magnetic property. It is thus advised not to heat or hammer a magnet.

Q. 2. *Why magnets should be kept away from mobiles, computer and compact disks (CDs)?*

Ans. Televisions, mobiles, CD, computers and many more devices are made up of magnetic materials and magnets inside. If you bring a magnet closer to it then it will spoil these devices.

Short Answer Type Questions

Q. 1. *Mention some important precautions to handle magnets.*

Ans. 1. Do not heat
2. Do not hammer
3. Do not drop

Q. 2. *It was observed that a pencil sharpener gets attracted by the poles of a magnet, although its body is made of plastic. Name a material that might have been used to make some part of it.*

Ans. The blade of a pencil sharpener is made of iron which is a magnetic material. Due to this a pencil sharpener gets attracted towards the poles of a magnet.

Q. 3. *What is the correct way of storing a bar magnet? Also support your answer with diagram.*

Ans. Bar magnet: Two-bar magnets should be placed inside a wooden box so that:

(*a*) the poles of two magnets lie opposite to each other.

(*b*) a wooden piece should be kept between the two magnets.

(*c*) two pieces of soft iron are placed across the ends of magnets.

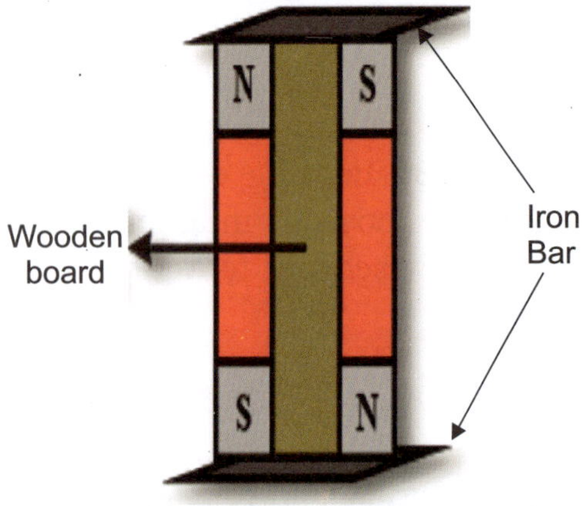

Long Answer Type Question

Q. 1. *What are the precautions to be taken while handling a magnet?*

Ans. When heated, hammered or dropped from a height, magnets tend to lose their properties. They become weak if they are not stored properly and hence:

- Bar magnets should be stored in pairs separated by a small block of wood and their unlike poles facing the same side with a soft iron across their ends.
- A piece of iron should be kept across the poles in case of a U-shaped magnet.
- Magnets should be kept away from computers, mobiles, televisions etc.

VI. OBJECTIVE TYPE QUESTIONS

1. *Match the following items given in Column A with that in Column B:*

Column A	Column B
(*a*) *Iron, nickel, cobalt*	(*i*) *Non-magnetic substances*
(*b*) *Leather, plastic, wax*	(*ii*) *Used to find out N-S directions*
(*c*) *Lodestone*	(*iii*) *Attract each other*
(*d*) *Compass*	(*iv*) *Repel each other*
(*e*) *Like poles of two magnets*	(*v*) *Naturally occurring magnet*
(*f*) *Opposite poles of two magnets*	(*vi*) *Magnetic substances*

2. *Fill in the blanks with appropriate words:*

(*a*) *When north-pole of one magnet is brought near the .... of another magnet, they attract one another.*

(*b*) *When the north-pole of one magnet is brought close to the .... of another magnet, they repel each other.*

(*c*) *Similar poles of two magnets .... one another.*

(*d*) *A compass needle always points in a .... direction.*

(*e*) *Magnetic poles always .... in pairs.*

(*f*) *Materials which get .... towards magnet are known as magnetic substances.*

(g) *The .... of magnet where maximum iron filings cling, are known as ....*

(h) *Hammering destroys the .... of small magnets.*

(i) *We should not drop the magnet, shouldn't heat it, shouldn't .... it.*

3. *State whether the statements given below are True or False:*

(i) *Lodestone is composed of oxides of iron.*

(ii) *North and south poles are found to exist separately.*

(iii) *Magnetite doesn't show magnetic properties.*

(iv) *If we cut a bar magnet in two halves we will have two magnets.*

(v) *Heat can destroy magnetic properties of a magnet.*

(vi) *Magnets are made up of different materials and in different shapes.*

(vii) *Compass needle is made of a magnet.*

(viii) *There is a maximum attraction in middle of a bar magnet.*

Multiple Choice Questions (MCQs)

Choose the correct option in the following questions

1. *Which is an example of a magnetic substance?*

(a) Iron (b) Nickel

(c) Cobalt (d) All of these

2. *Magnets have a shape*

(a) cylindrical (b) ball ended

(c) horseshoe (d) all of these

3. *When a bar magnet is brought near iron dust, most of the dust sticks*

(a) near the middle

(b) equally everywhere

(c) near two ends

(d) at the middle and ends

4. *A freely suspended bar magnet rests in*

(a) north-south directions

(b) east-west directions

(c) upside down

(d) any direction by chance

5. *Attraction is seen between the poles of two bar magnets in case of*

(a) N-pole of one magnet with N-pole of other

(b) N-pole of one magnet with S-pole of other

(c) S-pole of one magnet with S-pole of other

(d) all of these cases will show attraction

6. *Which is a natural magnet?*

(a) Lodestone

(b) Nickel

(c) Iron

(d) Copper

7. *Choose the wrong statement*

(a) Heat can destroy magnetic properties of a magnet.

(b) Magnets are made up of different materials and different shapes.

(c) There is a minimum attraction in middle of a magnet.

(d) Lodestone does not show magnetic properties.

8. *The magnetic properties of a magnet cannot be destroyed by*
   (*a*) hammering
   (*b*) heating
   (*c*) dropping on a hard surface
   (*d*) storing properly

9. *Two ends of a magnet are called*
   (*a*) North pole
   (*b*) South pole
   (*c*) North and South pole
   (*d*) Self demagnetisation

10. *Magnets attract*
   (*a*) wood
   (*b*) plastic
   (*c*) paper
   (*d*) iron

11. *A magnet which retains its magnetic properties for a long period is called a*
   (*a*) magnetic substance
   (*b*) non-magnetic substance
   (*c*) temporary magnet
   (*d*) permanent magnet

12. *North pole of a magnet can be identified by* (*NCERT Exemplar*)
   (*a*) Another magnet having its poles marked as North pole and South pole.
   (*b*) Another magnet no matter whether the poles are marked or not.
   (*c*) Using an iron bar.
   (*d*) Using iron filings.

13. *The substances that get attracted towards a magnet are called_____ substances.*
   (*a*) Magnetic
   (*b*) Non magnetic
   (*c*) Transparent
   (*d*) Luminous

14. *Maximum iron filings stick at the _____of a bar magnet when it is brought near them.*
   (*a*) Ends
   (*b*) Middle
   (*c*) Neither end nor middle
   (*d*) All around equally

15. *Like poles of a magnet*
   (*a*) Repel (*b*) Merge
   (*c*) Dissolve (*d*) Attract

16. *A bar magnet is immersed in a heap of iron filings and pulled out. The amount of iron filing clinging to the* (*NCERT Exemplar*)
   (*a*) North pole is almost equal to the south pole.
   (*b*) North pole is much more than the south pole.
   (*c*) North pole is much less than the south pole.
   (*d*) Magnet will be same all along its length.

17. *Observe the pictures A and B given in Fig. carefully.*

(NCERT Exemplar)

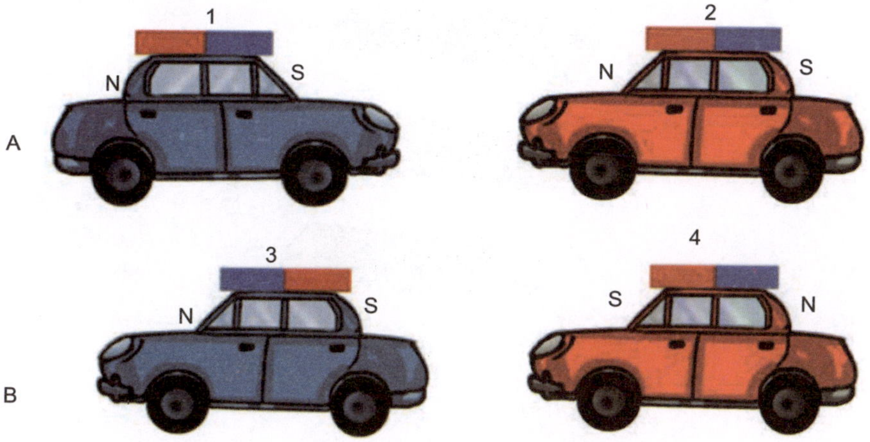

Fig.

Which of the following statement is correct for the above given pictures?

(a) *In A, cars 1 and 2 will come closer and in B, cars 3 and 4 will come closer.*

(b) *In A, cars 1 and 2 will move away from each other and in B, cars 3 and 4 will move away.*

(c) *In A, cars 1 and 2 will move away and in B, 3 and 4 will come closer to each other.*

(d) *In A, cars 1 and 2 will come closer to each other and in B, 3 and 4 will move away from each other.*

18. *The arrangement to store two magnets is shown by figures (a), (b), (c) and (d) in Fig. Which one of them is the correct arrangement?* *(NCERT Exemplar)*

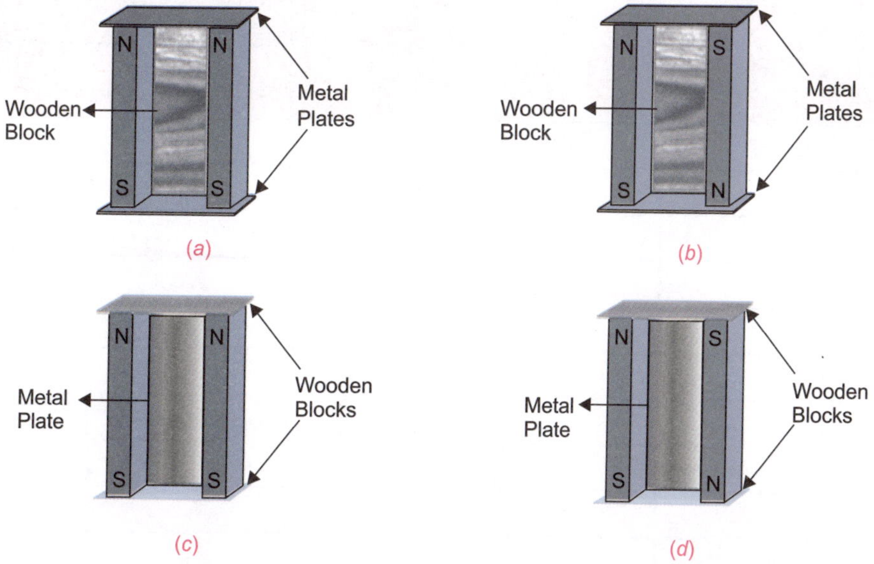

Fig.

19. *Three magnets A, B and C were dipped one by one in a heap of iron filing. Figure shows the amount of the iron filing sticking to them.* (*NCERT Exemplar*)

A
B
C

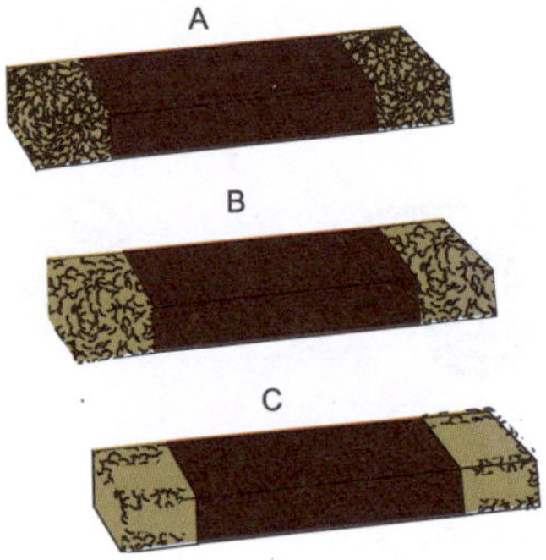

Fig.

The strength of these magnets will be

(*a*) A > B > C (*b*) A < B < C (*c*) A = B = C (*d*) A < B > C

ACTIVITY 4.1 (*Page 62*)

- *Collect a few objects made of different materials and also a magnet.*
- **Predict which of the objects will stick to the magnet. Write your prediction in Table 4.1.**
- *Now hold a magnet in your hand and bring it near the objects one by one* (See Textbook Fig. 4.3, *Page 63*). **Observe which of the objects stick to the magnet.**
- **Record your observations in Table 4.1.**

Ans.

Table 4.1: Identifying the materials attracted by a magnet

Name of the object	Material which the object is made of (plastic/wood/glass/iron/any other)	Attracted by the magnet (Yes/No)	
		Prediction	Observation
Pencil	Wood	No	No
Eraser	Rubber	No	No
Scale	Plastic	No	No
Pen	Plastic	No	No
Key	Steel	Yes	Yes
Stapler	Steel	Yes	Yes
Candle	Wax	No	No
Screw	Iron	Yes	Yes
Sharpener	Plastic & iron	No	Yes
Handkerchief	Cloth	No	No

ANSWERS

1. Match the items in Column A with Column B:

Column A	Column B
(*a*) Iron, nickel, cobalt	(*vi*) Magnetic substances
(*b*) Leather, plastic, wax	(*i*) Non-magnetic substances
(*c*) Lodestone	(*v*) Naturally occurring magnet
(*d*) Compass	(*ii*) Used to find out N-S directions
(*e*) Like poles of two magnets	(*iv*) Repel each other
(*f*) Opposite poles of two magnets	(*iii*) Attract each other

2. Fill in the blanks:

(*a*) south pole (*b*) north pole (*c*) repel (*d*) north-south
(*e*) exist (*f*) attracted (*g*) ends, poles (*h*) Magnetism
(*i*) hammer

3. True or False:

(*i*) True (*ii*) False (*iii*) False (*iv*) True
(*v*) True (*vi*) True (*vii*) True (*viii*) False

Multiple Choice Questions (MCQs)

1. (*d*) **2.** (*d*) **3.** (*c*) **4.** (*a*) **5.** (*b*) **6.** (*a*) **7.** (*d*) **8.** (*d*) **9.** (*c*) **10.** (*d*)
11. (*d*) **12.** (*a*) **13.** (*a*) **14.** (*a*) **15.** (*a*) **16.** (*a*) **17.** (*d*) **18.** (*b*) **19.** (*a*)

VII. EXERCISE FOR PRACTICE

1. Distinguish between magnetic and non-magnetic materials with suitable examples.

2. Classify the following as magnetic and non-magnetic material :

Iron, Plastic, Rubber, Glass, Mirror, Cobalt

3. What precautions you will take while handling the magnets?

4. What is lodestone?

5. Name two poles of a magnet.

6. How can we find the north-pole of a magnet?

7. Can the two poles of a magnet be separated?

8. What will be the result of cutting a magnet into two pieces?

9. You are given a bar magnet whose N and S poles are not marked. How would you find out which end is the north pole?

10. What do you observe when a bar magnet is hanged with a thread on a stand and the base of the stand is rotated?

11. How magnets lose their property?

12. How does a compass needle show directions?

13. What is the correct method to keep two bar magnets together?

14. In which condition do two magnets attract each other?

15. When do two magnets repel each other?

INTERESTING MIND MAP

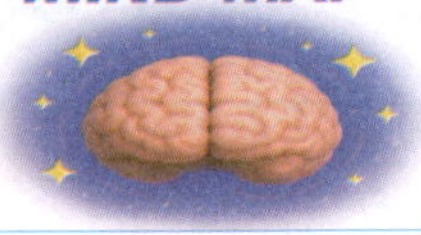

Measurement of Length and Motion

1 How do we Measure?

- Finger width, handspan, foot length, scales and measuring tapes.

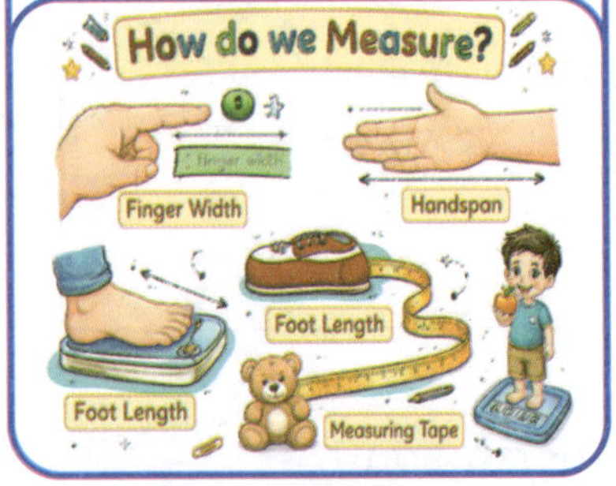

2 Standard Units

- The standard unit (SI) of length is metre whose symbol is m. Other units of length are centimetre (cm), millimetre (mm) and kilometre (km).

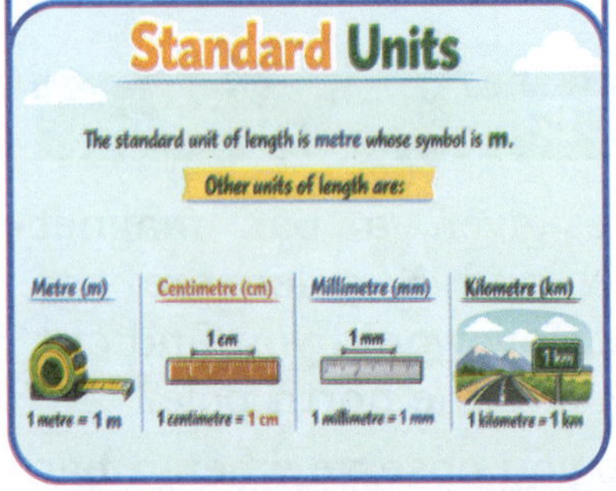

3 Correct Way of Measuring Length

- These two scales show the correct way of using scale to measure length.

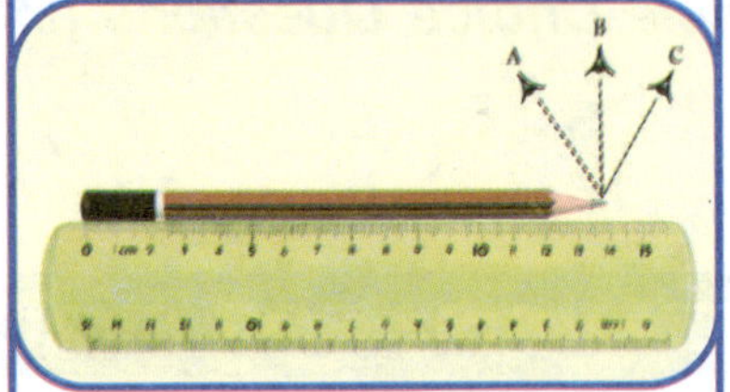

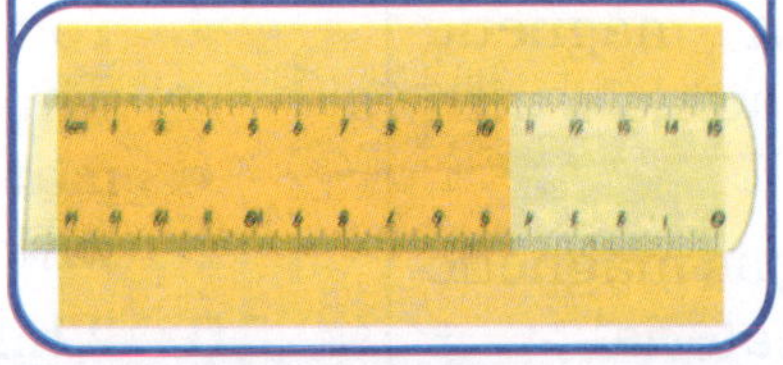

4 Measuring the Length of a Curved Line

- We measure the length of a curved line using a flexible measuring tape.

5 Describing Position

- We describe distance of an object with respect to a reference point.

6 Moving Things

- An object changing its position with respect to a reference point is a moving thing.

7 Types of Motion

- Linear motion
- Circular motion
- Oscillatory motion

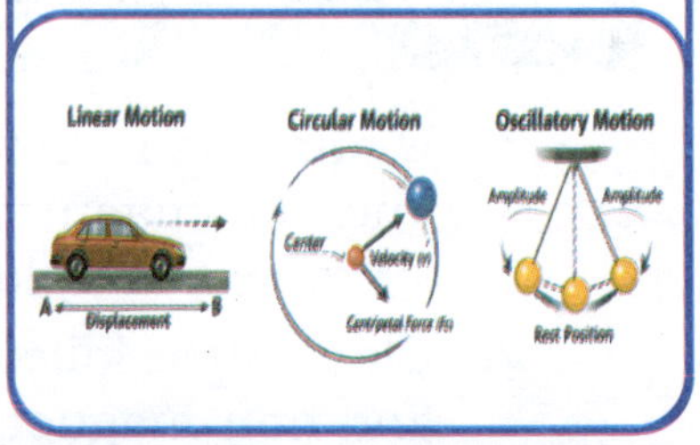

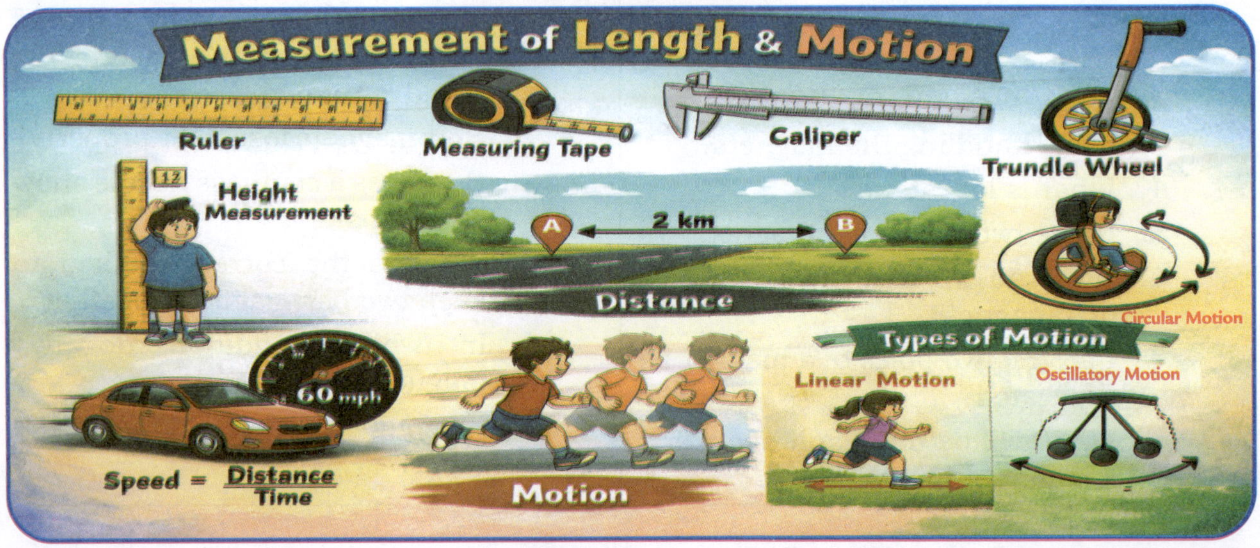

5 Measurement of Length and Motion

I. POINTS TO REMEMBER

1. We need to measure distances, length and breadth of objects, land and buildings.
2. Earlier, **Body parts** were used to measure the length. Common units were **handspan**, **cubit**, **foot length**, **angula**, **foot step** and **arm length**.
3. Small difference in the size of body parts of different persons resulted in difficulty in measuring lengths by primitive old methods like handspans, angula, cubit, etc. So there was a need for proper measuring units.
4. In 1790, French devised the **metric system** of **measurement**. The system of standard units is known as the **International System of Units** (SI).
5. In October 1960, the 12th general conference on weight and measures adopted the **International System of Units**. The International System of Units (**SI**) is the set of units to maintain uniformity all over the world.
6. **Metre:** It is the SI unit of length. The symbol of metre is **m**.

1 metre

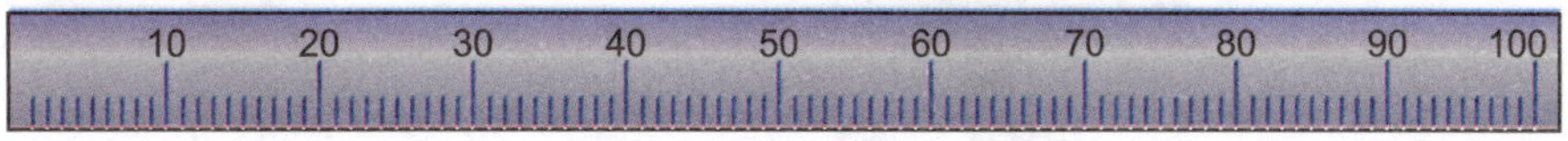

Fig. A metre scale

7. Each metre (m) is divided into 100 equal divisions, called **centimetre (cm)**. Each centimetre has ten equal divisions, called **millimetre (mm)**. Thus

$$1 \text{ m} = 100 \text{ cm}$$

$$1 \text{ cm} = 10 \text{ mm}$$

For measuring large distances, metre is not a convenient unit. We use a larger unit of length. It is called kilometre (km).

$$1 \text{ km} = 1000 \text{ m.}$$

8. On the 15 cm scale, there is also marking in inches, where **1 inch = 2.54 cm.** Inch and foot are also used for measuring length by some people.
9. For measuring any length, we need an **appropriate scale**. Scale should be **correctly placed** and while reading the scale, there should be **correct position of the eye.**
10. **Visually challenged** people use scales with raised marking that can be felt by touching them.
11. **Curved line** can be measured with the help of a **flexible measuring tape** or by using a thread. The thread can then be straightened and its length can be measured using a metre scale.

12. When distance is stated with respect to a fixed object or point, then this point is called a **reference point. It is important in deciding whether an object is at rest or in motion.**
13. An object is said to be in **motion** if its position changes with respect to a reference point with time.
14. **Motion:** It is a state of objects in which they are moving, that is, they are changing their place with time.
15. **Types of Motion:** Motion is classified into **linear**, **circular**, and **oscillatory**.
    (*i*) **Linear Motion:** Objects move along a straight path. Examples include a parade of N.C.C. cadets, a fruit falling from a tree or a heavy box pushed straight.

Fig. Linear motion

    (*ii*) **Circular Motion:** Objects move along a **circular path**, such as a merry-go-round or a whirling stone tied to a string.

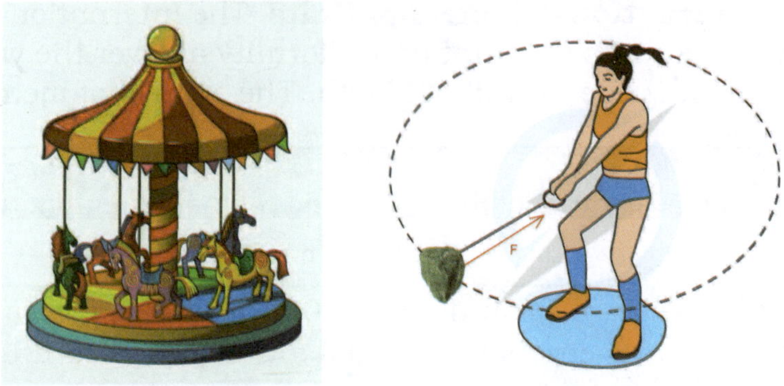

Fig. Circular motion

    (*iii*) **Oscillatory Motion:** Objects move **to and fro** around a fixed point, like a swing or a pendulum of a wall clock.

Fig. Oscillatory motion

16. If an object repeats its path after a fixed interval of time, its motion is said to be **periodic**. Both circular and oscillatory motion are **periodic in nature**.

II. KEYWORDS

1. **Centimetre:** A unit of length in the International System of Units, equal to one hundredth of a metre.
2. **Measurement:** The process of determining the size, length, or amount of something.
3. **Circular motion:** When an object moves along a circular path.
4. **Metre:** The SI unit of length, symbolised as **m**.
5. **Distance:** The amount of space between two points.
6. **Millimetre:** A unit of length in the International System of Units, equal to one thousandth of a metre.
7. **Kilometre:** A unit of length in the International System of Units, equal to one thousand metres.
8. **Motion:** The change in position of an object with respect to a reference point over time.
9. **Length:** The measurement of something from end to end.
10. **Oscillatory motion:** When an object moves **to and fro** about a fixed position.
11. **Linear motion:** When an object moves along a straight line.
12. **Reference point:** A fixed object or point used to describe the position of an object.
13. **SI Unit of Length:** The standard unit of length in the International System of Units is metre.

III. NCERT INTEXT QUESTIONS

Q. 1. ***Would it be convenient to use the unit metre to measure larger lengths, such as the length of a railway track between two cities, or to measure smaller lengths, such as the thickness of a page of a book?*** *(Page 83)*

Ans. Length and distance measurements are given in units and the number of units. For long distances if small units like meters are used the number of units will be very large. This becomes inconvenient. Therefore long distances like distances between two cities are measured in **kilometres**.

Small thicknesses or lengths like the thickness of a paper of book are measured in very small units like **mm**. If this is measured in metres or km then number of units become very small fractions which are difficult to handle.

Lengths like those of a room are measured in metres for convenience.

Q. 2. ***What do such kilometre stones indicate? How could Padma conclude that she was getting closer to her destination? (See fig. NCERT Textbook, Page 89)*** *(Page 89)*

Ans. Kilometre stones on the roads between cities and places indicate the distance left to reach a place or city (the reference point). Padma saw that earlier kilometre stone showed the distance to Delhi as 70 km and the next kilometre stone showed the distance to Delhi as 60 km. She concluded that she was in motion and moving towards Delhi (the reference point with respect to which she was changing her position with time). Decreasing numbers on kilometre stones indicate that **Padma** was getting closer to her destination.

Q. 3. *Does this mean that the position of Padma, with respect to the reference point, is changing with time? When does the position of an object change with respect to a reference point? Does it change when an object is moving?* *(Page 89)*

Ans. Padma saw from the kilometre stones that the distance to Delhi is decreasing with time. This means that with respect to Delhi (reference point here), she was changing position with time.

When the position of an object changes with time with respect to a reference point, the object is said to be in a state of motion or is moving.

Padma was changing her position with time with respect to Delhi, means that she was moving closer and closer to Delhi, her destination point with time.

IV. LET US ENHANCE OUR LEARNING (Pages 97–99)

Q. 1. *Some lengths are given in Column I of following Table. Some units are given in Column II. Match the lengths with the units suitable for measuring those lengths.*

Table

Column I	Column II
Distance between Delhi and Lucknow	centimetre
Thickness of a coin	kilometre
Length of an eraser	metre
Length of school ground	millimetre

Ans.

Column I	Column II
Distance between Delhi and Lucknow	**kilometre**
Thickness of a coin	**millimetre**
Length of an eraser	**centimetre**
Length of school ground	**metre**

Q. 2. *Read the following statements and mark True (T) or False (F) against each.*

(*i*) The motion of a car moving on a straight road is an example of linear motion. [ ]

(*ii*) Any object which is changing its position with respect to a reference point with time is said to be in motion. [ ]

(*iii*) 1 km = 100 cm [ ]

Ans. (*i*) T (*ii*) T (*iii*) F

Q. 3. ***Which of the following is not a standard unit of measuring length?***

(*i*) millimetre (*ii*) centimetre

(*iii*) kilometre (*iv*) handspan

Ans. (*iv*) handspan

Q. 4. ***Search for the different scales or measuring tapes at your home and school. Find out the smallest value that can be measured using each of these scales. Record your observations in a tabular form.***

Ans.

Type of Scale, Tape, Device	Smallest Value of Measurement
15 cm Scale	1 mm
Flexible Tape	1 mm, 1 inch
Long Tape Roll	1 mm, 1 cm, 1 inch
Vernier Calliper (from School Lab)	0.1 mm
Screw Gauge (from School Lab)	0.01 mm

Q. 5. ***Suppose the distance between your school and home is 1.5 km. Express it in metres.***

Ans.

$\because$ 1 km = 1000 metres

$\therefore$ 1.5 km = 1.5 × 1000

= 1500 metres

Q. 6. ***Take a tumbler or a bottle. Measure the length of the curved part of the base of glass or bottle and record it.***

Ans. Hint: Use a flexible measuring tape or a piece of string to measure the length of the curved part of the base of the tumbler, then measure the string using a metre scale.

Q. 7. ***Measure the height of your friend and express it in (i) metres (ii) centimetres and (iii) millimetres.***

Ans. Hint: Measure the height using a metre scale and express it in:

- Metres (e.g., 1.4 m)
- Centimetres (e.g., 140 cm)
- Millimetres (e.g., 1400 mm)

Q. 8. ***You are given a coin. Estimate how many coins are required to be placed one after the other lengthwise, without leaving any gap between them, to cover the whole length of the chosen side of a notebook. Verify your estimate by measuring the same side of the notebook and the size of the coin using a 15-cm scale.***

Ans. Hint: Measure the diameter of the coin and the length of the notebook. Divide the length of the notebook by the diameter of the coin to estimate the number of coins required. Say the diameter of the coin is 2 cm and the length of the notebook is 18 cm. Then $\frac{18}{2}$ = 9 coins can be placed side to side along the length of the notebook. Verify by placing the coins end-to-end and measuring again.

Q. 9. ***Give two examples each for linear, circular and oscillatory motion.***

Ans.
- **Linear motion:** A car moving on a straight road, an eraser dropping straight down.
- **Circular motion:** A merry-go-round, the motion of a whirling stone tied to a thread.
- **Oscillatory motion:** A swinging pendulum, the motion of a metal strip pressed and released.

Q. 10. ***Observe different objects around you. It is easier to express the lengths of some objects in mm, some in cm and some in m. Make a list of three objects in each category and enter them in the following Table.***

Table: Sizes of objects around us

Size	Objects
mm	
cm	
m	

Ans. Classify objects by the convenience of measuring in mm, cm, and m:

Size	Objects
mm	Thickness of a coin, thickness of a cardboard and diameter of a small screw
cm	Length of a pencil, width of a book, height of a water bottle, and length of an eraser.
m	Height of a room, width of a playground and height of a lamppost

Q. 11. ***A rollercoaster track is made in the shape shown in Fig. A ball starts from point A and escapes through point F. Identify the types of motion of the ball on the rollercoaster and corresponding portions of the track.***

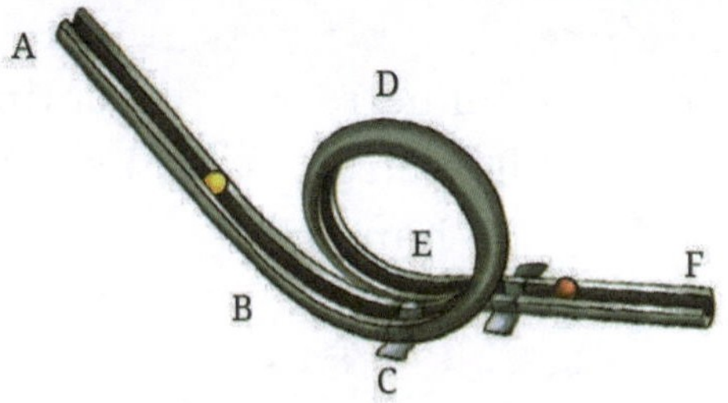

Fig. Rollercoaster track

Ans. Portions of the track and corresponding types of motion:

- A to B: Linear motion
- B to C: Circular motion (loop)
- C to D to E: Circular motion
- E to F: Linear motion

Q. 12. ***Tasneem wants to make a metre scale by herself. She considers the following materials for it—plywood, paper, cloth, stretchable rubber and steel. Which of these should she not use and why?***

Ans. Tasneem should not use stretchable rubber because it can change length when stretched, leading to inaccurate measurements. Plywood, cloth, paper, and steel are more suitable as they maintain consistent lengths.

Q. 13. ***Think, design and develop a card game on conversion of units of length to play with your friends.***

Ans. Create cards with different lengths and corresponding units (mm, cm, m, km). Each card can have a length in one unit and players must match it to its equivalent in another unit. For example, a card with "100 cm" would match with "1 m".

V. EXAM ORIENTED QUESTIONS

Very Short Answer Type Questions

Q. 1. ***What is the SI unit of length?***

Ans. Metre (m)

Q. 2. ***How many centimetres are there in a metre?***

Ans. 100 cm

Q. 3. ***How many millimetres are there in a centimetre?***

Ans. 10

Q. 4. ***Which body part do you and your friends use to measure the table?***

Ans. Handspan

Q. 5. ***Name a flexible tool used to measure the girth* of a tree.***

Ans. Flexible measuring tape

Q. 6. ***What is the unit used to measure long distances between different cities?***

Ans. Kilometre (km)

Q. 7. ***What type of motion is exhibited by a swing?***

Ans. Oscillatory motion

Q. 8. ***What is the smallest value that can be measured using a typical 15-cm scale?***

Ans. Millimetre (mm)

Q. 9. ***Which ancient Indian unit of measurement is mentioned as still being used by traditional craftspeople?***

Ans. Angula

Q. 10. ***What is the reference point used by a traveller to determine how close she/he is to Delhi?***

Ans. Delhi

Short Answer Type Questions

Q. 1. ***Why do people use standard units of measurement instead of body parts?***

Ans. People use standard units of measurement instead of body parts because body parts vary in size from person to person, leading to difference in measurements. Standard units ensure that measurements are uniform and accurate.

Q. 2. ***What is the significance of the metre in the International System of Units?***

Ans. The metre is an important International System of Units as it is the base unit of length. It provides a consistent standard for measuring length, which is essential for scientific and everyday measurements.

Q. 3. ***How can you measure the length of a curved line accurately?***

Ans. To measure the length of a curved line accurately, we can use a flexible measuring tape or a thread. Place the thread along the curve, then measure the length of the thread against a straight metre scale.

Q. 4. ***Explain the concept of a reference point in measuring distance.***

Ans. A reference point is a fixed object or location used to describe the position of another object. It helps in determining distances and positions accurately by providing a fixed point.

Q. 5. ***How does the position of the eye affect the accuracy of measuring with a scale?***

Ans. The position of the eye affects the accuracy of measuring with a scale because if the eye is not directly above the measurement mark, it can cause a parallax error. This error occurs when the measurement is viewed from an angle, leading to an incorrect reading.

Q. 6. ***Why are flexible measuring tapes preferred for measuring the girth* of objects?***

Ans. Flexible measuring tapes are preferred for measuring the girth of objects because they can easily wrap around curved surfaces. This flexibility allows for accurate measurements of objects with irregular shapes.

* *girth: Measurement around something, especially a person's waist or diameter of a tree.*

Q. 7. ***What do you and your friends discover when you compare the handspans?***

Ans. We discover that our handspans are different in size, leading to varying measurements of the same object. This highlights the inconsistency of using body parts for measurement and the need for standard units.

Q. 8. ***How is oscillatory motion different from linear and circular motion?***

Ans. Oscillatory motion is different from linear and circular motion in that it involves an object moving **to and fro** about a fixed position. Linear motion involves movement along a **straight path,** while circular motion involves movement along a **circular path**.

Q. 9. ***Describe the process of measuring an object using a scale with broken ends.***

Ans. To measure an object using a scale with broken ends, we can start from a full mark on the scale instead of the zero mark. Measure the length from this point and subtract the initial reading to get the correct length.

Q. 10. ***How can you measure the distance between two places using a bicycle?***

Ans. To measure the distance between two places using a bicycle, attach a flexible metal strip to the wheel spoke. The metal strip will produce a sound once in every completed circle of the wheel. To count, the number of rotations count the number of times the sound is produced. Measure the circumference of the wheel, multiply it by the number of rotations, and calculate the total distance travelled.

Q. 11. ***The photograph given as Fig. shows a section of a grill made up of straight and curved iron bars. How would you measure the length of the bars of this section, so that the payment could be made to the contractor?*** (NCERT Exemplar)

Fig.

Ans. The length can be measured using a thread which can be further measured with the help of a metre scale.

Q. 12. ***Three students measured the length of a corridor and reported their measurements. The values of their measurements were different. What could be the reason for difference in their measurements? (Mention any three)*** (NCERT Exemplar)

Ans. Main reasons for difference in their measurement could be:

1. Different measuring devices were used.
2. The smallest length that could be measured by different devices may be different.
3. Measurement may not be along the shortest length in all three cases.
4. The end of the corridor may not be easily accessible.

Long Answer Type Questions

Q. 1. ***Why is it important to use standard units of measurement in everyday life?***

Ans. It is important to use standard units of measurement in everyday life to ensure **consistency**, **accuracy**, **and reliability**. Standard units allow for clear communication and comparison of measurements, which is important in fields such as science, engineering, and trade. Without standard units, measurements would vary widely depending on the person taking the measurements. It leads to confusion and errors.

Q. 2. ***How the measurements using body parts to measure length were considered inconsistent?***

Ans. It was observed that using body parts like the handspans, foot spans or strides etc., to measure length was inconsistent. Each person's handspan resulted in a different measurement, because the body parts vary in size from person to person. This observation resulted in the need for standard units.

Q. 3. ***Describe the process of using a thread to measure the length of a curved line.***

Ans. To measure the length of a curved line using a thread, we place the thread along the entire length of the curve, following the shape precisely. After marking the endpoints on the thread, we straighten the thread and measure it against a straight metre ruler or measuring tape. This method gives accurate measurement of curves, which cannot be measured with rigid straight scales.

Q. 4. ***Explain the significance of the International System of Units (SI) and its impact on global measurements.***

Ans. The International System of Units (SI) provides a standard set of measurement units used globally, facilitating international trade, scientific studies, and technological development. By using SI units, countries can ensure that measurements are consistent and comparable, reducing errors. The SI system includes base units like the metre (for length), kilogram (for weight), and second (for time), which are fundamental to various scientific and practical applications.

Q. 5. ***Write the correct techniques for measuring length accurately. Explain why are they important?***

Ans. Correct techniques for measuring length include placing the scale in contact with the object, **aligning the scale properly along the object's length, and positioning the eye directly above the measurement mark** to avoid parallax errors. These techniques are important to ensure **accuracy** and **consistency** in measurements. For example, measuring a pencil with a broken scale requires starting from a full mark and subtracting the initial reading to obtain the correct length.

Q. 6. ***Discuss the historical units of measurement used in India and their relevance in modern times.***

Ans. Historical measurement units used in India, such as angula (finger width) and dhanusa (bow length), played a significant role in ancient architecture, town planning, and trade. These units are mentioned in ancient literature and are still used by traditional craftspeople like carpenters and tailors. Understanding these units provides insight into India's rich history of measurement and how it has evolved to incorporate modern standard units.

Q. 7. ***How does the concept of a reference point help in accurately describing the position of an object?***

Ans. The concept of a reference point is important for accurately describing the position of an object because it provides a fixed location from which measurements can be made. For example, when we see kilometre stones indicating distances from Delhi, Delhi acts as the reference point. Without a reference point, it would be difficult to determine exact locations.

It is essential for knowing the distances of our destination and estimating the time to reach there.

Q. 8. ***Describe an activity that demonstrates the difference between using body parts and standard units for measurement.***

Ans. An activity to demonstrate the difference between using body parts and standard units for measurement involves measuring the length of a classroom table using both methods. First, students can use their handspans and record the results, which will vary due to differences in hand size. Then, using a standard measuring tape or ruler, they can measure the table again, showing that **standard units provide consistent and reliable measurements regardless of the measurer.**

VI. OBJECTIVE TYPE QUESTIONS

1. *Match the following items given in Column A with that in Column B:*

(a)

	Column A		Column B
1	SI unit of length	A	Handspan
2	Measurement using body parts	B	Metre
3	Circular motion	C	Merry-go-round
4	Flexible measuring tool	D	Fixed object/location
5	Reference point	E	Measuring tape

(b)

	Column A		Column B
1	100 centimetres	A	Thread
2	Measuring curved lines	B	Avoids parallax error
3	Oscillatory motion	C	Kilometre
4.	Unit for measuring long distances	D	Swing
5	Positioning eye correctly	E	One metre

2. *Fill in the blanks with appropriate words:*

(a) The SI unit of length is the ....

(b) One metre is equal to .... centimetres.

(c) One centimetre is equal to ...... millimetres.

(d) A handspan is an example of a .... unit.

(e) A flexible measuring tape is ideal for measuring the .... of a tree.

(f) The length of a curved line can be measured accurately using a ....

(g) The position of the eye should be directly .... the measurement mark to avoid parallax error.

(h) The zero mark on a scale must be .... to the object being measured.

(i) When using a scale with broken ends, you should start measuring from another .... mark.

(*j*) *A .... is a fixed object or location used to describe the position of another object.*

(*k*) *An object is said to be in .... if its position changes with respect to a reference point over time.*

(*l*) *The .... system of units was adopted to avoid confusion from different measurement systems used globally.*

(*m*) *A .... marking on some scales represents units in inches, where 1 inch equals 2.54 centimetres.*

3. *State whether the statements given below are True or False:*

(*i*) *The SI unit of length is the metre.*

(*ii*) *One metre is equal to 10 centimetres.*

(*iii*) *A handspan is a standard unit of measurement.*

(*iv*) *Flexible measuring tapes are ideal for measuring the girth of trees.*

(*v*) *To measure a curved line, you can use a thread and then measure the thread against a straight scale.*

(*vi*) *The correct position of the eye when measuring is directly above the measurement mark.*

(*vii*) *If the zero mark on a scale is unclear, you cannot use the scale for measurement.*

(*viii*) *A reference point is necessary to describe the position of an object accurately.*

(*ix*) *An object at rest changes its position with respect to a reference point over time.*

(*x*) *Circular motion refers to movement along a straight path.*

(*xi*) *Linear motion can be observed in a car driving on a straight road.*

(*xii*) *Oscillatory motion involves an object moving to and fro about a fixed position.*

(*xiii*) *The length of a table measured in handspans will be the same for everyone.*

(*xiv*) *Standard units of measurement are necessary for consistency and accuracy.*

(*xv*) *Metres and inches are both units used in the International System of Units.*

Multiple Choice Questions (MCQs)

Choose the correct option in the following questions:

1. *If you do not have a measuring scale what will you use to measure the length of the table?*

(*a*) Ruler

(*b*) Measuring tape

(*c*) Handspan

(*d*) Yardstick

2. *Why did the measurements of the table differ among different people using their handspans to measure?*

(*a*) They measure different tables.

(*b*) Their handspans are of different sizes.

(*c*) They use different units.

(*d*) The table length changes with every measurement.

3. *What is the SI unit of length?*

(*a*) Foot (*b*) Inch

(*c*) Metre (*d*) Yard

4. *How many centimetres are there in one metre?*

(*a*) 10 (*b*) 100

(*c*) 1000 (*d*) 1

5. *Which of the following is NOT an SI unit of length?*
(*a*) Kilometre
(*b*) Centimetre
(*c*) Inch
(*d*) Millimetre

6. *Where should your eye be positioned when reading a measurement on a scale?*
(*a*) To the left of the mark
(*b*) To the right of the mark
(*c*) Directly above the mark
(*d*) Below the mark

7. *What should you do if the ends of your scale are broken?*
(*a*) Use a different scale.
(*b*) Use any other full mark on the scale to start measuring.
(*c*) Estimate the length.
(*d*) Ignore the broken ends and measure as usual.

8. *What tool can be used by visually challenged students to measure lengths?*
(*a*) Normal 15 - cm scale
(*b*) Digital scale
(*c*) Raised markings scale
(*d*) Normal measuring tape

9. *Which tool is best suited for measuring a curved line?*
(*a*) Ruler
(*b*) Metal rod
(*c*) Thread
(*d*) Yardstick

10. *After using a thread to measure a curved line, what should you do next?*
(*a*) Measure the length of the thread against a straight scale.
(*b*) Cut the thread.
(*c*) Mark the thread with a pen.
(*d*) Wrap the thread around the object again.

11. *What type of measuring tape/ scale is ideal for measuring curved lines?*
(*a*) Metal tape
(*b*) 15 cm scale
(*c*) Metre rod
(*d*) Flexible tape

12. *What is a reference point?*
(*a*) A random point
(*b*) A fixed object or location
(*c*) The start of a measurement
(*d*) The end of a measurement

13. *How will you and your friends decide to draw lines for a Kabaddi court?*
(*a*) By estimating the distances
(*b*) By using a reference point
(*c*) By using their handspans
(*d*) By guessing

14. *How can you determine if an object is in motion?*
(*a*) If it changes position with respect to a reference point over time.
(*b*) If it makes a sound.
(*c*) If it is heavy.
(*d*) If it is colourful.

15. *When we are on a moving bus and look at the other passengers on the bus, what do we conclude about their motion?*
(*a*) They are in motion.
(*b*) They are at rest.
(*c*) They are jumping.
(*d*) They are asleep.

16. *Why do we feel that all the passengers on a moving bus are in motion when we look outside?*

(*a*) The bus is shaking.

(*b*) The position of the passengers changes with respect to outside objects.

(*c*) The passengers are moving inside the bus.

(*d*) The driver announces the motion.

17. *What type of motion does a car moving on a straight road exhibit?*

(*a*) Circular motion

(*b*) Linear motion

(*c*) Oscillatory motion

(*d*) Rotational motion

18. *What type of motion does a swing exhibit?*

(*a*) Linear motion

(*b*) Circular motion

(*c*) Oscillatory motion

(*d*) Random motion

19. *What type of motion does a merry-go-round exhibit?*

(*a*) Linear motion

(*b*) Circular motion

(*c*) Oscillatory motion

(*d*) Irregular motion

20. *The distance between Delhi and Mumbai is usually expressed in units of* (*NCERT Exemplar*)

(*a*) decametre (*b*) metre

(*c*) centimetre (*d*) kilometre

21. *Fig. shows a measuring scale which is usually supplied with a geometry box. Which of the following distance cannot be measured with this scale by using it only once?* (*NCERT Exemplar*)

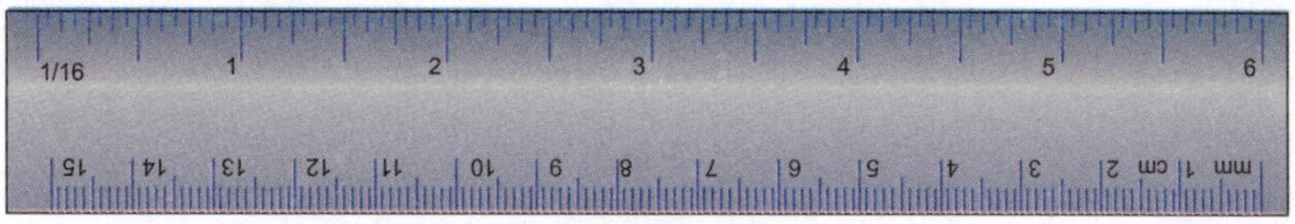

Fig.

(*a*) 0.1 m (*b*) 0.15 m (*c*) 0.2 m (*d*) 0.05 m

22. *A piece of ribbon folded five times is placed along a 30 cm long measuring scale as shown in Fig.* (*NCERT Exemplar*)

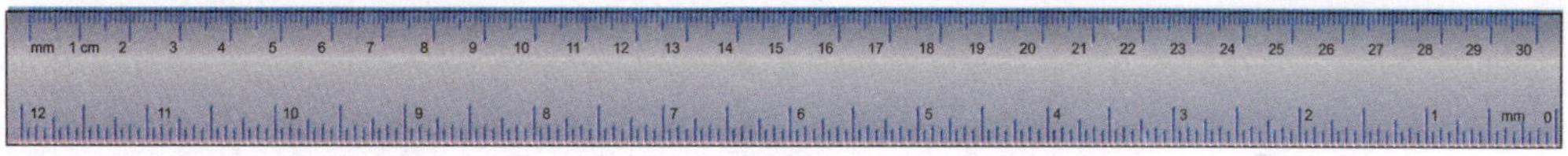

Fig.

The length of the ribbon is between

(*a*) 1.15 m – 1.25 m (*b*) 1.25 m – 1.35 m

(*c*) 1.50 m – 1.60 m (*d*) 1.60 m – 1.70 m

23. *Bholu and Golu are playing in a ground. They start running from the same point A in the ground and reach point B at the same time by following the paths marked 1 and 2 respectively as shown in Fig. Which of the following is/are true for the given situation.* (*NCERT Exemplar*)

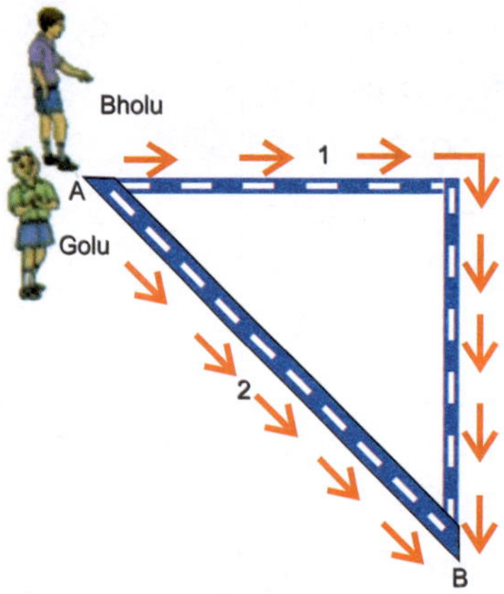

Fig.

As compared to Golu, Bholu covers a

(*a*) longer distance but with a lower speed.

(*b*) longer distance with a higher speed.

(*c*) shorter distance with a lower speed.

(*d*) shorter distance with a higher speed.

24. *Four pieces of wooden sticks A, B, C and D are placed along the length of 30 cm long scale as shown in Fig. Which one of them is 3.4 cm in length?* (*NCERT Exemplar*)

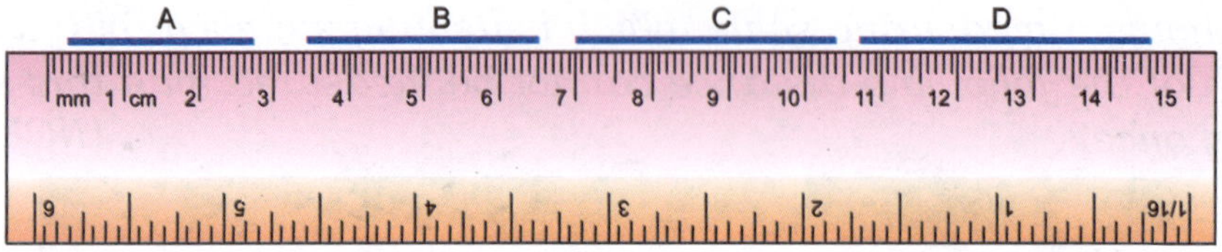

Fig.

(*a*) *A* (*b*) *B* (*c*) *C* (*d*) *D*

25. *You are provided three scales A, B and C as shown in Fig. to measure a length of 10 cm.* (*NCERT Exemplar*)

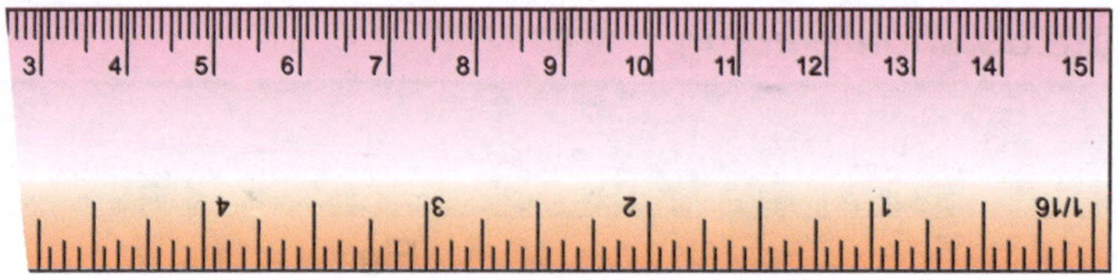

A

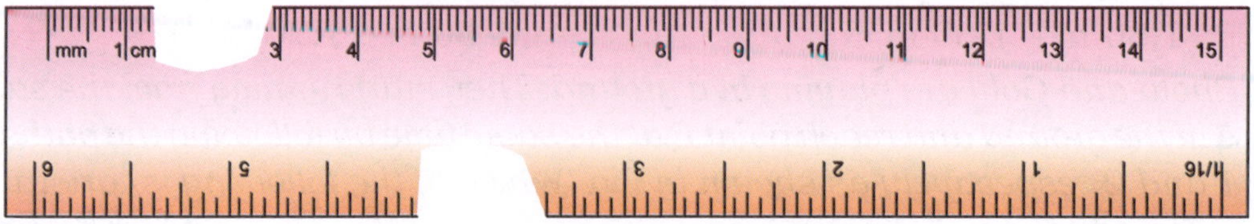

B

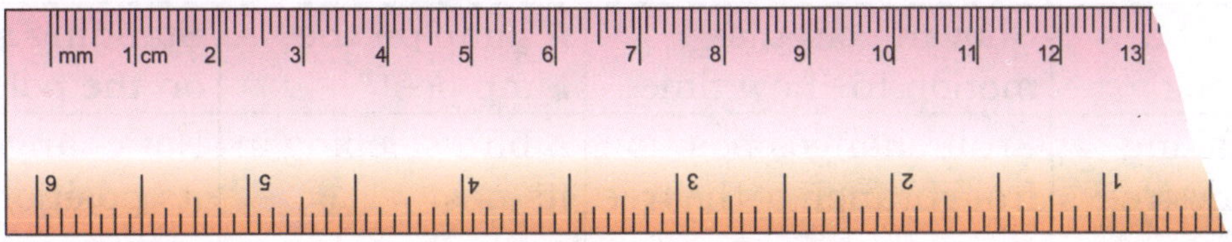

C

Fig.

For the correct measurement of the length you will use the scale

(*a*) *A only* (*b*) *B only*

(*c*) *C only* (*d*) *Any of the three scales.*

ACTIVITIES

ACTIVITY 5.1: Let us Measure (Page 86)

- Select some objects around you, such as a comb, a pen, a pencil, and an eraser to measure their lengths.
- Measure their lengths one by one using a metre scale and note down the measurements in **Table 5.2.**

Ans.

Table 5.2: Measuring lengths

Object	Length of the object
Comb	15 cm
Pen	14 cm
Pencil	18 cm

ACTIVITY 5.2: Let us Explore (Page 90)

- Look around and prepare a list of five objects that are in motion and five objects that are at rest.
- Record your observations in **Table 5.3.**
- Think about how you decided whether an object was in motion or at rest. Write your explanation (justification) in **Table 5.3.**

Ans.

Table 5.3: Observing things around you

Objects in motion	Justification	Objects at rest	Justification
Cow grazing in the field	Cow changes position with respect to grass in the field	Table in a classroom	Not moving
Switched on Fan	Blades of the fan rotate in a circular path	Chair with a teacher sitting	Stationary in the room
Car moving on the road	Car changes position with respect to objects on the road	Wall painting	Hanging at a fixed place on the wall

Hands of a wall clock	Showing circular motion to show time	A lamp on the lamp post	Standing still on the pole
Fruit falling from the tree	Fruit changes position from branch of the tree towards the ground below	A bird sleeping in its nest	Not changing its position with respect to the branches of the tree

ACTIVITY 5.7: Let us Identify (Page 94)

- Look at the picture of a children's park (Fig.) or visit a children's park.
- Observe different kinds of motions. Classify them as linear, circular or oscillatory motion.

List them in Table 5.4. Give your justification for why you put each in a certain category.

Fig. Types of motion observed in a children's park

Ans.

Table 5.4: Types of Motion

Object	Linear motion	Circular motion	Oscillatory Motion	Justification
Swing			Yes	Moves back and forth.
Slide	Yes			Moves straight down when sliding.
See saw			Yes	Moves up and down around a fixed point.

ANSWERS

1.

(a)

	Column A		Column B
1	SI unit of length	B	Metre
2	Measurement using body parts	A	Handspan
3	Circular motion	C	Merry-go-round
4	Flexible measuring tool	E	Measuring tape
5	Reference point	D	Fixed object/location

(b)

	Column A		Column B
1	100 centimetres	E	One metre
2	Measuring curved lines	A	Thread
3	Oscillatory motion	D	Swing
4.	Unit for measuring long distances	C	Kilometre
5	Positioning eye correctly	B	Avoids parallax error

2. Fill in the blanks:

(a) metre *(b)* 100 *(c)* 10 *(d)* traditional
(e) girth *(f)* thread *(g)* above *(h)* aligned
(i) full *(j)* reference point *(k)* motion
(l) International or SI *(m)* second

3. True or False:

(i) True *(ii)* False *(iii)* False *(iv)* True
(v) True *(vi)* True *(vii)* False *(viii)* True
(ix) False *(x)* False *(xi)* True *(xii)* True
(xiii) False *(xiv)* True *(xv)* False

Multiple Choice Questions (MCQs)

1. *(c)* **2.** *(b)* **3.** *(c)* **4.** *(b)* **5.** *(c)* **6.** *(c)* **7.** *(b)* **8.** *(c)* **9.** *(c)* **10.** *(a)*
11. *(d)* **12.** *(b)* **13.** *(b)* **14.** *(a)* **15.** *(b)* **16.** *(b)* **17.** *(b)* **18.** *(c)* **19.** *(b)* **20.** *(d)*
21. *(c)* **22.** *(c)* **23.** *(b)* **24.** *(c)* **25.** *(d)*

VII. EXERCISE FOR PRACTICE

1. Name any five units of measurement of length.
2. Why does the tailor need to take measurements while stitching your dress?
3. How does the measurement of length of a field differ if different farmers measure the same field with their strides?
4. Change the following measurements to km, m, cm and mm:
   (*i*) 0.5 km (*ii*) 250 m
   (*iii*) 1125 cm (*iv*) 80 mm
5. Name the SI unit of length. What are the units normally used for measuring smaller and larger lengths?
6. Define a 'Reference Point'. How is reference point important for determining the position of an object or a location?
7. Define motion. Name any three types of motion.
8. What do you mean by periodic motion? Which of the following is not a periodic motion?
   (*i*) Circular motion
   (*ii*) Oscillatory motion
   (*iii*) Motion in a straight line
9. What are the reference points for a passenger in a moving bus to observe that:
   (*i*) The co-passengers are at rest
   (*ii*) The co-passengers are moving
10. You are given a 1 m long thread and a potato. How can you demonstrate a circular motion?
11. Name the type of motion in each of the following cases:
    (*i*) A parade by N.C.C. cadets
    (*ii*) A boy in a roller coaster
    (*iii*) A girl on a moving swing
    (*iv*) A fruit falling from a tree
    (*v*) A car running on a straight road
12. How can you measure the length of a curved surface?
13. A coach has to measure the chest expansion of athletes. Which measuring scale, rod or tape will he use?
14. Explain the method to take accurate measurement of length while using a scale that has a broken end.
15. What precautions do we take for accurate measurement of length?

NOTES

INTERESTING MIND MAP

Materials Around Us

1 Observing Objects Around Us

- We see objects made up of some materials like paper, wood, cloth, glass, metal, plastic, clay, and so on.

2 How to Group Materials?

- We classify objects on the basis of their common property.

3 What are the Different Properties of Materials?

3a Observe and identify appearance of materials

- **Lustrous** materials have shiny surfaces.
- **Non-lustrous** materials don't have shiny surfaces.

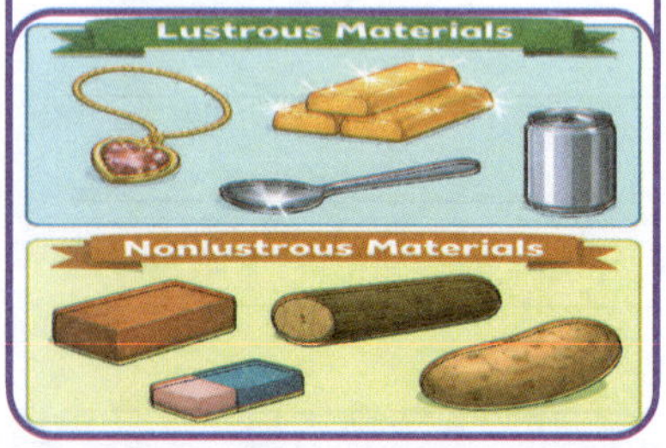

3b Which materials are hard?

- Materials which can be compressed or scratched easily are **soft.**
- Materials which cannot be compressed or scratched easily are **hard.**

3c Explore materials through which one can see or cannot see

- We can see through **transparent** materials.
- We can see partially through **translucent** materials, but not clearly.
- We cannot see through **opaque** materials at all.

3d What is soluble in water; what is not?

- **Soluble** materials disappear when mixed in water. E.g., **sugar.**
- **Insoluble** materials don't disappear when mixed in water even after stirring for a long time. E.g., **sand.**

3e How heavy or light?

- **Mass** is a property of an object by which we know how heavy or light it is.

3f Space and volume

- **Space** which an object occupies represents its **volume.**

4 What is Matter?

- A thing occupying space and having mass is called **matter.**
- Units of mass are gram (g) and kilogram (Kg).
- Units of volume are millilitre (mL) and litre (L).

TRANSPARENT

Can see through clearly.

Clear Glass | Clear Plastic

TRANSLUCENT

Can see through partially.

Frosted Glass | Wax Paper

OPAQUE

Cannot see through at all.

Wood | Metal

6

Materials Around Us

I. POINTS TO REMEMBER

- We use many things in our daily life. All things are made up of one or more types of materials. **Material** is a substance that is used to create an object.
- Different objects may be classified into different groups based on their properties such as shape, colour, hardness, softness, shine or materials they are made up of.
- **The method of arranging the objects into groups is called classification.** Different objects in a group have some common property.
- Materials possess different properties which determine their use. For example, gold is used for making ornaments because it is **lustrous**. A cloth bag cannot be used to carry water because water will pass through it.
- Objects can be classified on the basis of a common property that they have.
- Materials can be grouped based on appearance, such as **lustrous** or **non-lustrous** and based on the feel, such as hard or soft. The lustrous materials have shining surfaces whereas non-lustrous materials have dull surfaces. **Metals are generally lustrous.** Wood is non-lustrous.
- Not all materials that shine are metals. For example: Surfaces of some materials become shiny by polishing.
- Metals like silver and copper may become dull or non-lustrous due to the effect of air and moisture on them.
- Hard materials are difficult to compress or scratch. For example, steel, brick and wood are **hard** materials.

Fig. Hard materials

- **Soft** materials can be compressed or scratched easily. *For example,* wool, wax and sponge are soft materials.
- This property is relative in nature. For example, rubber is harder than sponge but softer than iron.

Fig. Soft materials

- Materials can be grouped as **transparent, translucent** or **opaque** depending on how much we can see through them.

  The materials, through which things can be seen clearly are called **transparent**. For example, glass, air, water, cellophane paper, etc. Materials through which we are not able to see at all are called **opaque**. Wood, metal sheets, plywood, rubber, etc., are examples of opaque materials. The materials through which objects can be seen, but not clearly, are known as **translucent**. Frosted glass and butter paper are examples of **translucent** materials.
- The materials which completely disappear when mixed in water are said to be **soluble** in water. On the other hand the materials which do not mix with water and do not disappear even after we stir them for a long time are said to be **insoluble** in water. For example, sugar and salt are soluble in water whereas sand and iron fillings are insoluble in water.

(a) (b)

Fig. (a) Some liquids mix well with water while (b) some others do not

- Water is known as universal solvent. It plays an important role in the functioning of our body because it can dissolve a large number of materials.
- Some liquids mix with water completely whereas some do not mix with water and form a separate layer. For example, milk mixes completely with water whereas mustard oil forms a separate layer. Some gases are soluble in water whereas others are not. **Oxygen, carbon dioxide, ammonia, etc., are soluble in water. Helium gas is almost insoluble in water.**
- Anything that occupies space and has mass is called **matter.** Thus all materials possess two properties. These are mass and volume. The amount of matter in an object is referred to as its **mass.** An object having more mass is heavier and the one which has less mass is lighter. **The units to measure mass are gram (g) and kilogram (kg).**
- The space occupied by an object is referred to as its volume. The units to measure the **volume** are litre (L) and millilitre (mL).
- **Kilogram** is the unit of mass in the International System of Units (SI). The SI unit for volume is cubic metre (m^3).

II. KEYWORDS

1. **Material:** Any substance that is used to create an object is called material.
2. **Classification:** The method of arranging the objects into groups, based on certain properties, is called classification.
3. **Lustrous:** The materials, that have shiny surfaces.
4. **Non-lustrous:** The materials, that do not have shiny surfaces.
5. **Soft materials:** The materials, which can be compressed or scratched easily, are called soft materials.
6. **Hard materials:** The materials, which are difficult to compress or scratch, are called hard materials.
7. **Transparent:** The materials, through which things can be seen clearly, are called transparent.
8. **Opaque:** The materials, through which we are not able to see at all, are called opaque.
9. **Translucent:** The materials, through which objects can be seen, but not clearly, are known as translucent.
10. **Soluble:** The materials, which completely disappear when mixed in water, are said to be soluble in water.
11. **Insoluble:** The materials, which when mixed with water, do not disappear even after we stir them for a long time, are insoluble in water.
12. **Matter:** Anything that occupies space and has mass is called matter.
13. **Mass:** The amount of matter in an object is referred to as its mass.
14. **Volume:** The space occupied by an object is referred to as its volume.

III. NCERT INTEXT QUESTIONS

Q. 1. ***Would it be a good idea to use paper-like materials for making cooking utensils?*** *(Page 104)*

Ans. No. Paper-like materials are not suitable for making cooking utensils. Such materials cannot withstand high temperature of the flame and will catch fire. The liquid contents of the food will also leak through the paper.

Q. 2. ***Are all lustrous materials metals?*** *(Page 107)*

Ans. All lustrous materials are not metals. Some materials can be made lustrous by polishing or coating them with a thin layer of plastic or any other material which makes them look shiny.

Q. 3. ***Is water transparent? Can it be made opaque?*** *(Page 110)*

Ans. Pure water is transparent. It can be made opaque by adding some mud etc. into the water. Muddy water is opaque.

Q. 4. ***Does everything you put in water disappear?*** *(Page 111)*

Ans. No. Everything we put in water does not disappear. Only the materials which are soluble in water disappear when mixed with water in limited amount.

Q. 5. ***Are there any properties which can be shown by all materials? If yes, what are those?*** *(Page 115)*

Ans. Yes, there are two properties which are shown by all materials. All material objects possess **mass** and have **volume**.

IV. LET US ENHANCE OUR LEARNING (*Pages 119-121*)

Q. 1. ***Visit your kitchen and observe how your parents have organised various edibles. Can you suggest a better sorting method? Write it in your notebook.***

Ans.
- Our parents have organised different food items in different groups in the kitchen.
- Pulses such as *moong dal, chana dal, urad dal, arhar dal,* etc., should be grouped together. Cereals such as rice, *dalia,* wheat flour, maize flour, etc., should be grouped together.
- Spices like red chilli powder, salt, clove, black pepper, *ajwain,* cumin (*jeera*), coriander seeds (*dhaniya*), turmeric powder, *garam masala* etc., should be grouped together.
- Cooking oils and ghee such as mustard oil, *soyabean oil,* olive oil, desi ghee, etc., should be grouped together.
- Jams and squashes should be placed together.

Q. 2. ***Unscramble the letters (Column I) and match with their properties (Column II).***

	Column I		Column II
(*i*)	T R E M A T	(*a*)	Objects can be seen clearly through it
(*ii*)	U L S B E L O	(*b*)	Occupies space and has mass
(*iii*)	T N E R P A S N A R T	(*c*)	Shiny surface
(*iv*)	E R U S T L	(*d*)	Mixes completely in water

Ans.

	Column I		Column II
(*i*)	*MATTER*	(*b*)	*Occupies space and has mass.*
(*ii*)	*SOLUBLE*	(*d*)	*Mixes completely in water.*
(*iii*)	*TRANSPARENT*	(*a*)	*Objects can be seen clearly through it.*
(*iv*)	*LUSTRE*	(*c*)	*Shiny surface.*

Q. 3. ***The containers which are used to store materials in shops and at home are usually transparent. Give your reasons for this.***

Ans. The containers which are used to store materials in shops and at home are usually transparent so that the materials stored in them can be seen through them and can be found easily.

Q. 4. ***State whether the statements given below are True [T] or False [F]. Correct the False statement(s).***

(*i*) Wood is translucent while glass is opaque. [ ]

(*ii*) Aluminium foil has lustre while an eraser does not. [ ]

(*iii*) Sugar dissolves in water whereas sawdust does not. [ ]

(*iv*) An apple is a matter because it occupies no space and has mass. [ ]

Ans. (*i*) F → Wood is opaque while glass is transparent.

(*ii*) T (*iii*) T (*iv*) F → An apple is a matter because it occupies space and has mass.

Q. 5. ***We see chairs made up of various materials, such as wood, iron, plastic, bamboo, cement and stones. Following are some desirable properties of materials which can be used to make chairs. Which materials used to make chairs fulfil these properties the most?***

(*i*) Hardness (does not bend or shake on sitting even after long use).

(*ii*) Lightweight (easy to lift or to move from one place to another).

(*iii*) Does not feel very cold when sitting during winters.

(*iv*) Can be cleaned regularly and made to look new even after long use.

Ans. (*i*) Iron, cement and stones

(*ii*) Plastic and bamboo

(*iii*) Wood and bamboo

(*iv*) Plastic, cement and stones

Q. 6. ***You need to have containers for collection of (i) food waste, (ii) broken glass and (iii) wastepaper. Which materials will you choose for containers of these types of waste? What properties of materials do you need to think of?***

Ans. We can use plastic containers for collection of (*i*) food waste (*ii*) broken glass and (*iii*) waste paper. These containers may have different colours. Food waste is biodegradable. The material of the container should not react with food and should be leak proof. For broken glass which is hazardous and recyclable the material of the container should be hard so that glass should not cut it. For storing waste paper which is recyclable the material of the container should be light and strong.

Q. 7. ***Air is all around us but does not hinder us from seeing each other. Whereas, if a wooden door comes in between, we cannot see each other. It is because air is .... and the wooden door is. .... Choose the most appropriate option:***

(*i*) transparent, opaque

(*ii*) translucent, transparent

(*iii*) opaque, translucent

(*iv*) transparent, translucent

Ans. (*i*) transparent, opaque

Q. 8. ***Imagine you have two mysterious materials, X and Y. When you try to press material X, it feels rigid and does not change its shape easily. On the other hand, material Y easily changes its shape when you press it. Now, when you mix both materials in water, only material X dissolves completely, while material Y remains unchanged. What can materials X and Y be? Can you identify whether material X is hard or soft? What about material Y? Justify your answer.***

Ans. X can be sugar crystal as it feels rigid and does not change its shape easily but dissolves in water and Y can be rubber block as it changes its shape easily when pressed but does not dissolve in water.

The material X is hard.

The material Y is soft.

Q. 9. ***(i) Who am I? Identify me on the basis of the given properties.***

(*a*) I have lustre.

(*b*) I can be easily compressed.

(*c*) I am hard and soluble in water.

(*d*) You cannot see clearly through me.

(*e*) I have mass and volume but you cannot see me.

(ii) Make your own 'Who am I?'

Ans. (i) (a) steel
(b) rubber
(c) sugar
(d) cardboard or plywood
(e) air

(ii) (a) You cannot see clearly through me
(b) I am hard
(c) I am non-lustrous
(d) I am solid and insoluble in water
(e) I cannot be compressed easily.

[**Ans.** (a) Wood, (b) Iron/Steel, (c) Stone/Brick, (d) Chalk, (e) Wood/Iron]

Q. 10. ***You are provided with the following materials—vinegar, honey, mustard oil, water, glucose and wheat flour.***

Make any two pairs of materials where one material is soluble in the other. Now, make two pairs of materials where one material remains insoluble in the other material.

Ans. Soluble pairs
(i) Water and glucose
(ii) Water and vinegar

Insoluble pairs
(i) Water and mustard oil
(ii) Water and wheat flour.

V. EXAM ORIENTED QUESTIONS

Q. 1. ***List any five objects and write the names of materials they are made up of.***

Ans.

Object	Materials it is made up of
1. Table	Wood, plastic, glass
2. Spoon	Steel, wooden, plastic, brass, silver
3. Spectacles	Glass, steel and plastic
4. Book	Paper
5. Toys	Plastic, rubber, wood

Q. 2. ***Name any four objects which can be made from wood.***

Ans. Table, chair, stool and door.

Q. 3. ***Group the objects given below on the basis of hardness/ softness:***

Earthen lamp, wooden scale, pencil, tennis ball, screw driver, wool, wax, eraser, sharpener, soap.

Ans.

Hard objects	Soft objects
Earthen lamp	Tennis ball
Wooden scale	Wool
Pencil	Wax
Screw driver	Soap
Sharpener	Eraser

Q. 4. ***Select the objects from the following which have lustre:***

Steel bowl, cotton shirt, glass bowl, brass lamp, bell, soap cake

Ans. Steel bowl, brass lamp and bell have lustre.

Q. 5. ***List any four materials which can be used to make a spoon.***

Ans. Steel, brass, wood and plastic can be used to make a spoon.

Q. 6. ***Can a cricket ball be used to play tennis?***

Ans. Cricket ball cannot be used to play tennis because it is heavy and has low bounce.

Q. 7. ***Which of the following objects can be classified as soft?***

Chalk, chair, brick, wax, wool, steel bowl and sponge

Ans. Chalk, wax, wool and sponge are soft.

Q. 8. ***What are transparent materials? Give three examples of transparent objects.***

Ans. The materials through which the things can be seen clearly, are called transparent. For example, glass, air and water.

Q. 9. ***Name three materials which are soluble in water and three which are insoluble.***

Ans. Sugar, salt and washing soda are soluble in water.

Sand, sawdust and wax are insoluble in water.

Q. 10. ***What are opaque materials? Give two examples of opaque objects.***

Ans. Materials, through which we are not able to see at all, are called opaque. For example, metal sheet and wooden board.

Q. 11. ***Which of the following liquids are soluble in water and which are insoluble? Honey, mustard oil, alcohol, kerosene, vinegar and petrol.***

Ans. Honey, alcohol and vinegar are soluble in water.

Mustard oil, kerosene and petrol are insoluble in water.

Q. 12. ***State whether the statements given below are True (T) or False (F)***

(*i*) Chalk dissolves in water
(*ii*) Spoon is opaque, while glass is transparent
(*iii*) Sand settles down in water
(*iv*) Oil is insoluble in water
(*v*) Glucose is insoluble in water

Ans. (*i*) F (*ii*) T (*iii*) T (*iv*) T (*v*) F

Q. 13. ***Oxygen gas is soluble in water. It dissolves in water present in various water bodies. What is the importance of the oxygen gas dissolved in water?***

Ans. Oxygen gas, dissolved in water, is important for the survival of animals and plants that live in water because they breath in oxygen gas dissolved in water.

Q. 14. ***Match the objects given below with the materials from which they could be made.***

Object	Materials
Chair	Leather
Book	Plastic
Toy	Paper
Tumbler	Wood
Shoes	Glass

Ans.

Object	Materials
Chair	Wood
Book	Paper
Toy	Plastic
Tumbler	Glass
Shoes	Leather

Q. 15. ***Give the units in which mass and volume are measured.***

Ans. Mass is measured in units of gram (g) and kilogram (kg).

The units to measure volume are litre (L), millilitre (mL) and cubic metre (m^3).

Q. 16. ***Why is water considered as matter?***

Ans. Water is considered as matter because it has mass and occupies space.

Q. 17. ***Name a material which is transparent and is not visible.***

Ans. Air

Q. 18. ***Why does a piece of wood float on water?***

Ans. A piece of wood floats on the surface of water as it is lighter than water.

VI. OBJECTIVE TYPE QUESTIONS

1. *Match the following terms given in Column I with the properties given in Column II:*

Column I	Column II
(i) Lustrous	(a) Has mass and occupies space.
(ii) Opaque	(b) Does not disappear when mixed in water.
(iii) Matter	(c) Can be compressed or scratched easily.
(iv) Insoluble	(d) Not able to see through it.
(v) Soft	(e) The materials that have shiny surfaces.

2. *Fill in the blanks with appropriate words:*
   (a) Pen is made up of ...., ... and ...... materials.
   (b) Any substance that is used to create an object is known as ....
   (c) The method of arranging the objects into groups is known as ....
   (d) A cricket ball bounces to .... height than a tennis ball.
   (e) Lustrous materials have .... surfaces.
   (f) Materials which are difficult to compress or scratch are ....
   (g) .... and .... are softer than iron.
   (h) .... and .... are two objects which are made up of baked clay.
   (i) The materials, through which things can be seen clearly, are called............... .
   (j) .... is opaque whereas .... is translucent.
   (k) Sugar is .... in water whereas chalk powder is .... .
   (l) Salt will __________ in water when mixed with water.
   (m) Sawdust is .... than water whereas sand is ...... than water.
   (n) .... is the measure of quantity of matter in an object.
   (o) .... is the measure of space occupied by an object.
   (p) SI unit of mass is .... and that of volume is ....

3. *State whether the statements given below are True or False:*
   (i) Wood is opaque while glass is transparent. [ ]
   (ii) Salt dissolves in water whereas chalk powder does not. [ ]
   (iii) Air is considered matter because it has mass and occupies space. [ ]
   (iv) Sand is lighter than water. [ ]
   (v) A lighter object occupies less space. [ ]
   (vi) SI unit of volume is litre (L). [ ]

Multiple Choice Questions (MCQs)

Choose the correct option in the following questions:

1. *Which of the following objects does not belong to the same group?*
   (a) Aluminium foil
   (b) Copper wire
   (c) Steel tumbler
   (d) Plastic cup
2. *Which of the following objects are soft?*
   (a) Pillow and rubber
   (b) Brick and table
   (c) Brick and pillow
   (d) Cricket bat and brick
3. *Which of the following materials is not transparent?*
   (a) Cellophane sheet
   (b) Air
   (c) Butter paper
   (d) Glass
4. *Which of the following objects is opaque?*
   (a) Frosted glass
   (b) Glass tumbler
   (c) Window glass
   (d) Wooden board
5. *Which of the following materials is not soluble in water?*
   (a) Sugar
   (b) Chalk powder
   (c) Salt
   (d) Vinegar
6. *Which of the following is not an example of matter?*
   (a) Water (b) Air
   (c) Thought (d) Diamond

ACTIVITIES

ACTIVITY 6.1: Let us Identify (Page 102)

Make a list of objects you see around and also write the names of the materials they are made up of in Table.

Ans. Table: Identify materials

I Observe (Objects)		Materials they are made up of
1.	Books	Paper
2.	Table	Wood, glass, plastic
3.	Tumbler	Glass, steel, plastic
4.	Notebook	Paper
5.	Pen	Plastic, metal and ink
6.	Pencil	Wood and carbon (graphite)
7.	Scale	Plastic, iron
8.	Sharpener	Plastic and metal
9.	Chair	Wood, plastic
10.	Shirt	Cloth and plastic (buttons)

ACTIVITY 6.3: Let us think (Page 104)

Let us think what materials we can use to make a tumbler. Fill in the names of the materials in the spaces provided in Fig. 6.2.

(See Textbook, Page 104)

Ans. To study the various materials that can be used to make a tumbler

The material selected for making an object depends on the properties of material and the purpose for which the object is to be used. We may use different materials for making an object. The materials that are required to make a tumbler should be capable of holding water or some other beverage which is put into it. We cannot use cloth for making a tumbler because water would leak through it.

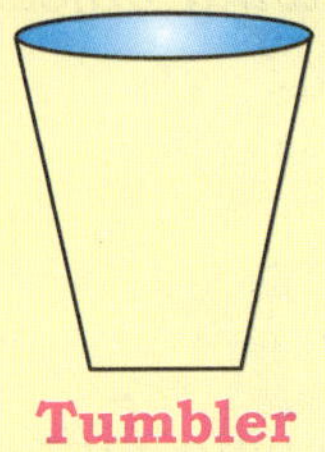

Tumbler

	Materials used to make tumbler
1.	Steel
2.	Brass
3.	Plastic
4.	Glass
5.	Paper
6.	Baked clay

It may be concluded that material used for making tumbler should be able to hold the liquid substance such as milk, water, tea, etc., in the tumbler. The porous materials such as cloth cannot be used for making tumbler because it will not be able to hold the liquid.

ACTIVITY 6.4: Let us Explore

(Page 105)

Fig. illustrates a variety of balls that are of the same size but made up of different materials.

Tennis ball Cricket ball Hand exercise ball

Fig. Different types of balls used for various purposes

- Take each ball and drop it from a fixed height.
- Note the height to which the ball bounces and record.
- Identify the ball that achieves the highest bounce.

Ans. To explore the bouncing level of the balls used for various purposes. Balls used for different purposes are made up of different materials. Bouncing levels of these balls are different depending on the material used to make them.

- Take different balls that are of the same size but made up of different materials.
- Take each ball and drop it from a fixed height (about 2 m).
- Observe the height to which the ball bounces and record it.
- Identify the ball that achieves the highest and the lowest bounce.

Table: Bouncing level of the balls

Ball	Bounce (high, medium or low)
Tennis ball	High
Cricket ball	Medium
Hand exercise ball	Low

It is observed that balls made up of different materials bounce back to different levels. The cricket ball has medium bouncing level whereas tennis ball has high bouncing level. Bouncing level of tennis ball is high.

It may be concluded that a level to which the ball bounces back depends upon the type of material used for *making* it.

ACTIVITY 6.5: Let us Observe

(Page 107)

- Hold the objects given in Table 6.3 with your hands. Feel whether the objects are hard or soft. Find out the materials they are made up of. Enter your observations in Table 6.3. (See Textbook, page 108)
- Compare your observations with the observations of your friends and discuss.

Ans. To study whether the given objects are hard or soft and to find the materials the objects are made up of. Materials which can be compressed or scratched easily are classified as **soft**, while the materials which are difficult to compress or scratch are classified as **hard**.

Table: Classification of objects as hard or soft and study of materials they are made up of

Objects		Hard/ Soft	Material(s)
1.	Brick	Hard	Baked clay
2.	Water bottle	Hard	Plastic/glass
3.	Pillow	Soft	Cloth and cotton
4.	Tumbler	Hard	Glass/steel/ plastic
5.	Table	Hard	Wood, plastic and glass
6.	Sweater	Soft	Wool
7.	Spoon	Hard	Steel, wood, silver
8.	Pen	Hard	Plastic, metal and ink

From the above observations it may be concluded that an object may be hard or soft depending on the nature of the material it is made up of. Hardness or softness property is relative in nature. For example, rubber is harder than sponge but softer than iron.

ACTIVITY 6.6: Let us Classify

(Page 109)

Classify the following objects as transparent, translucent or opaque in Table. (See Fig. NCERT Textbook, Page 109)

Ans. The materials through which the things can be seen clearly are called **transparent**.

The materials through which we are not able to see at all are called **opaque**. The materials through which the objects can be seen, but not clearly are called **translucent**.

- Record the results in tabular form.

Table: Classification of objects

Transparent	Translucent	Opaque
Glass tumbler	Butter paper	Eraser
Window glass	Frosted glass	Wooden board

It may be noted that depending on the extent to which we can see through an object, the objects may be classified as transparent, translucent or opaque.

ANSWERS

1.

Column I	Column II
(*i*) *Lustrous*	(*e*) *The materials that have shiny surfaces.*
(*ii*) *Opaque*	(*d*) *Not able to see through it.*
(*iii*) *Matter*	(*a*) *Has mass and occupies space.*
(*iv*) *Insoluble*	(*b*) *Does not disappear when mixed in water.*
(*v*) *Soft*	(*c*) *Can be compressed or scratched easily.*

2. Fill in the blanks:

(a) plastic, metal, ink (b) material (c) classification
(d) less (e) shiny (f) hard
(g) sponge, rubber (h) brick, pitcher (i) transparent
(j) wooden board, frosted glass (k) soluble, insoluble
(l) dissolve (m) lighter, heavier (n) mass
(o) volume (p) kilogram (or kg), cubic metre (or m^3)

3. True or False:

(i) True (ii) True (iii) True (iv) False
(v) False (vi) False

Multiple Choice Questions (MCQs)

1. (d) 2. (a) 3. (c) 4. (d) 5. (b) 6. (c)

VII. EXERCISE FOR PRACTICE

1. Give two examples of objects which are made up of more than one type of materials. Name the materials present in them.
2. Group the following objects based on any common property:
   Water, spoon, notebook, keys, cricket ball, air, glass, and milk.
3. List any four materials which can be used to make a chair.
4. Why are different materials used for making balls for various sports?
5. Observe the following figure and group the objects in as many different ways as possible.

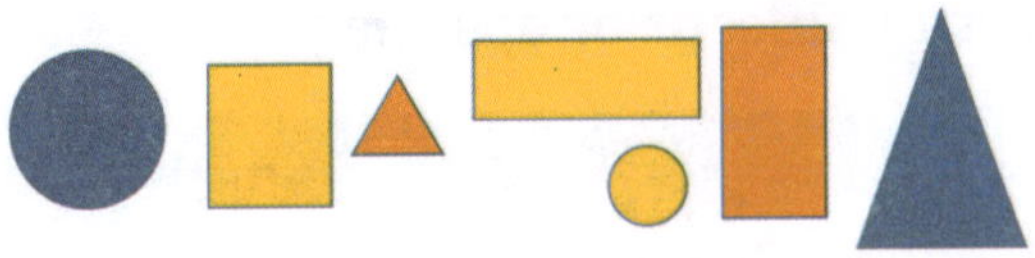

Fig.: Grouping of objects

6. Give two examples of lustrous materials and two examples of non-lustrous materials.
7. Classify the following objects as hard and soft:
   Glass rod, wax, rubber, tile, stone
8. Define the followings:
   (i) matter (ii) lustrous
   (iii) volume (iv) mass
   (v) classification
   (vi) non-lustrous.
9. State whether the statements given below are True [T] or False [F]. Correct the false statement(s).
   (i) Air is transparent and has mass. [ ]
   (ii) Salt dissolves in water whereas sand does not. [ ]
   (iii) Milk is transparent whereas water is opaque. [ ]
   (iv) Rubber is soft and aluminium is hard. [ ]
10. Complete the following sentences:
    (i) ________ is soluble in water whereas _____ is insoluble in water.
    (ii) All materials have ________ and occupy ________.
11. Identify me on the basis of given properties.
    (i) I am liquid and insoluble in water.
    (ii) I am hard and insoluble in water.
    (iii) I have mass and lustre.
    (iv) I can be compressed but you cannot see me.
    (v) I am hard and you can see clearly through me.

NOTES

INTERESTING MIND MAP

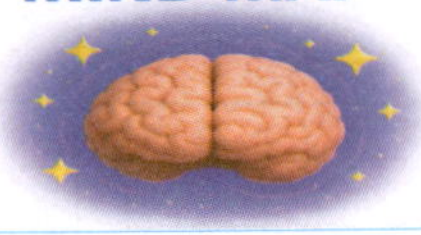

Temperature and its Measurement

1 Hot or Cold?

- We can use our sense of touch to differentiate between a hot object and a cold object.

2 Temperature

- Temperature measured by a thermometer helps us to know hotness or coldness of a body.

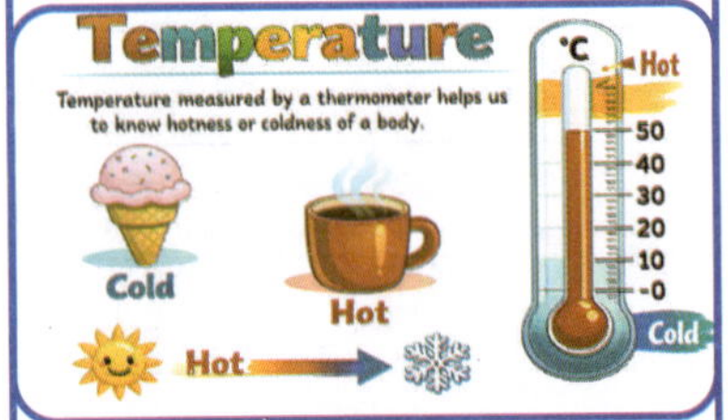

3 Measuring Temperature

3a Clinical Thermometer

- Also called digital clinical thermometer measures temperature of a person's body.
- Unit of temperature on the Celsius scale is degree Celsius denoted by °C.
- Unit of temperature on Fahrenheit scale is degree Fahrenheit denoted by °F.
- Unit of temperature on Kelvin scale is kelvin denoted by K.
- The SI unit of temperature is kelvin.

3b Laboratory Thermometer

- It has a liquid column that rises or falls with change in temperature.
- It measures temperature from –10°C to 110°C.
- The smallest value it can measure is 1°C.

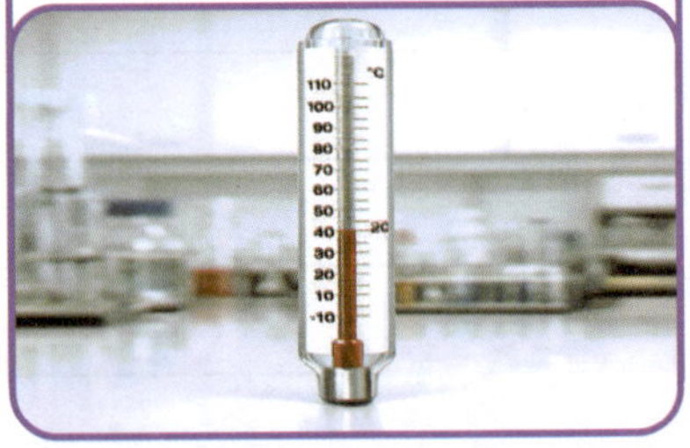

3c Air Temperature

- Room thermometer helps to measure air temperature.

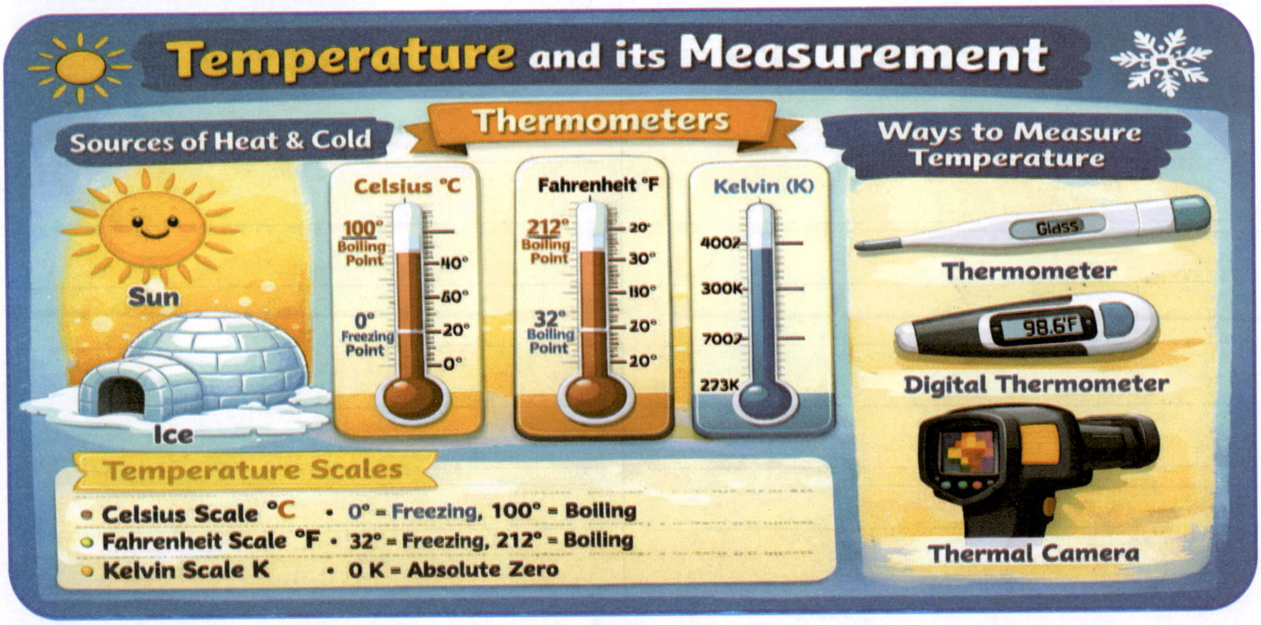

7

Temperature and its Measurement

I. POINTS TO REMEMBER

1. **Hot or Cold:** We can feel the difference between warm water and ice-cold water only by **touch** and tell whether an object is hot or cold.
2. When the sun is shining directly above us, usually we say that it is very hot outside.

Fig. Hot or Cold

3. **Temperature:** Hotness (or coldness) of a body is known from its temperature. A body 'A' is hotter in comparison to another body 'B' means the temperature of body 'A' is more than the temperature of body 'B'.
4. Hotter bodies have higher temperatures compared to colder bodies.
5. Boiling water is hot and has a high temperature compared to normal tap water while ice-cold water is cold and has a low temperature compared to normal tap water.
6. **Measuring Temperatures:** The device used to measure temperatures is called a **thermometer.**
7. **Clinical thermometers** are used to measure human body temperatures which are usually measured using **Celsius** scale in **degrees Celsius denoted by °C.** Earlier mercury was used in clinical thermometers. Mercury has the properties of good expansion and shine. It helps in correct measurement of temperature. But mercury is toxic and difficult to dispose of in case the thermometer breaks.
8. **Digital clinical thermometers** use **heat sensors** and are easy to measure the temperature and take readings.

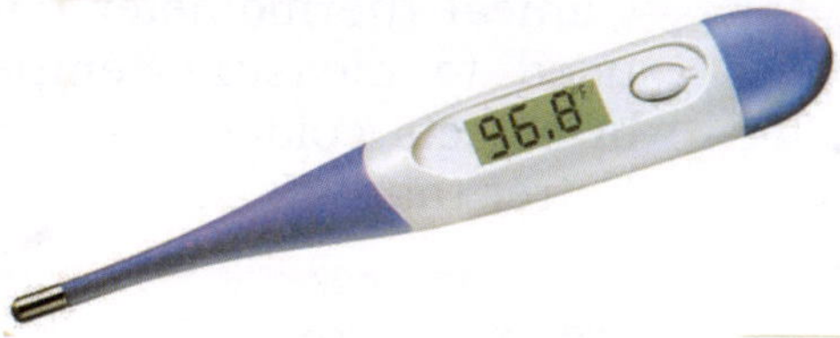

Fig. Clinical thermometer

9. Since **COVID 19** time non-**contact infrared thermometers** are used. These measure the body temperature **without touching** the human body.

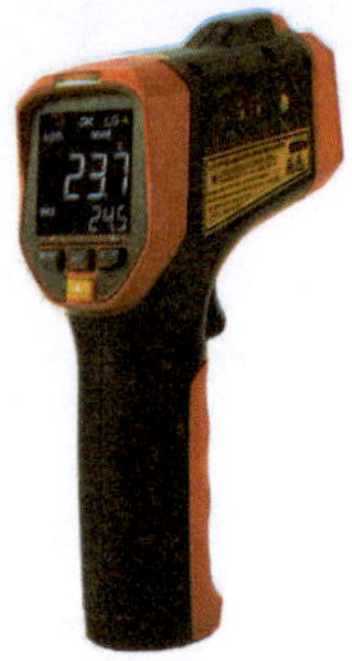

Fig. Non-contact infrared thermometer

10. **Human body temperature:** Normal temperature of a healthy human body is 37 °C. This is nearly equal to 98.6°F on the Fahrenheit scale. There can be small variations in the normal body temperatures of healthy persons with age, with time of the day and activity level etc.

11. Normal body temperature of healthy children is a little higher (37° C to 37.5°C).

12. For older adults, normal temperature is a little lower for a healthy human body (36.2°C to 36.8°C).

13. The range of a clinical thermometer is 35°C to 42°C. There are normally 10 divisions between any two consecutive degrees. Thus, the smallest value of reading on a clinical thermometer is 0.1°C.

14. Clinical thermometer cannot be used to measure temperatures of objects colder than 35°C and hotter than 42°C.

15. **Laboratory thermometers:** These are used to measure the temperatures of objects, air around us and for many other scientific purposes. Coloured **alcohol (usually red)** or **mercury** is used in the laboratory thermometers.

Fig. Laboratory thermometers

16. Usual range of laboratory thermometer is from –10° C to 110°C.

17. **Different scales to measure temperature:** Scales used in laboratories to measure temperatures of objects are **Kelvin, Celsius** and **Fahrenheit** scales. These are easily convertible to each other.

Temperature in Kelvin Scale = Temperature in Celsius scale + 273.15

Temperature in Fahrenheit scale = 9/5 of Temperature in Celsius scale + 32

Temperature in Celsius scale = 5/9 of (temperature in Fahrenheit scale – 32)

18. The name of a temperature scale e.g. Celsius scale, Fahrenheit scale and Kelvin scale start with a capital letter. The symbols of all units (°C, °F, K) are Capital letters. The degree sign (°) is not written with K.

19. **Correct way of measuring temperature using a laboratory thermometer:**
    - When a thermometer is immersed in a liquid, its bulb should not touch the bottom or walls of the container.
    - The thermometer should be held vertically and not tilted.
    - Reading of temperature must be taken when the bulb is immersed in the liquid.

- While reading the temperature, the eye should be directly in line with the level of the liquid column of the thermometer.

Fig. Measuring temperature of warm water

20. Temperature of air around us: To know the temperature of the air during the day, thermometers are hung on the walls of our laboratories. We can read the temperature of air at any time during the day from these thermometers. Sometimes a special thermometer called **Maximum-minimum thermometer** is used which keeps the two readings of the maximum and minimum temperatures reached during the 24 hours.

II. KEYWORDS

1. **Air Temperature:** The temperature of air around us at a given time.
2. **Celsius Scale:** A scale for measuring temperature in degrees Celsius, named after a scientist.
3. **Clinical Thermometer:** A device used for measuring human body temperatures.
4. **Degree Celsius:** The unit of temperature measured on Celsius scale.
5. **Degree Fahrenheit:** The unit of temperature measured on Fahrenheit scale.
6. **Fahrenheit Scale:** A scale for measuring temperature in degrees Fahrenheit, named after a scientist.
7. **Kelvin:** The unit of temperature measured on Kelvin scale.
8. **Kelvin Scale:** A scale for measuring temperature in kelvin, named after a scientist.
9. **Laboratory Thermometer:** Thermometer used to measure the temperatures of objects, air around us and for many other scientific purposes.
10. **SI Unit of Temperature:** The SI unit of temperature is kelvin.
11. **Temperature:** The degree of hotness (or coldness) is called temperature.

III. NCERT INTEXT QUESTIONS

Q. 1. ***Can it always be correctly judged, that a person has fever, only by touching the person?*** ***(Page 123)***

Ans. 1. Sense of touch varies from person to person. One person may feel by touch that the other person is hot and has fever while other may not feel that hot. Our sense of touch is not accurate so it cannot observe small differences in hot or less hot body of a person due to fever.

2. It cannot always be correctly judged that a person has fever, only by touching the person.

3. For correct judgement that a person has fever or not, we must use clinical thermometer correctly.

Q. 2. ***Do small children generally have slightly higher body temperatures as compared to adults? (Page 128)***

Ans. Yes, small children usually have slightly higher body temperatures compared to adults. For kids, a normal body temperature is usually between 37.0°C and 37.5°C. For adults, it's a bit lower, usually between 36.1°C and 37.2°C.

Q. 3. ***Do old people, even when healthy, generally have lower body temperatures than young adults? (Page 128)***

Ans. Yes, even healthy older people generally have lower body temperatures than young adults. As people age, their bodies slow down. For older adults, normal body temperature is often around 36.2°C to 36.8°C, which is slightly lower than the typical range for younger adults.

Q. 4. ***Can a clinical thermometer be used for measuring the temperature of boiling water? Or for measuring the temperature of ice? (Page 129)***

Ans. A clinical thermometer has a range of 35 °C to 42 °C. The temperature of boiling water is 100 °C and is beyond the range of a clinical thermometer. Also the temperature of ice is 0 °C and is beyond the range of clinical thermometer.

Therefore a clinical thermometer cannot be used for measuring the temperatures of boiling water or of ice.

IV. LET US ENHANCE OUR LEARNING *(Pages 137–140)*

Q. 1. ***The normal temperature of a healthy human being is close to***

(*i*) 98.6 °C (*ii*) 37.0 °C
(*iii*) 32.0 °C (*iv*) 27.0 °C

Q. 2. ***37 °C is the same temperature as***

(*i*) 97.4 °F (*ii*) 97.6 °F
(*iii*) 98.4 °F (*iv*) 98.6 °F

Q. 3. ***Fill in the blanks:***

(*i*) The hotness or coldness of a system is determined by its ....

(*ii*) The temperature of ice-cold water cannot be measured by a .... thermometer.

(*iii*) The unit of temperature is degree ....

Q. 4. ***The range of a laboratory thermometer is usually ....***

(*i*) 10 °C to 100 °C
(*ii*) –10 °C to 110 °C
(*iii*) 32 °C to 45 °C
(*iv*) 35 °C to 42 °C

Q. 5. ***Four students used a laboratory thermometer to measure the temperature of water as shown in the given figure***

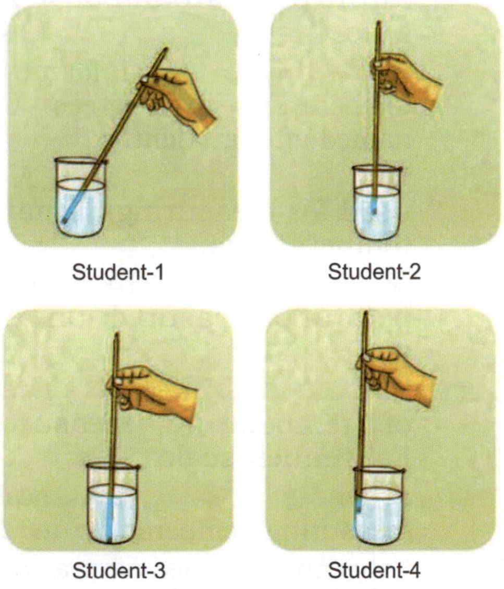

Who do you think followed the correct way for measuring temperature?

(*i*) Student 1 (*ii*) Student 2
(*iii*) Student 3 (*iv*) Student 4

Answers

1. (*ii*) 37.0 °C **2.** (*iv*) 98.6 °F
3. (*i*) temperature (*ii*) clinical (*iii*) Celsius
4. (*ii*) –10 °C to 110 °C
5. (*ii*) Student 2

Q. 6. ***Colour to show the red column on the drawings of thermometers (Fig. below) as per the temperatures written below:***

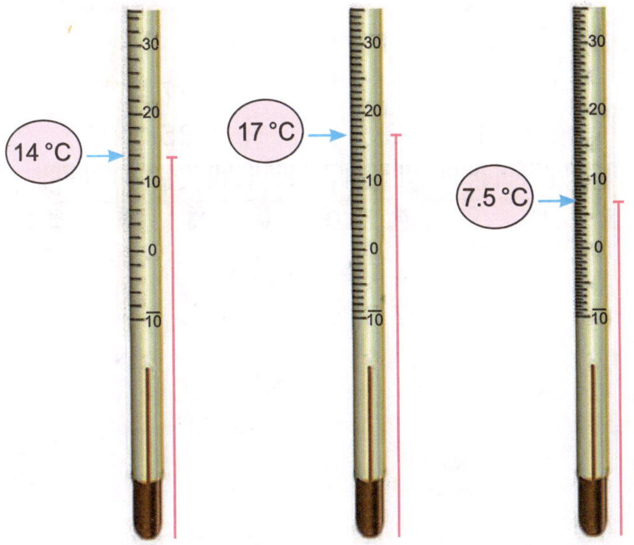

Ans. Hint: In the first thermometer for 14 °C colour up to two small lines above mark 10 (each small line indicates 2 degrees Celsius).

In the **second** thermometer for 17°C colour up to seven small lines above mark 10 (each small line indicates 1 degree Celsius).

In the **third** thermometer colour up to fifteen small lines above mark 0 (each small line indicates 0.5 degree Celsius). Red lines are marked alongside the respective thermometers for information.

Q. 7. ***Observe the part of thermometer shown in Fig. and answer the following questions:***

(*i*) What type of thermometer is it?

(*ii*) What is the reading of the thermometer?

(*iii*) What is the smallest value that this thermometer can measure?

Ans.

(*i*) The lowest mark on the thermometer is '–10' so this is a laboratory thermometer that has a measuring range of –10 °C to 110 °C.

(*ii*) The reading of the thermometer is 26 °C.

(*iii*) There are 10 small line marks between any 10 degrees (0–10, 10–20 and so on) on the thermometer. One small division can read 10/10 = 1 degree celsius. So the thermometer can measure the smallest value of 1°C.

Q. 8. ***A laboratory thermometer is not used to measure our body temperature. Give a reason.***

Ans. A laboratory thermometer is not used to measure human body temperature for two reasons:

(*i*) The bulb of the laboratory thermometer has to be kept inside the liquid for taking the reading and it is not convenient for measuring human body temperature.

(*ii*) The smallest value of reading required for body temperature is 0.1 °C which is not possible in laboratory thermometer.

Q. 9. ***Vaishnavi has not gone to school as she is ill. Her mother has kept a record of her body temperature for three days as shown in Table below***

Table: Body temperature record of Vaishnavi

	Temperature at					
DAY	**7 am**	**10 am**	**1 pm**	**4 pm**	**7 pm**	**10 pm**
One	38.0 °C	37.8 °C	38.0 °C	38.0 °C	40.0 °C	39.0 °C
Two	38.6 °C	38.8 °C	39.0 °C	39.0 °C	39.0 °C	38.0 °C
Three	37.6 °C	37.4 °C	37.2 °C	37.0 °C	36.8 °C	36.6 °C

(*i*) What was Vaishnavi's highest recorded temperature?

(*ii*) On which day and at what time was Vaishnavi's highest temperature recorded?

(*iii*) On which day did Vaishnavi's temperature return to normal?

Ans. (*i*) 40.0 °C (*ii*) Day one 7 pm (*iii*) Day three

Q. 10. ***If you have to measure the temperature 22.5 °C, which of the following three thermometers will you use (Fig.)? Explain.***

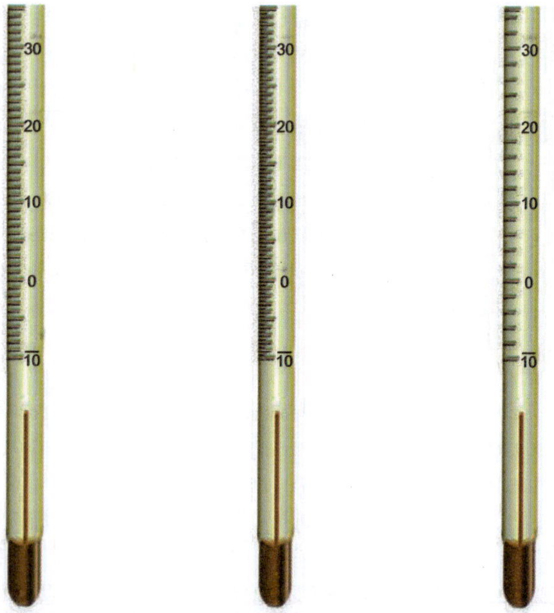

Fig. Three thermometers

Ans. We will use thermometer (*b*). Thermometer (*a*) can measure the smallest value of 1°C and thermometer (*c*) can measure the smallest value of 2°C as per the small line markings on these. Only thermometer (*b*) has the markings on it to measure the smallest value of 0.5°C which is necessary for measuring a temperature of 22.5 °C.

Q. 11. **The temperature shown by the thermometer in Fig. is**

(*i*) 28.0 °C (*ii*) 27.5 °C

(*iii*) 26.5 °C (*iv*) 25.3 °C

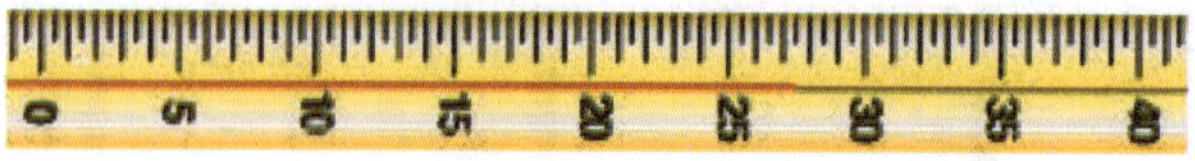

Fig. Thermometer

Ans. (*ii*) 27.5 °C

Q. 12. ***A laboratory thermometer has 50 divisions between 0°C and 100°C. What does each division of this thermometer measure?***

Ans. 2°C

Q. 13. ***Draw the scale of a thermometer in which the smallest division reads 0.5 °C. You may draw only the portion between 10°C and 20°C.***

Ans.

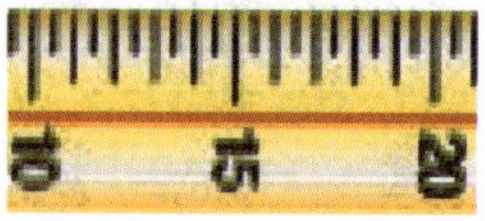

Q. 14. ***Someone tells you that she has a fever of 101 degrees. Does she mean it on the Celsius scale or Fahrenheit scale?***

Ans. She means the temperature on the Fahrenheit scale. Human body temperature does not normally go below 35 °C or above 42 °C. In the Fahrenheit scale this range is between 95 degrees to 107.8 degrees.

V. EXAM ORIENTED QUESTIONS

Very Short Answer Type Questions

Q. 1. ***What is a reliable measure of hotness or coldness of a body?***

Ans. Temperature.

Q. 2. ***What device measures temperature?***

Ans. Thermometer.

Q. 3. ***Name two types of thermometers.***

Ans. Clinical and laboratory thermometers.

Q. 4. ***What scale is commonly used in clinical thermometers?***

Ans. Celsius scale.

Q. 5. *What is the normal temperature of a healthy human body on Celsius and on Fahrenheit scale?*

Ans. 37.0 °C, 98.6 °F.

Q. 6. *What substance was traditionally used in thermometers but is now avoided due to toxicity?*

Ans. Mercury.

Q. 7. *Which type of thermometer uses heat sensors to measure temperature?*

Ans. Digital thermometer.

Q. 8. *How much lower is the temperature measured in the armpit compared to the actual body temperature?*

Ans. About 0.5 °C to 1 °C lower.

Q. 9. *What is the unit of temperature in the Kelvin scale?*

Ans. Kelvin (K).

Q. 10. *Can a clinical thermometer measure the temperature of boiling water?*

Ans. No. Boiling water has a temperature of 100°C, while the clinical thermometer has a range of 35 °C to 42 °C only.

Q. 11. *What is the temperature range of a typical laboratory thermometer?*

Ans. –10 °C to 110 °C.

Q. 12. *Which liquid is commonly used in laboratory thermometers?*

Ans. Coloured alcohol (usually red) or mercury.

Q. 13. *At what temperature does the Celsius scale mark the boiling point of water and the freezing point of water?*

Ans. 100 °C, 0 °C.

Q. 14. *What is the smallest value a laboratory thermometer can read according to the text?*

Ans. 1°C

Q. 15. *What is the SI unit of temperature?*

Ans. Kelvin (K).

Q. 16. *What should be done to the digital thermometer before and after use?*

Ans. Wash the tip with soap and water.

Short Answer Type Questions

Q. 1. *Why is it important to measure temperature accurately?*

Ans. Accurate temperature measurement is important because wrong measurements can lead to incorrect conclusions. Inaccurate measure of body temperature may lead to suggest a fever when there is no fever and when there is fever it may suggest no fever.

Q. 2. *How does a digital clinical thermometer work?*

Ans. A digital clinical thermometer measures temperature using heat sensors and displays the temperature digitally. It runs on batteries and provides an easy-to-read digital display. There is no risk in using a digital clinical thermometer.

Q. 3. *What is the normal range of human body temperature? Can it vary?*

Ans. The normal range of human body temperature is around 37.0 °C but it can vary slightly due to factors like age, time of the day, and activity level. A perfectly healthy person's temperature might be a bit higher or lower than 37.0 °C.

Q. 4. *Why is it necessary to wash the tip of the thermometer before and after use?*

Ans. Washing the tip of the thermometer before and after use helps prevent the spread of germs and ensures accurate readings. It is essential for maintaining hygiene, especially when measuring the temperature of different individuals.

Q. 5. *How do non-contact thermometers work, and what are their benefits?*

Ans. Non-contact thermometers, or infrared thermometers, measure temperature from a distance using infrared sensors. They reduce the risk of spreading infections and are particularly useful in medical settings for quick and safe temperature measurements.

Q. 6. ***What did people use to detect fever before thermometers were developed?***

Ans. Before thermometers, people used to detect fever by checking the pulse rate, as fever affects the pulse rate of a person. However, this method was not very reliable since conditions other than fever could also influence the pulse rate.

Q. 7. ***How do you measure temperature using a laboratory thermometer? What precautions should be taken when using a laboratory thermometer?***

Ans. To measure temperature with a laboratory thermometer, immerse the bulb in the liquid without touching the sides or bottom of the container. Hold the thermometer vertically and read the temperature while it is still immersed. Ensure your eye level is in line with the liquid column in the thermometer.

Q. 8. ***How is the Kelvin scale related to the Celsius scale?***

Ans. The Kelvin scale is related to the Celsius scale by the formula: Temperature in Kelvin = Temperature in Celsius + 273.15.

Q. 9. ***What is the role of weather stations in measuring air temperature?***

Ans. Weather stations monitor air temperature along with other parameters to gather data used for weather forecasting. This data collection helps predict weather patterns and informs the public about daily temperature variations and climate trends.

Q. 10. ***What smallest value of temperature can we measure on a laboratory thermometer?***

Ans. Different laboratory thermometers give different measures of the smallest value of temperature. This depends on the markings on the scale of thermometer. In some thermometers 5 small lines are marked between any 10 (10 - 20 or 20 - 30 degrees) degrees. The smallest value of temperature of 2 degrees is measured on these. When a thermometer has 20 small lines between any 10 degrees. The smallest value of temperature of 0.5 degrees is measured on these.

Long Answer Type Questions

Q. 1. ***Describe the differences between clinical and laboratory thermometers in terms of their use and range.***

Ans.

Clinical Thermometers	Laboratory Thermometers
• Clinical thermometers are designed specifically for measuring human body temperature.	• Laboratory thermometers are used for a variety of scientific purposes.
• Typically these have a limited range, from around 35 °C to 42 °C, which is sufficient for detecting fevers and other health-related temperature variations.	• Laboratory thermometers can measure a much wider range of temperatures, usually from –10 °C to 110 °C.
• Clinical thermometers are used to take readings of human body temperatures on Celsius or sometimes on Fahrenheit scale.	• Laboratory thermometers are used to take readings of temperatures on Celsius scale or on Kelvin scale.
• Clinical thermometers can be mercury thermometers, digital thermometers or non-contact infrared thermometers.	• Laboratory thermometers use coloured alcohol or mercury as liquids that expand to show the temperature readings.

Q. 2. *Explain why digital clinical thermometers are preferred over earlier mercury thermometers.*

Ans. Mercury thermometers have mercury in the thin glass tubes. Mercury was used because of its shining and good expansion properties. But mercury is a highly toxic substance and it is difficult to dispose of mercury in case the thermometer breaks.

Digital clinical thermometers are preferred over mercury thermometers because:

(*i*) Digital thermometers do not use mercury. These use heat sensors to detect the body temperature.

(*ii*) The numbers on display on the digital thermometers are easy to read.

Q. 3. *Explain the principle of the Kelvin scale and its significance in scientific measurements.*

Ans. Scientifically there is no limit on the higher temperature that can exist. The highest temperature known is about 15 million degrees Celsius at the core of the Sun. There can be more celestial objects having higher temperatures.

The lowest temperature that can exist, till date known to the scientists, is close to −273 °C.

On the Kelvin scale this lowest temperature of −273 °C is taken as 0 kelvin. 0 kelvin is also called absolute zero.

Q. 4. *Describe the process and precautions necessary for using a laboratory thermometer.*

Ans. The thermometer should be handled carefully, avoiding any impact that could break it.

The bulb of the thermometer should be immersed in the liquid to measure its temperature.

The bulb of the thermometer should not touch the sides or bottom of the container.

The thermometer must be held vertically straight and it should not be tilted.

The temperature should be read keeping the eye in line with the level of the thermometer in the liquid.

The reading of the temperature must be taken immediately after the level of liquid in the column of the thermometer stops moving up. Temperature of the liquid may change if we delay taking reading.

After taking the reading, it should be cleaned and stored properly to maintain its accuracy and longevity.

Q. 5. *Describe how air temperature data is used in making weather forecasts.*

Ans. Air temperature data is an important component in weather forecasting as it influences atmospheric pressure, humidity, and wind patterns. Temperature data from various sources, including weather stations, satellites, and weather balloons is collected. This data is used in computer models to analyse atmospheric conditions.

Accurate temperature measurements allow forecasting of changes in weather, such as cold and heat waves, and rain. This information is very useful for agriculture, transportation, and public safety.

Q. 6. *Name the three scales of measuring temperatures known to you. Write down the correct ways to write the names and units of these scales.*

Ans. The three scales of measuring temperature are the Celsius scale, the Fahrenheit scale and the Kelvin scale.

- The names of temperature scales—Celsius scale, Fahrenheit scale and Kelvin scale, start with a capital letter.

- For the units of temperature, degree Celsius and degree Fahrenheit, the word degree starts with a lower-case letter while Celsius and Fahrenheit start with a capital letter.
- The unit kelvin starts with a lower-case letter.
- The symbols of all units (°C, °F, K) are capital letters. The degree sign (°) is not written with K.
- A full stop is not written after the symbol, except at the end of a sentence.
- While writing the temperature, a space is left between the number and the unit.
- For temperatures more than one degree, we use the plural of 'degree', that is, 'degrees', while writing the full form of the unit.

Q. 7. *Explain the role of Anna Mani in the field of meteorology and her contributions to temperature measurement.*

Ans. Anna Mani was a great Indian scientist known as the **'Weather Woman of India.'** She made significant contributions in the field of meteorology by developing and building a large number of weather measurement instruments. Her work reduced India's reliance on foreign instruments.

India has grown to lead the world in renewable energy due to the contributions of Anna Mani in this field.

VI. OBJECTIVE TYPE QUESTIONS

1. *Match the following items given in Column A with that in Column B:*

Column A	Column B
(*a*) *Clinical thermometer*	(*i*) *Measures temperature without contact*
(*b*) *Mercury*	(*ii*) *98.6 °F in Fahrenheit scale*
(*c*) *Digital thermometer*	(*iii*) *–273.15 °C*
(*d*) *Normal body temperature in Celsius*	(*iv*) *Weather Woman of India*
(*e*) *Infrared thermometer*	(*v*) *Used to measure human body temperature*
(*f*) *37°C in Celsius scale equals*	(*vi*) *Highly toxic substance used in old thermometers*
(*g*) *Laboratory thermometer*	(*vii*) *Provides easy-to-read digital display*
(*h*) *Absolute zero*	(*viii*) *Typically has a range from –10 °C to 110 °C*
(*i*) *Anna Mani*	(*ix*) *37.0 °C*
(*j*) *Heat sensors*	(*x*) *Used in digital thermometers*

2. *Fill in the blanks with appropriate words :*

   (a) *The device that measures temperature is called a ....*

   (b) *Clinical thermometers generally use a scale called the .... scale.*

   (c) *The normal temperature of a healthy human body is taken to be ..... °C.*

   (d) *The liquid used in laboratory thermometers is generally alcohol or ....*

   (e) *A digital clinical thermometer measures temperature using .... sensors.*

   (f) *Non-contact thermometers are also known as .... thermometers.*

   (g) *The unit of temperature in the Kelvin scale is ....*

   (h) *Mercury thermometers are being replaced by .... thermometers due to safety concerns.*

   (i) *The temperature difference between the two bodies tells us how .... one body is in comparison to another.*

   (j) *The Fahrenheit scale is not commonly used in .... studies.*

   (k) *The normal temperature of a human body in Fahrenheit is .... °F.*

   (l) *Laboratory thermometers typically have a temperature range from –10 °C to .... °C.*

   (m) *The lowest and the highest temperature a laboratory thermometer can measure is known as its ....*

   (n) *The temperature of a body tells us how .... or cold it is.*

   (o) *During the COVID-19 pandemic, special thermometers called .... were used to measure temperature from a distance.*

3. *State whether the statements given below are True or False:*

   (i) *Clinical thermometers are used for measuring the temperature of boiling water.*

   (ii) *Digital thermometers are safer than mercury thermometers because they do not contain toxic substances.*

   (iii) *The Kelvin scale is primarily used for everyday temperature measurements.*

   (iv) *The normal temperature of a healthy human body is 37.0 °C.*

   (v) *Infrared thermometers can measure temperature without making contact with the body.*

   (vi) *Laboratory thermometers typically have a temperature range from 0 °C to 100 °C.*

   (vii) *The Fahrenheit scale sets the freezing point of water at 0 °F.*

   (viii) *Anna Mani made significant contributions to the field of meteorology in India.*

   (ix) *Mercury thermometers are being replaced by digital thermometers due to ease of reading and safety concerns.*

   (x) *Lowest temperature limit is close to –273.15 °C (0 kelvin) and it is called absolute zero.*

Multiple Choice Questions (MCQs)

Choose the correct option in the following questions

1. *What device measures temperature?*
   (*a*) Barometer
   (*b*) Thermometer
   (*c*) Hygrometer
   (*d*) Anemometer
2. *What is the normal temperature of a healthy human body in Celsius?*
   (*a*) 35.0 °C (*b*) 36.0 °C
   (*c*) 37.0 °C (*d*) 38.0 °C
3. *Which substance was traditionally used in thermometers but is now avoided due to toxicity?*
   (*a*) Alcohol (*b*) Mercury
   (*c*) Water (*d*) Glycerin
4. *Digital thermometers measure temperature using which sensors?*
   (*a*) Light sensors
   (*b*) Sound sensors
   (*c*) Heat sensors
   (*d*) Pressure sensors
5. *Which scale is commonly used in clinical thermometers?*
   (*a*) Kelvin (*b*) Fahrenheit
   (*c*) Rankine (*d*) Celsius
6. *What is the unit of temperature in the Kelvin scale?*
   (*a*) Degree Kelvin
   (*b*) Kelvin
   (*c*) Degree Celsius
   (*d*) Degree Fahrenheit
7. *What is the normal temperature of a healthy human body in Fahrenheit?*
   (*a*) 97.6 °F (*b*) 98.6 °F
   (*c*) 99.6 °F (*d*) 100.6 °F
8. *Which type of thermometer measures temperature without making contact with the human body?*
   (*a*) Digital thermometer
   (*b*) Mercury thermometer
   (*c*) Infrared thermometer
   (*d*) Alcohol thermometer
9. *What is the typical range of a laboratory thermometer?*
   (*a*) –10 °C to 50 °C
   (*b*) –10 °C to 100 °C
   (*c*) –10 °C to 110 °C
   (*d*) –10 °C to 150 °C
10. *There is a limit to the lowest temperature that can be achieved and is called absolute zero.*
    (*a*) 0°C (*b*) – 100 °C
    (*c*) –273.15 °C (*d*) – 500 °C
11. *What was Anna Mani known for?*
    (*a*) Developing the Kelvin scale
    (*b*) Creating the first digital thermometer
    (*c*) Contributions in the field of meteorology and weather instruments
    (*d*) Discovering infrared thermometers
12. *How should a laboratory thermometer be held when measuring temperature?*
    (*a*) Horizontally
    (*b*) Vertically
    (*c*) At a 45-degree angle
    (*d*) Upside down
13. *What should be done to the digital thermometer before and after use?*
    (*a*) Boil it
    (*b*) Clean it with alcohol
    (*c*) Wash the tip with soap and water
    (*d*) Freeze it

14. *Which scale is primarily used for very low scientific temperature measurements?*

(*a*) Celsius
(*b*) Fahrenheit
(*c*) Kelvin
(*d*) Both (*a*) and (*b*)

15. *What is the freezing point of water on the Celsius scale?*

(*a*) −273.15 °C (*b*) 0 °C
(*c*) 32 °C (*d*) 100 °C

16. *What is the boiling point of water on the Fahrenheit scale?*

(*a*) 100 °F (*b*) 180 °F
(*c*) 212 °F (*d*) 373 °F

17. *What should be avoided when handling a laboratory thermometer?*

(*a*) Holding it by the bulb
(*b*) Immersing it in the substance
(*c*) Reading it at eye level
(*d*) Keeping it vertical

18. *Which type of thermometer was used during the COVID-19 pandemic for non-contact measurement?*

(*a*) Digital thermometer
(*b*) Mercury thermometer
(*c*) Infrared thermometer
(*d*) Alcohol thermometer

19. *Why is it important to measure temperature accurately in scientific experiments?*

(*a*) To save time
(*b*) To ensure reliability of results
(*c*) To use expensive equipment
(*d*) To make experiments faster

20. *Why are digital thermometers replacing mercury thermometers?*

(*a*) They are cheaper
(*b*) They are easier to break
(*c*) They pose no risk of mercury exposure and are easier to read
(*d*) They are less accurate

Assertion-Reason Questions

For the following questions, two statements are given- one labelled Assertion (A) and the other labelled Reason (R). Select the correct answer to questions from the codes (a), (b), (c) and (d) as given below- (a) Both A and R are true and R is correct explanation of the assertion. (b) Both A and R are true but R is not the correct explanation of the assertion. (c) A is true but R is false. (d) A is false but R is true

1. **Assertion (A):** Clinical thermometers are used for measuring the temperature of boiling water.

Reason (R): Clinical thermometers have a limited range suitable only for measuring human body temperature.

2. **Assertion (A):** Digital thermometers are replacing mercury thermometers.

Reason (R): Mercury is a toxic substance, and digital thermometers provide easier-to-read displays.

3. **Assertion (A):** Infrared thermometers were widely used during the COVID-19 pandemic.

Reason (R): Infrared thermometers can measure temperature without direct contact with the body.

ACTIVITIES

ACTIVITY 7.3: ***Let us Observe (Page 130)***

- Take a laboratory thermometer and observe it carefully.

Q. 1. *What is the lowest temperature it can measure?*

Ans. The lowest temperature a laboratory thermometer can measure is –10 °C.

Q. 2. *What is the highest temperature it can measure?*

Ans. The highest temperature a laboratory thermometer can measure is 110 °C.

So the range of this thermometer is from –10 °C to 110 °C.

ACTIVITY 7.7: ***Let us Analyse (Page 134)***

- Read or listen to the weather reports for a place for 10 successive days.
- Record the maximum and minimum air temperature for each day in Table.
- Analyse the data in the Table.

Ans. Table: Maximum and minimum air temperature in New Delhi

S. No	Date	Maximum air Temperature	Minimum air Temperature
1.	14 July, 2024	40 °C	34 °C
2.	15 July, 2024	39 °C	34 °C
3.	16 July, 2024	38 °C	31 °C
4.	17 July, 2024	40 °C	32 °C
5.	18 July, 2024	39 °C	31 °C
6.	19 July, 2024	36 °C	30 °C
7.	20 July, 2024	38 °C	30 °C
8.	21 July, 2024	38 °C	31°C
9.	22 July, 2024	38 °C	31 °C
10.	23 July, 2024	35 °C	29 °C

Analysis: From the analysis of the data on temperatures we observe that:

1. The maximum and minimum temperatures keep changing day to day.
2. The gap between the maximum and minimum temperatures in New Delhi in these ten days varied from 5 to 8 °C.
3. The highest temperature during these 10 days in New Delhi was noted at 40 °C.
4. The lowest temperature during these 10 days in New Delhi was noted at 29 °C.
5. Both maximum and minimum temperatures during these 10 days in New Delhi were the lowest on 23 July, 2024.

ANSWERS

1.

Column A	Column B
(*a*) *Clinical thermometer*	(*v*) *Used to measure human body temperature*
(*b*) *Mercury*	(*vi*) *Highly toxic substance used in old thermometers*
(*c*) *Digital thermometer*	(*vii*) *Provides easy-to-read digital display*
(*d*) *Normal body temperature Celsius*	(*ix*) *37.0 °C*
(*e*) *Infrared thermometer*	(*i*) *Measures temperature without contact*
(*f*) *37° C in Celsius scale equals*	(*ii*) *98.6 °F in Fahrenheit scale*
(*g*) *Laboratory thermometer*	(*viii*) *Typically has a range from –10 °C to 110 °C*
(*h*) *Absolute zero*	(*iii*) *–273.15 °C*
(*i*) *Anna Mani*	(*iv*) *Weather Woman of India*
(*j*) *Heat sensors*	(*x*) *Used in digital thermometers*

2. Fill in the blanks:

(*a*) Thermometer (*b*) Celsius (*c*) 37 (*d*) Mercury
(*e*) Heat (*f*) Infrared (*g*) Kelvin (*h*) Digital
(*i*) Hot (*j*) Scientific (*k*) 98.6 (*l*) 110
(*m*) Range (*n*) Hot (*o*) infrared

3. True or False:

(*i*) False (*ii*) True (*iii*) False (*iv*) True (*v*) True
(*vi*) False (*vii*) False (*viii*) True (*ix*) True (*x*) True

Multiple Choice Questions (MCQs)

1. (*b*) **2.** (*c*) **3.** (*b*) **4.** (*c*) **5.** (*d*) **6.** (*b*) **7.** (*b*) **8.** (*c*) **9.** (*c*) **10.** (*c*)
11. (*c*) **12.** (*b*) **13.** (*c*) **14.** (*c*) **15.** (*b*) **16.** (*c*) **17.** (*a*) **18.** (*c*) **19.** (*b*) **20.** (*c*)

Assertion–Reason Questions

1. (*d*) **2.** (*a*) **3.** (*a*)

VII. EXERCISE FOR PRACTICE

1. We can observe the fever of a person by touching his forehead or by noting his/her pulse rate. Why do doctors then use clinical thermometers for knowing and recording the body temperatures of a patient?
2. Give two shortcomings of earlier clinical thermometers in which readings were taken from the mercury expansion in a narrow tube inside the thermometer.
3. Convert the following:
   (*i*) 55 °C to °F
   (*ii*) 113 °F to °C
   (*iii*) 10 °C to K
   (*iv*) 300.15 K to °C
4. Can we measure the body temperature of a person without touching the body? What device do we use for this?
5. Give the normal range of body temperature of a healthy child, a healthy adult and a healthy old person.
6. We have to measure the temperature of hot water. Why should we take the reading on the laboratory thermometer immediately after the liquid inside the thermometer stops rising?
7. What is the range of temperature measurement in:
   (*i*) A clinical thermometer
   (*ii*) A laboratory thermometer
   Also give the smallest values of temperatures that these thermometers can measure.
8. 10 students are made to take readings on a laboratory thermometer of the temperature of hot water in an experiment already set up by a teacher. There are small variations in the temperatures observed by the students. Give any two reasons for these variations.
9. Make a list of the precautions for measuring temperature of a liquid using a laboratory thermometer.
10. Give five precautions for measuring human body temperature using earlier clinical thermometers (that have mercury inside).
11. Write down the temperatures in °C and °F, that you will observe in the following cases:
    (*i*) Boiling water
    (*ii*) Crushed ice
    (*iii*) A healthy adult human being
    (*iv*) A child of 5 years
    (*v*) Air on a hot summer day at 3:00 p.m.in New Delhi

NOTES

A Journey through States of Water

1 Investigating Water's Disappearing Act

- Water converts into water vapour, even at room temperature.
- This process of conversion of water into its vapour state is known as **evaporation.**

2 Another Mystery

- Water vapour converts into water droplets when it comes in contact with a cold surface.
- The process of conversion of water vapour into its liquid state is called **condensation.**

3 What are the Different States of Water?

- Ice (solid state)
- Water (liquid state)
- Water vapour (gaseous state)

4 How can we Change the States of Water?

- Heating or cooling changes states of substances.
- Cooling changes water into ice. It's called freezing.
- Heating changes water into water vapour (evaporation).
- Heating changes ice into water **(melting).**

5 How can Water be Evaporated Faster or Slower?

- Fan, windy day, and hot day make evaporation of water faster.
- Cold day makes evaporation of water slower.

6 Cooling Effect

- Water seeping through the surface of the earthen pot evaporates and gives a cooling effect on the water.

7 How do Clouds give us Rain?

- Clouds bring rain when their water droplets become very heavy.
- Rise of water as vapour and fall as rain, hail or snow is called **water cycle.**

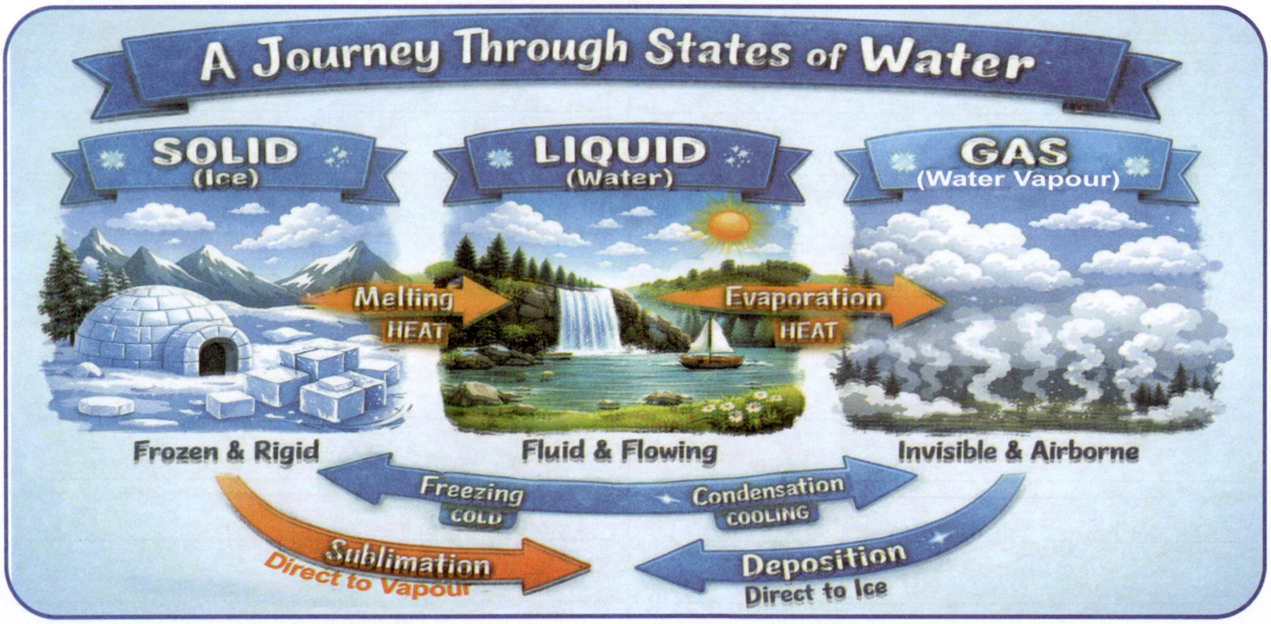

8

A Journey through States of Water

I. POINTS TO REMEMBER

1. **Water:** Water exists on the Earth in all the three states—solid, liquid and gas.

Fig. States of water

2. **Three States of Water**

   (*i*) **Liquid state:** The water that we use in everyday life is a liquid. It is called liquid state of water.

   (*ii*) **Gaseous state:** On heating, water evaporates to form its vapour. Water vapour is its gaseous state.

   (*iii*) **Solid state:** Water turns into ice on cooling. Ice is the solid form of water. These three states of water are interconvertible, that is, we can change it from one state to another.

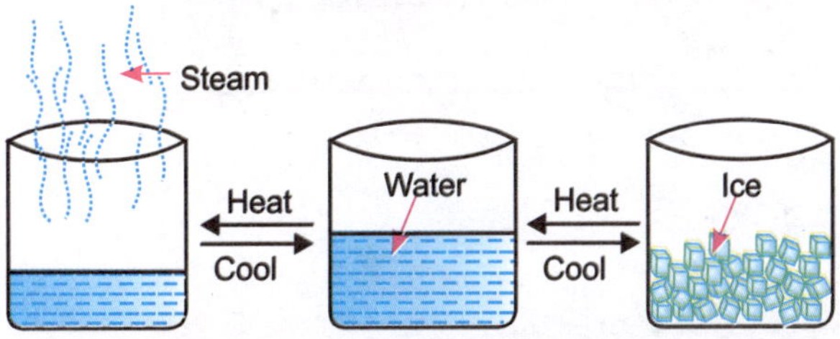

Fig. Three states of water are interconvertible

3. **Evaporation**

   (*i*) The process of changing water to its vapour form is known as evaporation.

   (*ii*) Evaporation takes place from open surfaces of water all the time—day and night.

   (*iii*) Evaporation causes cooling.

   (*iv*) The rate of evaporation depends on

   — surface area of the liquid exposed to air.

   — movement of air

   — humidity

   — temperature.

4. **Condensation**

   (*i*) The process of conversion of vapour into liquid form of water is called condensation.

   (*ii*) The process of condensation is opposite to the process of evaporation.

5. **Cloud formation:** The climate close to the earth's surface is warm. It gets cooler as one goes up in atmosphere. Water vapour being lighter, rise up in the atmosphere. At the upper layer of atmosphere, where the temperature is lower, the vapour get condensed into tiny water droplets and forms clouds.

Fig. Cloud formation

6. **Water cycle:** Due to evaporation, water from oceans and other water bodies is converted into vapour. Due to condensation, these vapour change into clouds and return as rain or snow. This circulation of water is called water cycle.

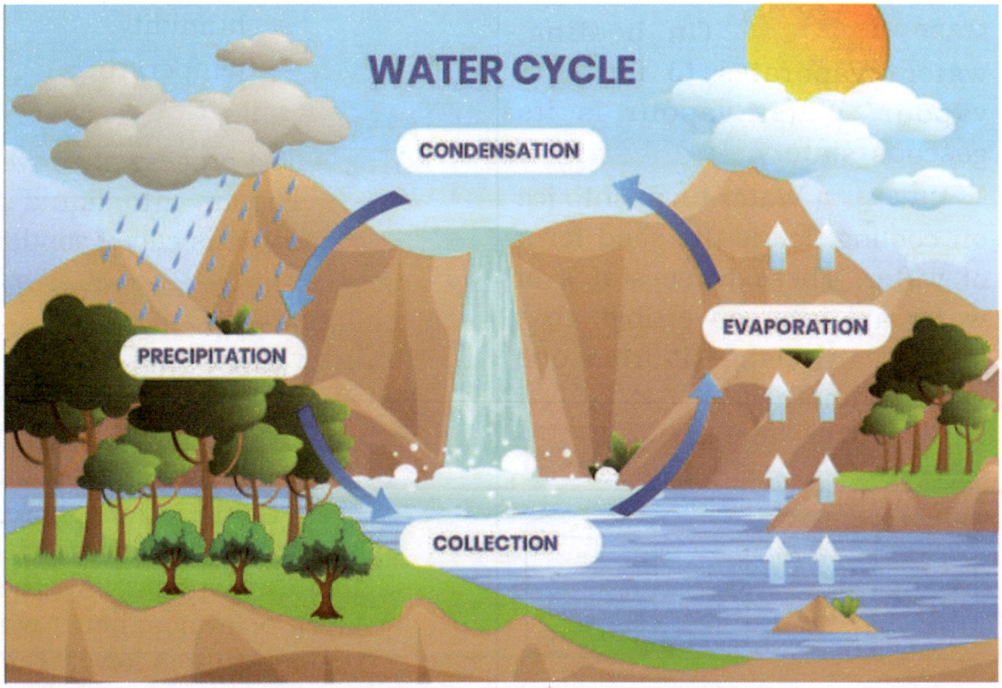

Fig. Water Cycle

II. KEYWORDS

1. **Condensation:** Conversion of vapour into liquid state.
2. **Evaporation:** Conversion of liquid into vapour.
3. **Freezing:** Conversion of liquid into solid.
4. **Melting:** Conversion of solid into liquid.
5. **Humidity:** Presence of water vapour in the air.
6. **Water cycle:** Interconversion of water from the ocean and the earth into the atmosphere and back to the earth as rain, hail or snow.
7. **Gas:** Gaseous state of water or any matter has the property of spreading and occupying available space. Gases do not possess a fixed shape.
8. **Liquid:** Liquid state of water or any matter has the property of spreading with a fixed volume but no definite shape.
9. **Solid:** Solid state of water or any matter has fixed shape and volume. Solids do not flow or spread.

III. NCERT INTEXT QUESTIONS

Q. 1. ***Reflect on what you did really well in this activity.*** *(Page 154)*

Ans. We increased the exposed area in the case of water in the plate. Water in the cap of a bottle had lesser exposed area. It was found that water evaporates faster as the exposed area increases.

Q. 2. ***What did I do well? Was I able to label all the parts of the water cycle? Which parts of the water cycle were unclear to me?*** *(Page 159)*

Ans. We could label some parts of water cycle. It was difficult to distinguish between lake and river water. Also labelling ground water is difficult.

IV. LET US ENHANCE OUR LEARNING *(Pages 161-162)*

Q. 1. ***Which of the following best describes condensation?***

(*i*) The conversion of water into its vapour state.

(*ii*) The process of water changing from a liquid into gaseous state.

(*iii*) The formation of clouds from tiny water droplets.

(*iv*) The conversion of water vapour into its liquid state.

Ans. (*iv*) The conversion of water vapour into its liquid state describes condensation.

Q. 2. ***Identify in which of the given processes, evaporation is very important—***

(*i*) Colouring with

(*a*) crayons

(*b*) water colours

(*c*) acrylic colours

(*d*) pencil colours

(*ii*) Writing on paper with

(*a*) pencil (*b*) ink pen

(*c*) ball point pen

Ans. (*i*) (*b*) water colours

(*ii*) (*b*) ink pen

Q. 3. ***We see green coloured plastic grass at many places these days. Space around natural grass feels cooler than space around the plastic grass. Can you find out why?***

Ans. Space around natural grass feels cooler because it contains water and evaporation of water from its surface causes cooling.

Q. 4. ***Give examples of liquids other than water, which evaporate.***

Ans. Milk, alcohol, ether, eye drops, sanitizer.

Q. 5. ***Fans move air around, creating a cooling sensation. It might seem strange to use a fan to dry wet clothes since fans usually make things cooler, not warmer. Normally, when water evaporates, it requires heat, not cold air. What do you think about this?***

Ans. Movement of air by fans helps in displacing the air containing evaporated moisture around wet clothes with dry air. This increases the rate of evaporation and helps in drying wet clothes.

Q. 6. ***Usually, when sludge is removed from drains, it is left in heaps next to the drain for 3–4 days. Afterward, it is transported to a garden or a field where it can be used as manure. This approach reduces transportation cost of the sludge and enhances the safety of individuals handling it. Reflect upon it and explain how.***

Ans. Water (moisture) from the sludge evaporates with time making it light and dry. This reduces the transportation cost and makes its handling safer and easier.

Q. 7. ***Observe the activities in your house for a day. Identify the activities that involve evaporation. How does understanding the process of evaporation help us in our daily activities?***

Ans. We perform various activities where process of evaporation help us.

(*i*) We dry our clothes by spreading them in open.

(*ii*) We can smell the food being cooked even without entering the kitchen.

(*iii*) Washed utensils dry up after some time.

Q. 8. ***How is water present in the solid state in nature?***

Ans. Ice, snow and frost are the solid state of water present in nature.

Q. 9. ***Reflect on the statement "Water is our responsibility before it is our right." Share your thoughts.***

Ans. Only a small portion of water available on earth is fit for use by plants, animals and humans. Most of the water is available in the oceans which we cannot use directly. We need water for drinking and many other activities. With increasing population the availability of safe water is decreasing. Though it is our right to get water for our existence but at the same time it is our responsibility to conserve it and keep water bodies free from pollution.

Q. 10. ***The seat of a two-wheeler parked on a sunny day has become very hot. How can you cool it down?***

Ans. To cool down the hot seat of a two-wheeler parked on a sunny day, we can:

- **Cover it with a wet cloth:** Place a damp cloth or towel over the seat. The water will absorb heat as it evaporates, cooling the seat.
- **Sprinkle water on it:** Lightly sprinkle water directly on the seat. The evaporating water will help to lower the temperature.

V. EXAM ORIENTED QUESTIONS

8.1. INVESTIGATING WATER'S DISAPPEARING ACT

Q. 1. ***After rain water puddles appear in the playground. After some time these disappear. Where does the water go?***

Ans. Water gets absorbed by the soil on the playground. It also evaporates.

Q. 2. ***After washing the utensils, water remains on the surface of utensils. After sometime it dries. Where does the water disappear?***

Ans. Water from the surface of utensils evaporates with time.

Q. 3. ***Give three examples of evaporation.***

Ans. (*i*) Drying of wet clothes

(*ii*) Drying of mopped floor

(*iii*) Drying of sweat from our body.

Q. 4. ***Where does hand sanitizer disappear as you rub it in your hands.***

Ans. It disappears in air due to evaporation.

Q. 5. ***While making dosa, we sprinkle some water on the hot pan. Soon it disappears. Where does it go?***

Ans. It gets converted into steam and water vapour and disappears.

8.2. ANOTHER MYSTERY

Q. 1. ***Take a tumbler with cold water. Keep it for some time. What do you observe?***

Ans. Some water droplets appear on the outer surface of tumbler.

Q. 2. ***Suggest possible reasons explaining the appearance of water droplets on the outer surface of the glass tumbler containing lemonade.***

Ans. Water droplets appear on the outer surface of the glass tumbler due to condensation of water vapour (moisture) present in the air.

Q. 3. ***Give another example of condensation similar to water droplets on the outside tumbler containing cold water.***

Ans. Appearance of dew drops on the plants in the morning.

8.3. WHAT ARE THE DIFFERENT STATES OF WATER?

Q. 1. ***Name a substance that can be observed in three different states.***

Ans. Water

Q. 2. ***How do you get three states of water?***

Ans. Take some ice. Heat it. It melts and gets converted into water. On further heating water gets converted into its gaseous state, *i.e.*, vapours.

Q. 3. ***Compare the properties of ice, liquid water and water vapour.***

Ans. The shape and volume of ice does not change when shifted from one container to another. In case of water, shape depends on the container but volume remains the same. In case of water vapour, both shape and volume change. It occupies all available space.

Property	Ice (solid state)	Water (liquid state)	Water vapour (gaseous state)
1. Ability to flow	No	Yes	Yes
2. Ability to spread	No	Yes	Yes

Q. 4. ***State some examples where three states are exhibited.***

Ans. Wax, water and ghee.

8.4. HOW CAN WE CHANGE THE STATES OF WATER?

Q. 1. ***What is melting?***

Ans. The process of conversion of a solid into liquid is called melting.

Q. 2. ***What is freezing?***

Ans. The process of conversion of liquid into solid state is called freezing.

Q. 3. ***How can you change ice to liquid state and then to vapour?***

Ans. By supplying heat slowly and continuously we can change ice to liquid water and then to vapour.

Q. 4. ***How do you change water to ice?***

Ans. By placing water in a cold environment such as freezer.

Q. 5. ***Name two examples other than water where you observe liquid to solid change and vice versa.***

Ans. Wax and coconut oil.

Q. 6. ***What is atmospheric water generator (AWG)?***

Ans. This machine collects water from humid air through the process of condensation and gives drinkable water.

8.5. HOW CAN WATER BE EVAPORATED FASTER OR SLOWER?

Q. 1. ***In which case evaporation is faster–water in a bottle cap or water on a plate?***

Ans. The water on a plate will evaporate faster as its area exposed to air is larger.

Q. 2. ***Why do wet clothes placed on a clothes line get dry after some time? Explain.*** (*NCERT Exemplar*)

Ans. Wet clothes placed on a clothes line get dry after some time because water present in wet clothes is converted into water vapour due to evaporation and leaves them dry.

Q. 3. ***Water kept in sunlight gets heat from sun and is evaporated.* But how does water kept under the shade of a tree also get evaporated? Explain.** (*NCERT Exemplar*)

Ans. Air around us gets heated by sunlight. This warm air provides heat for evaporation of water kept in the shade.

Q. 4. ***How do the areas covered with concrete affect the availability of ground water?*** (*NCERT Exemplar*)

Ans. Areas covered with concrete reduce the seepage of rain water into the ground and this reduces the availability of ground water.

8.6. COOLING EFFECT

Q. 1. ***Which of the two— water in an earthen pot or water in a stainless steel pot will give cold water after being left for some time? Explain.***

Ans. Water in the earthen pot will be cold. It is because water in an earthen pot seeps through it and comes to the outer surface. From the surface it evaporates and imparts a cooling effect on water. On the other hand, water in stainless steel pot cannot seep through it and does not undergo evaporation. Hence, it will not give cold water.

8.7. HOW DO CLOUDS GIVE US RAIN?

Q. 1. ***Name the process which helps to bring evaporated water back to the earth's surface.***

Ans. Condensation.

Q. 2. ***How does condensation help to form clouds? What causes rain?***

Ans. When air moves higher above the earth's surface, it becomes cooler and cooler. At certain heights, the cooled vapour turns into water droplets which are generally formed around dust particles. These droplets float in the air in the form of clouds. When these droplets join together, the drops become bigger and heavier, and start falling as rain.

Q. 3. ***What is water cycle?***

Ans. The water from the oceans and Earth's surface evaporates into the atmosphere as vapour. In due course of time it forms heavy clouds of water droplets and dust due to condensation. This then falls as rain, hail or snow, ultimately flowing to the oceans. This cycle of water is called water cycle.

Q. 4. ***Name the natural processes leading to water cycle.***

Ans. Evaporation and condensation.

Q. 5. ***Why is there a need for conserving water? Give two reasons.***

(*NCERT Exemplar*)

Ans. The two reasons for the need for conserving water are:

(*i*) Increasing population needs more water.

(*ii*) Only a small portion of water available on the Earth is fit for use by humans.

VI. OBJECTIVE TYPE QUESTIONS

1. *Match the following items given in Column A with that in Column B:*

Column A	Column B
(*a*) *Water cycle*	(*i*) *Conversion of water into vapour*
(*b*) *Ocean*	(*ii*) *Feeds nearly all other water sources*
(*c*) *Evaporation*	(*iii*) *Formed during winters due to condensation of atmospheric moisture*
(*d*) *Transpiration*	(*iv*) *Suspended water droplets in the air*
(*e*) *Condensation*	(*v*) *Evaporation of water from oceans and Earth's surface into the atmosphere and return in the form of rain and snow.*
(*f*) *Melting*	(*vi*) *Ice, water and steam*
(*g*) *Rain*	(*vii*) *Conversion of water vapours into water*
(*h*) *Dew*	(*viii*) *Change of state from solid to liquid*
(*i*) *Fog*	(*ix*) *The major source of water*
(*j*) *Three states of water*	(*x*) *Water loss by plants*

2. *Fill in the blanks with appropriate words:*

(*a*) *............. is needed for drinking, bathing, washing our clothes and many more functions.*

(*b*) *Large part of the earth is covered by ....*

(*c*) *The water in the oceans is very .... in taste.*

(*d*) *Ice, water and .... are the three states of same material.*

(*e*) *Water vapours get continuously added to atmosphere due to evaporation and ....*

(*f*) *The process of conversion of vapours into liquid is known as ....*

(*g*) *Ice can be changed into water by ....*

(*h*) *Evaporation increases with .... in temperature.*

(*i*) *Water vapour is .... than air.*

(*j*) *Water drops present on grass during winter morning is called ....*

(*k*) *........... carry the water which mainly serves the purpose of drinking.*

3. *State whether the statements given below are True or False:*

(*i*) *Water is needed in producing almost all materials and goods that we use in our everyday life.*

(*ii*) *Oceans are the major sources of sweet water.*

(*iii*) *Water from wet roads, rooftops and other places disappears some time after the rains.*

(*iv*) *The process of condensation is opposite to the process of evaporation.*

(*v*) *Clouds are the mixture of opaque gases.*

(*vi*) *Condensation near the surface of earth results in fog.*

(*vii*) *Evaporation takes place only in presence of sunlight.*

(*viii*) *Cloud formation occurs only at higher temperatures.*

(*ix*) *Rains feed almost all other sources of water.*

(*x*) *We should take bath by as much water as we can.*

Multiple Choice Questions (MCQs)

Choose the correct option in the following questions

1. *Which one is not hard to touch?*
   (*a*) ice (*b*) wood
   (*c*) water (*d*) stone
2. *Which pair represents different states of the same matter?*
   (*a*) green grass–plastic grass
   (*b*) ice-water
   (*c*) wax-stone
   (*d*) mountain-stone
3. *In which case does water seep through?*
   (*a*) utensil (*b*) plastic
   (*c*) sand
   (*d*) human body
4. *In which case water does not evaporate?*
   (*a*) covered earthen pot
   (*b*) covered plastic bottle
   (*c*) sweat on our body
   (*d*) wet clothes kept in sunlight
5. *Increase in which of the following factors does not increase the rate of evaporation?*
   (*a*) Temperature
   (*b*) Humidity
   (*c*) Surface area exposed to air
   (*d*) Movement of air
6. *Which of the following can be converted into liquid form?*
   (*a*) stone (*b*) wax
   (*c*) wood (*d*) coal
7. *Choose an example of condensation:*
   (*a*) disappearance of water from puddles in the ground
   (*b*) deposition of water droplets over outside surface of glass tumbler containing ice cold water
   (*c*) smell of yummy food from kitchen
   (*d*) rubbing of sanitizer with hands

8. *Which of the following does not exhibit spreading properly?*

(*a*) oxygen
(*b*) carbon dioxide
(*c*) water vapour
(*d*) wood

9. *Which one will have highest rate of evaporation?*

(*a*) water in a plate kept in shade
(*b*) water in plate kept in sunlight
(*c*) water in plate kept on a rainy day
(*d*) water in a small cap of bottle

10. *Which process represents condensation?*

(*a*) water from oceans to clouds
(*b*) falling of rain
(*c*) water from lakes to clouds
(*d*) water from river to clouds

ACTIVITY 8.6 (*Page 152*)

Fill up the blank boxes in Fig. (*See Page 152*) marked as A, B, C and 1, 2, 3, 4 for conversion of different states of water using the words—liquid, freezes, evaporates, gas, condenses. Two words have been filled for you.

Liquid, Freezes, Evaporates, Gas, Condenses

Ans.

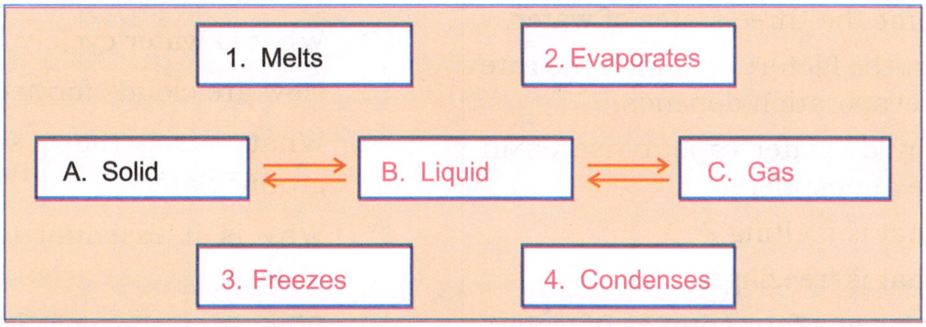

Fig. Conversion of different states of water

ANSWERS

1.

Column A	Column B
(*a*) *Water cycle*	(*v*) *Evaporation of water from oceans and Earth's surface into the atmosphere and its return in the form of rain and snow*
(*b*) *Ocean*	(*ix*) *The major source of water*
(*c*) *Evaporation*	(*i*) *Conversion of water into vapour*
(*d*) *Transpiration*	(*x*) *Water loss by plants*
(*e*) *Condensation*	(*vii*) *Conversion of water vapours into water*
(*f*) *Melting*	(*viii*) *Change of state from solid to liquid*
(*g*) *Rain*	(*ii*) *Feeds nearly all other water sources*
(*h*) *Dew*	(*iii*) *Formed during winters due to condensation of atmospheric moisture*
(*i*) *Fog*	(*iv*) *Suspended water droplets in the air.*
(*j*) *Three states of water*	(*vi*) *Ice, water and steam*

2. Fill in the blanks:

(a) Water (b) ocean and seas (c) salty
(d) steam (e) transpiration (f) condensation
(g) heating (h) increase (i) lighter
(j) dew (k) Rivers

3. True or False:

(i) True (ii) False (iii) True (iv) True (v) False
(vi) True (vii) False (viii) False (ix) True (x) False

Multiple Choice Questions (MCQs)

1. (c) 2. (b) 3. (c) 4. (b) 5. (b) 6. (b) 7. (b) 8. (d) 9. (b) 10. (b)

VII. EXERCISE FOR PRACTICE

1. Which human activity consumes the largest amount of water?
2. Write the importance of water for us.
3. Name the three states of water.
4. List the factors on which the rate of evaporation depends.
5. Why do water vapour rise up in the atmosphere?
6. What is melting ?
7. What is freezing?
8. Name any four sources of water.
9. Mention one way in which sea water differs from river water.
10. Name the phenomenon by which water is converted into water vapour.
11. What is condensation?
12. What is water cycle?
13. How are clouds formed?
14. What is the source of groundwater?
15. Why is it essential to conserve water?
16. What are the various ways in which you can conserve water at home?

NOTES

NOTES

Methods of Separation in Everyday Life

1 Handpicking

- Separation of components of a mixture by hand is called handpicking. E.g. picking of small stones from rice.

2 Threshing

- The process of separating grains from the stalks is called threshing.

3 Winnowing

- This method of separation helps to separate heavier and lighter components of a mixture by wind or blowing air. E.g. husk from grains.

4 Sieving

- This method uses a sieve to separate the fine flour particles from the bigger particles like bran and small stones.

5 Evaporation

- This is used to separate salt from seawater.

6 Sedimentation

- This method makes heavier insoluble component of a mixture settle down at the bottom. E.g. tea leaves of prepared tea.

7 Decantation

- Removal of water (liquid) by tilting the vessel is called decantation.

8 Filtration

- The process of separating tea leaves from tea by strainer is known as filtration.

9 Churning

- It is a method to separate butter from curd by the use of churner.

10 Magnetic Separation

- This method helps to separate magnetic substances from non-magnetic substances by using a magnet.

9

Methods of Separation in Everyday Life

I. POINTS TO REMEMBER

1. **Mixture:** Mixture is a substance obtained by mixing two or more substances. A mixture can be solid, liquid or gas.
2. **Handpicking:** Handpicking is the method to separate slightly large sized impurities like the pieces of stones and husk from wheat, rice and pulses by manual picking.

Fig. Handpicking of stones from pulses

3. **Threshing:** Threshing is the process to separate grains of wheat, rice, etc. from stalks.

Fig. (A): Manual threshing

Fig. (B): Mechanised threshing

4. **Winnowing:** Winnowing is the method of separation of heavier and lighter components of a mixture by wind or by blowing air. Grains are separated from husk by this method.

Fig.: Winnowing by wind

5. **Sieving:** Sieving is done to separate solid components of a mixture which differ in their sizes.

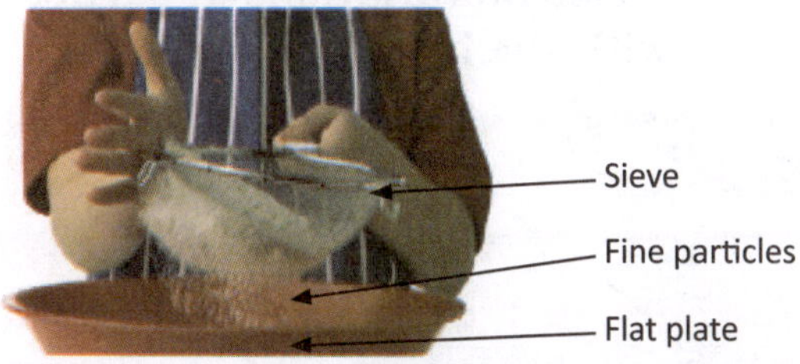

Fig. Sieving

6. **Sedimentation:** Sedimentation is the process of settling of heavier insoluble components at the bottom of a liquid.

7. **Decantation:** Decantation is used to separate insoluble solids from liquid by tilting the vessel. Two immiscible liquids are also separated by this process.

8. **Evaporation:** The process of conversion of water into its vapours (gas) is called evaporation. It can be used to separate solids dissolved in a liquid.

9. **Filtration:** The process of removal fine insoluble solids from a liquid-solid mixture is called filtration.

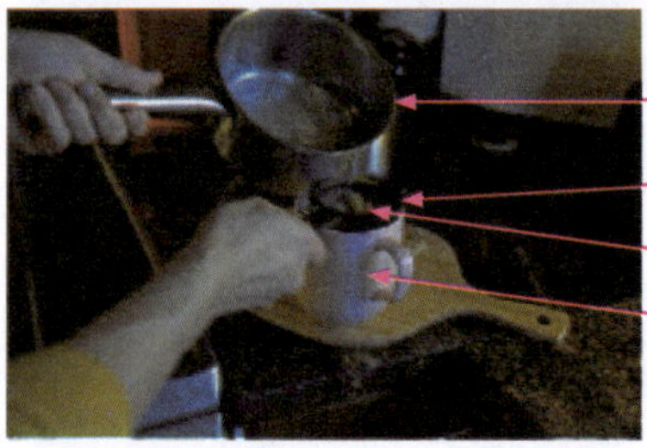

Fig. : Filtration of tea by strainer or sieve

10. **Magnetic Separation:** Magnetic separation is the process of separating magnetic and non-magnetic components of mixtures by using a magnet.

II. KEYWORDS

1. **Churning (or centrifugation):** It is the process of separation of the lighter particles of a suspended solid from a liquid. For example, to obtain butter from the curd or milk.
2. **Evaporation:** It is the process of conversion of a liquid into its vapour or gaseous state.
3. **Decantation:** It is the process of transferring a liquid from one container to another by tilting the container without disturbing the materials settled at the bottom.
4. **Filtration:** Process of removing impurities from a liquid by means of a filter.
5. **Sieving:** The process of separating components of a solid mixture, based on variations in particle size, with the help of a sieve.
6. **Handpicking:** Removing of undesirable components from a mixture by hand.
7. **Mixtures:** Substances consisting of two or more types of different substances.
8. **Sedimentation:** Settling of heavier insoluble component at the bottom of a liquid.
9. **Threshing:** The process of separation of grains or seeds from the stalks of wheat, rice or pulses manually or by using bullocks or by using mechanised threshers.
10. **Winnowing:** It is the process of separation of lighter husk from heavier grains or seeds by wind or by blowing air.
11. **Magnetic Separation:** Magnetic separation is a process that uses magnets to separate materials based on their magnetic properties.

III. NCERT INTEXT QUESTIONS

Q. 1. ***A small amount of puffed rice is mixed with chana dal. Can you think of separating the mixture by any method other than handpicking? (Page 165)***

Ans. Puffed rice and *chana dal* can be separated by winnowing.

Q. 2. ***Valli is unable to separate husk from rice in a closed room. How can you help her?*** ***(Page 166)***

Ans. We can help her by placing a fan for blowing the light husk.

Q. 3. ***Have you ever observed sieves being used at construction sites to separate pebbles and stones from the sand?*** ***(Page 167)***

Ans. Yes, large sieves are used for this purpose. Sand passes through the sieve whereas pebbles and stones are left on the sieve.

Q. 4. ***Have you ever observed white patches on the dark coloured clothes you wear during hot summers? How are these patches formed?*** ***(Page 168)***

Ans. Yes, these patches are formed due to evaporation of water from sweat leaving behind salts present in the sweat.

Q. 5. ***Observe the figure. Does it answer the question? Can you name the process involved?*** ***(Page 169)***

Ans. Yes, it answer the question. The process is condensation.

Q. 6. ***In the chapter 'Materials Around Us', you have studied that oil does not mix with water and forms a separate layer when left undisturbed for some time. Which method of separation would you use to separate oil and water?*** ***(Page 170)***

Ans. Decantation process.

IV. LET US ENHANCE OUR LEARNING (*Pages 178–180*)

Q. 1. ***What purpose does hand-picking serve in the process of separation?***

(*i*) Filtration

(*ii*) Sorting

(*iii*) Evaporation

(*iv*) Decantation

Q. 2. ***Which of the following substances are commonly separated using the churning method?***

(*i*) Oil from water

(*ii*) Sand from water

(*iii*) Cream from milk

(*iv*) Oxygen from air

Q. 3. ***Which factor is usually essential for the filtration?***

(*i*) Apparatus size

(*ii*) Presence of air

(*iii*) Pore size

(*iv*) Temperature of the mixture

Answers

1. (*ii*) Sorting

2. (*iii*) Cream from milk

3. (*iii*) Pore size

Q. 4. ***State with reason(s) whether the following statements are True [T] or False [F]. Also, correct the False statement(s).***

(*i*) Salt can be separated from salt solution by keeping it under the Sun. [ ]

(*ii*) Handpicking should be used only when the quantity of one component is small. [ ]

(*iii*) A mixture of puffed rice and rice grains can be separated by threshing. [ ]

(*iv*) A mixture of mustard oil and water can be separated by decantation. [ ]

(*v*) Sieving is used to separate a mixture of rice flour and water. [ ]

Answers

(*i*) True

Reason : Water will evaporate leaving the salt behind.

(*ii*) True

Reason: It is easier to handpick small quantities.

(*iii*) False

Reason: Process of threshing is used to separate the grains from the stalks.

Correct statement: This mixture can be separated by handpicking or winnowing.

(*iv*) True

Reason: Oil and water will form separate layers which can be decanted.

(*v*) False

Reason: Sieving is done to separate solid-solid mixture of different particles size.

Correct Statement: Filtration is used to separate a mixture of rice flour and water.

Q. 5. ***Match the mixtures in Column I with their method of separation in Column II.***

Column I		Column II	
(*i*)	Gram flour mixed with black gram	(*a*)	Handpicking
(*ii*)	Chalk powder mixed with water	(*b*)	Magnetic separation
(*iii*)	Corn mixed with potatoes	(*c*)	Decantation
(*iv*)	Iron filings mixed with sawdust	(*d*)	Sieving
(*v*)	Oil mixed with water.	(*e*)	Filtration

Ans.

Column I		Column II	
(*i*)	Gram flour mixed with black gram	(*d*)	Sieving
(*ii*)	Chalk powder mixed with water	(*e*)	Filtration
(*iii*)	Corn mixed with potatoes	(*a*)	Handpicking
(*iv*)	Iron filings mixed with sawdust	(*b*)	Magnetic separation
(*v*)	Oil mixed with water.	(*c*)	Decantation

Q. 6. ***In what situations would you use decantation instead of filtration to separate solids from liquids?***

Ans. Decantation is used when the solid particles are heavy and settle down at the bottom of the container, allowing the clear liquid to be poured off without disturbing the solid sediment. For example separating sand from water.

Q. 7. ***Can you relate the presence of nasal hair to any separation process?***

Ans. Nasal hair acts like a natural filter, trapping dust, pollens, and other particles from the air we breathe, similar to how a filtration process works to remove solid impurities from a liquid.

Q. 8. ***During the COVID-19 pandemic, all of us wore masks. Generally, what material are they made of? What is the role of these masks?***

Ans. Masks are generally made of materials like cotton, synthetic fibers, or polypropylene. Their role is to filter out airborne particles, including viruses and bacteria, to prevent their inhalation and spread.

Q.9. ***A mixture containing potatoes, salt and sawdust has been given to you. Outline a stepwise procedure for separating each component from this mixture.***

Ans.

Step-1 : Handpick the potatoes

Step-2 : Add water to the remaining mixture to dissolve the salt

Step-3 : Filter the mixture to separate the sawdust from the salt solution.

Step-4 : Evaporate the water from the salt solution to obtain the salt.

Q. 10. ***Read the following story titled 'Intelligent Leela' and tick the most appropriate options. Provide a suitable title of your choice for the paragraph.***

Leela was working in the farm with her father when she realised that they left their drinking water at home. Before her father felt ***thirsty/hungry***, she went to the nearby pond to fetch some ***water/ grains***. After obtaining some water in the container, she noticed that the water was muddy and ***fit/unfit*** for drinking. To purify the water, she kept it for some time and then she ***filtered/churned*** the muddy water using a piece of ***paper/ muslin cloth***. Leela, then, **cooled/ boiled** the water for about 10 minutes in a covered pan. After ***cooling/boiling***, she ***filtered/churned*** it again and made it ***fit/unfit*** for drinking. She served this water to her father while having food, who blessed her and appreciated her efforts.

Ans. 1. Thirsty 2. Water
3. Unfit 4. Filtered
5. Muslin Cloth 6. Boiled
7. Cooling 8. Filtered
9. Fit

Title – Leela's Clever Solution for Clean Water

V. EXAM ORIENTED QUESTIONS

Q. 1. ***When is handpicking used?***

Ans. Handpicking is used when the particles to be removed are present in small quantity and have different size, colour or shape from the particles of the other component.

Q. 2. ***What is threshing? How is it done?***

Ans. The process that is used to separate the grains from stalks is **threshing**. In this process, the stalks are beaten to free the grains from stalks.

Q. 3. ***Give one example of sieving used in everyday life.***

Ans. Separation of barn (*choker*) from flour.

Q. 4. ***Name some materials that are used as filters.***

Ans. Cotton, filter cloth, filter paper.

Q. 5. ***What is the use of decantation?***

Ans. Decantation is used to separate insoluble solids from liquids. Two immiscible liquids are also separated by this process.

Q. 6. ***What is the drawback of evaporation?***

Ans. The liquid component in the mixture is evaporated off into the air and is not recovered.

Q. 7. ***Name the process to obtain salt from seawater.***

Ans. Evaporation.

Q. 8. ***What are sedimentation and decantation?***

Ans. Decantation is a process of separating insoluble solids from liquids. A suspension of solid particles in liquid is allowed to stand for some time. Solid particles settle down at the bottom, due to their weight. This is called sedimentation. The clear water is transferred into another beaker, by tilting the beaker, without disturbing the settled particles. This type of separation is called decantation (Fig.).

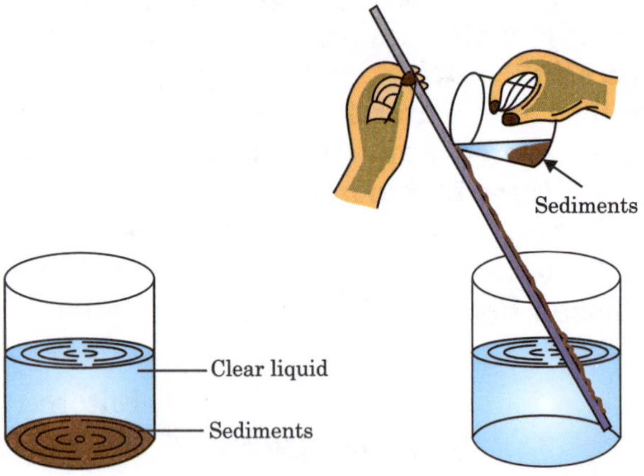

Fig. Decantation

Q. 9. *Which types of mixtures are separated by evaporation?*

Ans. Evaporation is used to separate solids dissolved in liquid.

Q. 10. *Describe the method to obtain pure salt from rock salt.*

Ans. First, the mixture is crushed and grinded. Water is then added and filtered. Pure salt is collected as filtrate which is heated for evaporation. Water evaporates off and pure salt is left.

Q. 11. *What is the importance of centrifugation? How is it done?*

Ans. Centrifugation is the process of separating suspended particles from a liquid by rotating the liquid at a high speed.

The mixture is taken in a closed tube and rotated at a high speed. The heavy particles settle at the bottom of the tube. The liquid component is removed by decantation.

This method is also used to separate cream from milk. Cream collects at the centre and being lighter than milk, it floats at the top of the mixture.

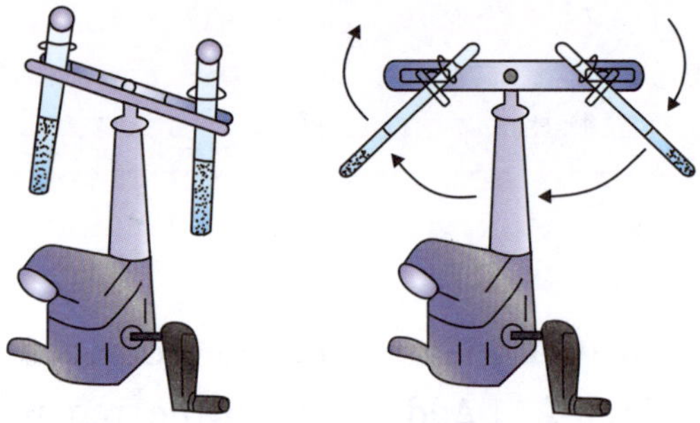

Fig. Hand centrifugal machine

Q. 12. *Name the property of the components used for separating the following mixtures:*

(*i*) *salt and water*

(*ii*) *wheat and husk*

(*iii*) *iron filings and saw-dust*

Ans. (*i*) One of the components is volatile and hence can undergo evaporation.

(*ii*) One of the components is light and can be blown away by wind.

(*iii*) One of the components is magnetic and is attracted by a magnet.

Q. 13. *Write various methods of separation of compounds from their mixture.*

Ans. (*i*) Handpicking

(*ii*) Threshing and winnowing

(*iii*) Sedimentation and Decantation

(*iv*) Evaporation

(*v*) Filtration

(*vi*) Centrifugation

(*vii*) Magnetic separation

Q. 14. *Name and describe briefly a method which can be helpful in separating a mixture of husk from grains. What is the principle of this method?* (*NCERT Exemplar*)

Ans. Winnowing can be used to separate lighter and heavier components of a mixture.

Husk is lighter than wheat. When the mixture is allowed to fall down from a height, the wind carries the lighter husk with it and the heavy wheat grains fall vertically down on the ground.

Principle of this method is that the lighter particles are carried away by the wind.

Q. 15. ***How will you separate pure water from a solution of salt in water?***

Ans. We can separate pure water from a solution of salt in water, by the process of distillation that is by evaporation, followed by condensation of water vapour.

Q. 16. ***What is the opposite process of condensation ?***

Ans. Evaporation.

Q. 17. ***How is common salt obtained from seawater?***

Ans. When seawater is allowed to evaporate in shallow pits, water gets heated by sunlight and changes into water vapour by the process of evaporation leaving behind impure solid salts. Now, the lumps of impure common salt are crushed to get powdered salt. The powdered common salt is dissolved in water to prepare a solution. The solution of common salt is filtered to remove insoluble impurities. The clear solution is evaporated by heating to reduce the water content to obtain a concentrated solution of common salt. The hot and concentrated solution is allowed to cool. On cooling, crystals of pure common salt are obtained.

Q. 18. ***During centrifugation, which particles settle down at the bottom?***

Ans. Heavy particles settle down at the bottom during centrifugation.

Q. 19. ***Name the method by which you can separate butter from milk.***

Ans. Centrifugation.

Q. 20. ***Name the device by which cream can be separated from milk at home.***

Ans. A mixer-grinder is the very important device by which cream can be separated from milk by the process of centrifugation. (Fig.)

Fig. : Mixer-grinder

Q. 21. ***Mention the methods that can be used for the separation of the following mixtures:***

(*i*) *wheat, sugar and husk*

(*ii*) *rice, gram and iron filings*

(*iii*) *sand, black gram and husk.*

Ans.

(*i*) Mixture of wheat, sugar and husk.

1. For separating husk from the mixture, we should follow the winnowing method as husk is lighter than the other two components.
2. Wheat and sugar can be separated by sieving as they have different sizes.

(*ii*) Mixture of rice, gram and iron filings.

1. For separating iron filings, we can use a magnet.
2. Rice and gram can be separated either by sieving or by handpicking.

(*iii*) Mixture of sand, black gram and husk.

1. For separating sand from the mixture, we can sieve the mixture.
2. Black gram and husk can be separated by the method of winnowing.

VI. OBJECTIVE TYPE QUESTIONS

1. *Match the following items given in Column A with that in Column B:*

Column A	Column B
(a) *Handpicking*	(i) *Conversion of water vapour into liquid*
(b) *Threshing*	(ii) *Separating fine particles from flour*
(c) *Winnowing*	(iii) *Separating larger size impurities*
(d) *Sieving*	(iv) *Separating butter from milk*
(e) *Sedimentation*	(v) *Conversion of water into its vapour*
(f) *Evaporation*	(vi) *Separating grains from its stalks*
(g) *Condensation*	(vii) *Settling of heavier components at bottom*
(h) *Churning*	(viii) *Separation by wind or by blowing air*

2. *Fill in the blanks with appropriate words:*

(a) *Peanuts are separated from a mixture of wheat and peanut by ....*

(b) *................ is used to separate husk from wheat.*

(c) *Fine sand can be separated from larger particles by ....*

(d) *Sea salt is a ....*

(e) *A mixture of chalk powder and iron filings can be separated by ....*

(f) *When a mixture containing fine sand and water is subjected to centrifugation, ... settles at the bottom of the tube.*

(g) *Conversion of vapour into liquid is known as ....*

(h) *Mixture may be solid, liquid or ....*

3. *State whether the statements given below are True or False:*

(i) *Butter is separated from butter milk by churning.*

(ii) *Separation of components of a mixture is a useful process.*

(iii) *Ink loses its properties when mixed in water.*

(iv) *'Sharbat' is a mixture of sugar and water.*

(v) *Rocks are pure substances.*

(vi) *Milk is a mixture.*

(vii) *Common salt is a pure substance.*

(viii) *Components of a mixture retain their properties in the mixture.*

Multiple Choice Questions (MCQs)

Choose the correct option in the following questions

1. *Butter is separated from milk by*

(a) sedimentation (b) filtration

(c) churning (d) decantation

2. *Threshing is done by*

(a) beating (b) bullocks

(c) machines (d) all of these

3. *Which method is used to separate pebbles and stones from sand?*

(a) Handpicking

(b) Winnowing

(c) Sieving

(d) Decantation

4. *The components of a solution (say sugar in water) can be separated by*
(*a*) filtration (*b*) evaporation
(*c*) sedimentation (*d*) decantation

5. *Sand from water is separated by*
(*a*) sieving
(*b*) evaporation
(*c*) condensation
(*d*) sedimentation and decantation

6. *The process of conversion of water vapours into liquid is called*
(*a*) condensation (*b*) decantation
(*c*) sedimentation (*d*) evaporation

7. *The process of conversion of water into its vapours is called*
(*a*) evaporation
(*b*) condensation
(*c*) sublimation
(*d*) transpiration

8. *Paheli bought some vegetables such as french beans, lady's finger, green chillies, brinjals and potatoes all mixed in a bag. Which of the following methods of separation would be most appropriate for her to separate them?* (*NCERT Exemplar*)
(*a*) Winnowing (*b*) Sieving
(*c*) Threshing
(*d*) Handpicking

9. *Boojho's grandmother is suffering from diabetes. Her doctor advised her to take 'Lassi' with less fat content. Which of the following methods would be most appropriate for Boojho to prepare it?* (*NCERT Exemplar*)
(*a*) Filtration (*b*) Decantation
(*c*) Churning (*d*) Winnowing

10. *Which of the following mixtures would you be able to separate using the method of filtration?* (*NCERT Exemplar*)
(*a*) Oil in water
(*b*) Cornflakes in milk
(*c*) Salt in water
(*d*) Sugar in milk

11. *Which amongst the following methods would be most appropriate to separate grains from bundles of stalks?* (*NCERT Exemplar*)
(*a*) Handpicking
(*b*) Winnowing
(*c*) Sieving
(*d*) Threshing

12. *Four mixtures are given below:*
(*i*) Kidney beans and chick peas
(*ii*) Pulses and rice
(*iii*) Rice flakes and corn
(*iv*) Potato wafers and biscuits
Which of these can be separated by the method of winnowing? (*NCERT Exemplar*)
(*a*) (*i*) and (*ii*) (*b*) (*ii*) and (*iii*)
(*c*) (*i*) and (*iii*) (*d*) (*iii*) and (*iv*)

13. *While preparing chapatis, Chinky found that the flour to be used was mixed with wheat grains. Which out of the following is the most suitable method to separate the grains from the flour?* (*NCERT Exemplar*)
(*a*) Threshing (*b*) Sieving
(*c*) Winnowing (*d*) Filtration

14. *You might have observed the preparation of ghee from butter and cream at home. Which method(s) can be used to separate ghee from the residue?* (*NCERT Exemplar*)
(*i*) Evaporation (*ii*) Decantation
(*iii*) Filtration (*iv*) Churning
Which of the following combination is the correct answer?
(*a*) (*i*) and (*ii*) (*b*) (*ii*) and (*iii*)
(*c*) (*ii*) and (*iv*) (*d*) (*iv*) only

ANSWERS

1.

Column A	Column B
(a) *Handpicking*	(iii) *Separating larger size impurities*
(b) *Threshing*	(vi) *Separating grains from its stalks*
(c) *Winnowing*	(viii) *Separation by wind or by blowing air*
(d) *Sieving*	(ii) *Separating fine particles from flour*
(e) *Sedimentation*	(vii) *Settling of heavier components at bottom*
(f) *Evaporation*	(v) *Conversion of water into its vapour*
(g) *Condensation*	(i) *Conversion of water vapour into liquid*
(h) *Churning*	(iv) *Separating butter from milk*

2. Fill in the blanks:
(a) handpicking (b) Winnowing (c) sieving (d) mixture
(e) magnetic separation (f) sand (g) condensation
(h) gas

3. True or False:
(i) True (ii) True (iii) False (iv) True
(v) False (vi) True (vii) True (viii) True

Multiple Choice Questions (MCQs)

1. (c) 2. (d) 3. (c) 4. (b) 5. (d) 6. (a) 7. (a) 8. (d) 9. (c) 10. (b)
11. (d) 12. (d) 13. (b) 14. (b)

VII. EXERCISE FOR PRACTICE

1. Name the method used to separate husk from wheat.
2. Name the process by which water is separated from rice and pulses after washing them.
3. Define sedimentation.
4. Explain decantation.
5. How do jewellers separate the pearls of different sizes?
6. What is a mixture?
7. Why do we separate substances in a mixture?
8. Name the process used to separate tea leaves from prepared tea.
9. How can we separate a mixture of water and kerosene ?

NOTES

1 What Sets the Living Apart from the Non-living?

- Movement, growth, nutrition, respiration, excretion, response to stimuli, reproduction and death. Non-living things lack these characteristics.

2 Essential Conditions for Germination of a Seed

- Availability of air, sunlight, and water.

3 Growth and Movement in Plants

- Shoot of a plant grows upward towards sunlight and root grows downwards.

Living Creatures: Exploring their Characteristics

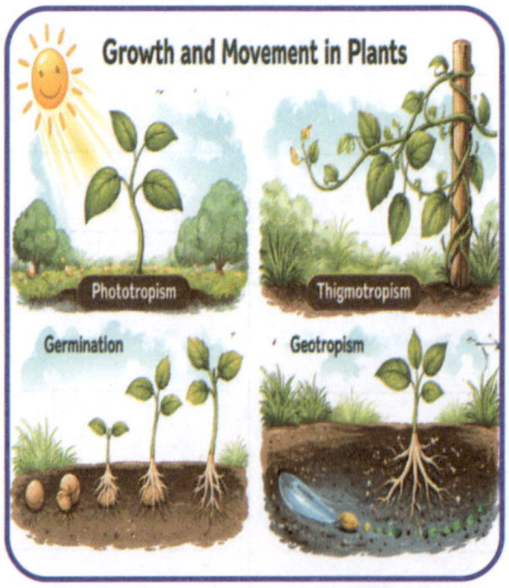

4 Life Cycle of a Plant

- The entire process from a seed to a plant, and then, to the next generation of seeds is known as the life cycle of a plant.

5 Life Cycle of Animals

5a Life cycle of a mosquito

- Egg → Larva → Pupa → Adult

5b Life cycle of a frog

- Egg stage (Embryo stage) → tadpole stage → froglet stage → Adult frog stage

10

Living Creatures: Exploring their Characteristics

I. POINTS TO REMEMBER

1. **Living beings:** These are the organisms which need water, air and nutrients for their survival.
2. **Non-living things:** These are the objects which do not need water, air and nutrients for their survival.
3. **Life:** It is a process seen only in living beings in the form of growth, movement, feeding or nutrition, sensitivity, respiration, excretion and reproduction.
4. **Characteristics of the living beings:** All living beings on this earth possess certain basic characteristics. These are:
   1. Growth
   2. Movement
   3. Nutrition
   4. Response to stimuli
   5. Excretion
   6. Respiration
   7. Reproduction
   8. Adaptations.
5. **Growth:** It is defined as the increase in the size and total weight of the living organism over time.
   (*i*) Animals grow for a certain period.
   (*ii*) In case of trees, growth takes place throughout the life.
   (*iii*) Growth in plants and animals is influenced by several factors like food, climate, life style, etc.
6. **Life span:** Each animal lives for a certain period. This period is known as life span.
7. **Movement:** Change in the position from one place to other is called movement.
   (*i*) **Locomotion:** The movement involving change of place in animals is called locomotion.
   (*ii*) Animals use wings (bird), fins (fish), limbs (cow, horse, buffalo, man) for locomotion.
   (*iii*) Plants do not move from one place to another. They generally show movements of various parts, *e.g.,* flower buds open, roots grow away from light. Mimosa leaves (touch-me-not), fold themselves when we touch them.

8. **Nutrition:** The process of taking food by organisms is generally referred to as nutrition or nourishment.

(*i*) Living beings need food (nutrition) for their growth and development.

(*ii*) Food and water are essential for life.

(*iii*) Food provides energy that helps in the growth of body and its repair.

9. **Respiration:** All living things **respire**.

(*i*) Breathing is part of a process called **respiration**.

(*ii*) In the process of **breathing**, when we **inhale**, the air moves from outside to inside our body. When we **exhale** (breathe out), the air moves from inside our body to outside.

(*iii*) Respiration is a process in which oxygen taken by an organism combines with food, and releases energy, carbon dioxide and water.

(*iv*) We inhale oxygen (O_2) and exhale carbon dioxide (CO_2).

10. **Excretion**

(*i*) The removal of waste products from the body of a living being is called excretion. Urine is formed as a product of excretion in animals.

(*ii*) Latex, resin and gum are wastes for the plant but useful for us.

(*iii*) Plants excrete excess water and minerals in the form of small droplets on leaves.

(*iv*) The sweat consists of water and salts removed by the body as waste products.

11. **Response to Stimuli**

(*i*) Living beings respond to changes in their surroundings.

(*ii*) **Stimuli:** The factors like food, water, light, touch, gravitational force, etc., are stimuli (stimulus) to which plants and animals respond.

12. **Reproduction**

(*i*) Reproduction is the process of producing new ones of one's own kind.

(*ii*) Reproduction is necessary for the continuity of life.

(*iii*) Plants reproduce by seeds and spores. Some plants also reproduce by vegetative methods.

13. **Alive or Dead**

When a living being is not able to exhibit the above mentioned characteristics, despite the availability of food, air and water which are needed for being alive, it is said to be **dead**.

14. **Seed Germination**

(*i*) Soil, air, water, light and/or dark conditions help in seed germination.

(*ii*) Seeds of **Coleus** and **Petunia** plants require light for germination while seeds of **Calendula** and **Zinnia** need darkness to germinate.

15. Life Cycle of a Plant

(*i*) Seed give rise to new generation of plants. For example: Bean plant.

(*ii*) A seed grows into a young plant which matures to produce flowers and fruits.

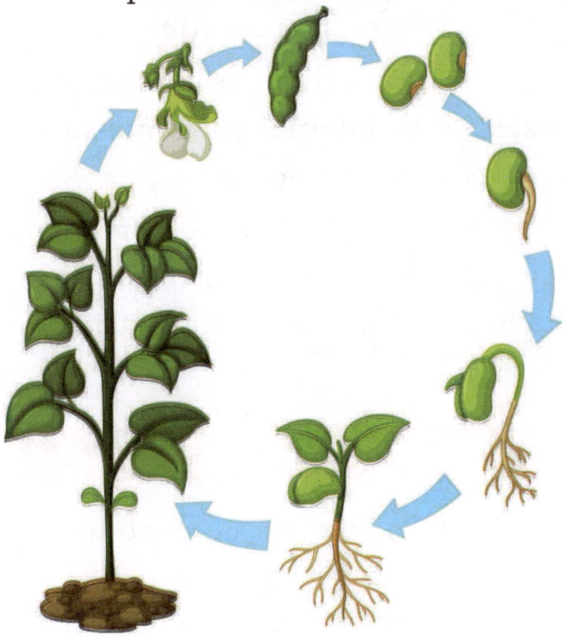

Fig: Bean Life Cycle

(*iii*) The fruits (pods) give rise to new generation of bean plants.

(*iv*) The whole process from a seed to a plant, and then, to the next generation of seeds is called the **life cycle of a plant.**

(*v*) When a plant stops growing and all life processes come to an end, even after the availability of all the necessary conditions, the plant is considered **dead**.

16. Life Cycle of Mosquitoes

Mosquitoes pass through four stages in their life cycle— egg, larva, pupa and adult.

17. Life Cycle of Frog

Stages in the life cycle of frog include eggs, tadpoles, froglets and adults.

18. Spawn

White jelly–like substance on the surface of water towards the edge of the pond is actually a cluster of eggs of a frog and is known as **spawn**.

19. We should take care of plants and animals so that the living world flourishes well.

II. KEYWORDS

Breathing: It is a process in which air rich in oxygen is inhaled and air rich in carbon dioxide is exhaled with the help of respiratory organs.

Death: The meaning of death is a stoppage of all vital functions and the end of life.

Excretion: Excretion is the process of removal of metabolic waste material and other non-useful substances from the body of a living being.

Froglet: When the tadpole reaches the froglet stage, it is almost a full adult. At this point, the tadpole's gills have disappeared, and its lungs have enlarged.

Germination: Germination is the process by which seeds develop into new plants.

Growth: Growth is an increase in dry weight, size, mass, or volume of cell, organ, or organism with time.

Larva: A larva is a worm-like creature that hatches from an egg. When the egg hatches, the larval stage begins.

Life cycle: A life cycle is the series of stages in the life of an organism, beginning with life and ending with death.

Living: Living means alive. Living beings can grow, move, reproduce, respire and carry out various activities.

Movement: The process of moving or being moved from one place to another.

Non-living: A non-living thing is which do not need water, air and nutrients for its survival.

Nutrition: Nutrition is required by living beings for their growth and development. We get nutrition from food we eat.

Pupa: A pupa is the stage of development between a larva and a fully grown adult in the life cycle of an insect.

Reproduction: Reproduction is the process by which organisms produce young ones of their own kind.

Respiration: The process in which the food that we eat (nutrition) is broken down inside the cells which results in the release of energy.

Response: A response is the behavior of a living organism which is the result of an external or internal stimulus.

Stimulus: A stimulus is a change in the external or internal environment which brings about a response.

Tadpole: Tadpole is the stage in the life cycle of a frog when it hatches from egg. A tadpole has gills as well as a tail.

III. NCERT INTEXT QUESTIONS

Q. 1. ***How would you now categorise a seed, as living or non-living?*** *(Page 191)*

Ans. Seed is a living thing. Seed can grow into a plant under right conditions of soil, air, water and light/dark.

Q. 2. ***How can the life cycle of a mosquito be disrupted?*** *(Page 197)*

Ans. Life cycle of a mosquito can be disrupted by spraying **kerosene oil** on stagnant water. Kerosene oil forms a thin layer over the water surface. This layer separates water from air, and does not allow larvae and pupae to inhale air. This results in the death of the larvae of mosquito.

IV. LET US ENHANCE OUR LEARNING *(Pages 203–204)*

Q. 1. ***List the similarities and differences in life cycles of plants and animals.***

Ans. **(A) Similarities in Life Cycles of Plants and Animals**

(*i*) **Developmental Stages:** Both have distinct stages of development (e.g., germination, flowering in plants; egg, larva, adult in animals).

(*ii*) **Growth:** Both plants and animals grow from a small initial stage (seed or embryo) into a mature form.

(*iii*) **Reproduction:** Both plants and animals undergo reproduction to produce offspring (seeds for plants and young ones for animals).

(B) Differences in Life Cycles of Plants and Animals

Characteristics	Plants	Animals
Growth pattern	Plants can grow throughout their life **(Indeterminate growth)**	Animals stop growing after reaching maturity. **(determinate growth)**
Respiration	Plants respire by **stomata** and **lenticels**.	Animals use **lungs** or **skin** or **gills** for respiration.
Movement	Plants **do not** move from one place to another. Their parts show certain movements.	Animals move from one place to another in search of food and to escape from enemies.
Reproduction	Plants reproduce by flowers, cones or spores.	Animals have specialised organs for reproduction.

Q. 2. ***The table (See NCERT Textbook, Page 204) shows some data. Study the data and try to find out examples appropriate for the conditions given in the second and third columns. If you think that an example for any of the conditions given below is not possible, explain why?***

Ans.

S. no.	Does it Grow?	Does it respire?	Example	Remarks
1.	No	No	Rock	Non-living, No growth or respiration
2.	No	Yes	Virus	Viruses are non-living outside host cells but respire in host
3.	Yes	No	Crystals (salt) or clouds	Non-living can perform tasks but does not respire
4.	Yes	Yes	Humans, Plants	Living beings can grow and respire

Q. 3. ***You have learnt that different conditions are required for seed germination. How can we use this knowledge for proper storage of grains and pulses?***

Ans. To ensure proper storage of grains and pulses and prevent their germination:

- Keep them Dry
- Cold Storage
- Keep them in airtight containers

Q. 4. ***You have learnt that a tail is present in a tadpole but it disappears as it grows into a frog. What is the advantage of having a tail in the tadpole stage?***

Ans. The tail present in the tadpole stage of a frog helps in swimming and maintaining balance.

(i) **Swimming:** Tail helps the tadpole swim efficiently in water to find food and escape predators.

(ii) **Balance and Stability:** Tail helps in maintaining balance while moving in water.

Q. 5. ***Charan says that a wooden log is non-living as it cannot move. Charu counters it by saying that it is living because it is made of wood obtained from trees. Give your arguments in favour or against the two statements given by Charan and Charu.***

Ans. Against Charan: The wooden log was once part of a living tree, which was alive and showed characteristics of living beings.

Against Charu: Once the wood is separated from the tree, it no longer shows growth, reproduction, or other life processes, so it is non-living.

Q. 6. ***What are the similarities and distinguishing features in the life cycles of a mosquito and a frog?***

Ans. Similarities

- Both begin life as eggs.
- Both have a larval stage (tadpole in frogs, larvae in mosquitoes) that is aquatic.

Distinguishing Features in the life cycle of mosquitoes and frogs

	Mosquitoes	Frogs
1.	Adult female mosquito lays **eggs** directly on or near water.	Frogs lays **cluster of eggs** in the form of **white jelly** – like **substance** on the surface of water towards the edge of the pond. This cluster of eggs is known as **spawn**.
2.	Egg develops into **larva.**	Egg develops into **tadpole stage** which has a tail, gills and no legs.
3.	The larva grows into **pupa**.	Late stage of tadpole is called **froglet stage** which has hind legs.
4.	**Pupa** transforms into **adult mosquito** which rests briefly on the surface of water and then flies away.	Froglet transforms into **adult frog,** which lives both in water and on land.
5.	Thus mosquitoes pass through four stages in their life cycle: **egg**, **larva**, **pupa** and **adult**.	Thus different stages in the life cycle of frog are **eggs** (spawn), **tadpole larva**, **froglet stage** and **adult frog**.
6.	Larvae and pupae come to the surface of water for air (to respire)	Tadpoles have gills to respire while adult frog respires through lungs and skin.

Q. 7. ***A plant is provided with all the conditions suitable for its growth (Fig. below). Draw what you expect to see in the shoot and the root of the plant after one week. Write down the reasons.***

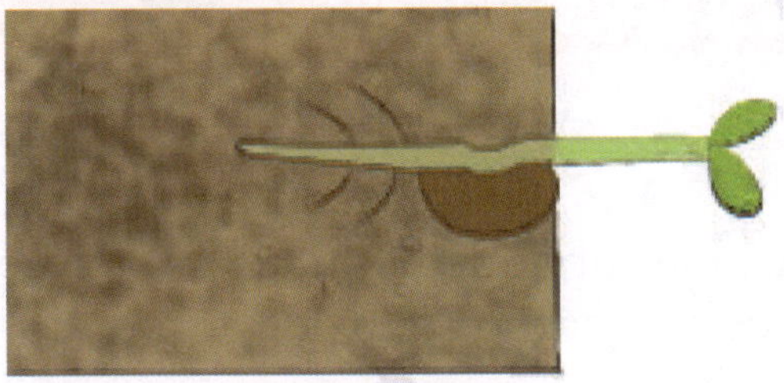

Fig: Pot kept horizontally along the ground

Ans.

Expected observations

- **Shoot:** Grows upwards towards the light source.
- **Root:** Grows downwards into the soil for stability and nutrient absorption.

Reasons

- Shoots grow towards light (phototropism) for photosynthesis.
- Roots grow downwards (geotropism and hydrotropism) for nutrient and water absorption.

Q. 8. ***Tara and Vijay set up the experiment shown in the picture (Fig. below). What do you think they want to find out? How will they know if they are correct?***

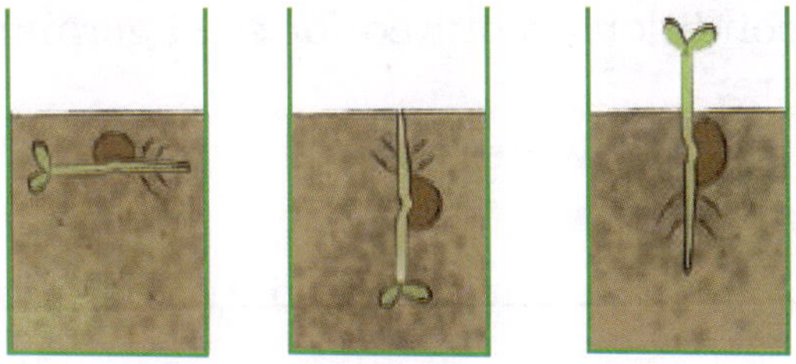

Fig. Experimental set-up

Ans. Tara and Vijay are trying to understand the orientation of a seed which affects the growth and direction of the shoot (the green part above ground) and the root (part below ground).

Observation: The shoot always grows upwards (towards the light) and the root always grows downwards (into the soil), regardless of how the seed is placed. This shows that plants have natural growth movement (like phototropism and geotropism) that control their growth direction.

Q. 9. ***Design an experiment to check if temperature has an effect on seed germination.***

Ans. AIM: To Check the Effect of Temperature on Seed Germination.

Materials required: Identical pots, soil, seeds, thermometers, and different temperature-controlled environments (e.g., refrigerator, room temperature, heated environment).

Procedure

(*i*) Fill each pot with the same type of soil.

(*ii*) Plant seeds in each pot.

(*iii*) Place each pot in a different environment with controlled temperatures (e.g., cold, room temperature, warm). For example, keep one pot outside in balcony to get sunlight. Put another in shade in the room. Keep the third one in basement or at coldest part of the house.

(*iv*) Water each pot regularly.

(*v*) Observe the number of seeds germinated in each environment regularly for two weeks.

Observation: Measure and compare the rate of germination and growth in different temperatures.

Conclusion: The optimal temperature for seed germination based on observations can be determined.

V. EXAM ORIENTED QUESTIONS

10.1 WHAT SETS THE LIVING APART FROM THE NON-LIVING?

Q. 1. *What is movement?*

Ans. Movement can be defined as the change in physical position or location. It means moving from one place to another.

Q. 2. *Do plants show any kind of movement?*

Ans. Plants do not move from one place to another but they do show certain types of movements.

For example

(*i*) Opening of flowers

(*ii*) Movement of hairs in insectivorous plant like **Drosera**.

(*iii*) Climbers twine around any object placed close by.

Q. 3. *What are insectivorous plants?*

Ans. Insectivorous plants are special plants that catch insects and digest them to get nutrients. e.g. **Drosera**, **Pitcher plant** and **Venus-fly-trap**.

Q. 4. *Write the examples of insectivorous plants.*

Ans. Venus fly trap, pitcher plant, and sundews.

Q. 5. *What is growth? Or Define growth.*

Ans. Growth is the process of increase in size, mass or overall development of living beings.

Q. 6. *Define nutrition.*

Ans. Nutrition is the process by which organisms obtain and utilize nutrients from food for growth, development and energy.

Q. 7. *What is respiration?*

Ans. Respiration is the process by which organisms take in oxygen and release carbon dioxide to obtain energy from food.

Q. 8. *What is excretion?*

Ans. Excretion is the process by which waste is removed from body. Urine, sweat and salts are called excretory products.

Q. 9. *Define stimulus.*

Ans. Anything or any event that prompts living beings to respond is called a stimulus.

Q. 10. *What is reproduction?*

Ans. Reproduction is the process of producing new young ones of one's own kind.

10.2 ESSENTIAL CONDITIONS FOR GERMINATION OF A SEED

Q. 1. *What is germination?*

Ans. Germination is the process by which a seed develops into a new plant.

Q.2. *Write the essential things/ conditions required for seed germination.*

Ans. The essential things/ conditions required for seed germination are:

(*i*) Water

(*ii*) Air and soil

(*iii*) Light and/or dark condition

10.3 GROWTH AND MOVEMENT IN PLANTS

Q. 1. *How do plants respond to sunlight?*

Ans. The plants respond to sunlight when their shoots move towards the sunlight due to phototropism.

Q. 2. *What is geotropism movement in plants?*

Ans. Geotropism means - The movement of plant roots towards the gravity.

Q. 3. *What is tropism in plant?*

Ans. Tropism in plants is the growth movement which they respond to external stimuli by growing or showing movement in certain way.

Q. 4. *Write the types of tropic movements in plants.*

Ans. Types of tropic movements in plants are:

(*i*) **Phototropism:** Movement towards sunlight

(*ii*) **Geotropism:** Movement towards gravity

(*iii*) **Hydrotropism:** Movement towards water

(*iv*) **Chemotropism:** Movement towards chemicals

(*v*) **Thigmotropism:** Movement towards touch or external stimuli.

10.4 LIFE CYCLE OF A PLANT

Q. 1. *What is life cycle of a plant?*

Ans. The whole process, starting from a seed to the formation of a plant and then to the next generation of seeds is called the life cycle of a plants.

Q. 2. *What is seed?*

Ans. A seed is a small structure that contain a baby plant inside it. It grows into a young plant.

Q. 3. *What is flower?*

Ans. A flower is a part of plant that matures into fruit after pollination. The seeds are present inside the fruit.

Q. 4. *Write the stages in the life cycle of the plant.*

Ans. Stages in the life cycle of a plant are:

(*i*) **Seeds:** Seeds grow into young plants by **germination**.

(*ii*) **Young plant:** It has stem, leaves and roots. Young plant grows into a mature plant.

(*iii*) **Mature plant:** Mature plant bear flowers and fruits.

(*iv*) **The fruit:** The fruit has seeds which give rise to a new generation of plants.

10.5 LIFE CYCLE OF ANIMALS

Q. 1. *How long does it take for a tadpole to become frog?*

Ans. Time taken by a newly hatched tadpole to become a frog is **around 14 weeks**.

Q. 2. *What are frog eggs called?*

Ans. The white jelly like substance that is a cluster of eggs of a frog in water is known as spawn.

Q 3. *What is metamorphosis?*

Ans. The development of larvae **(an immature form that hatches from an egg)** to the adult form is called metamorphosis.

Q. 4. *Explain the life cycle of a frog.*

Ans. The life cycle of a frog begins with a fertilized egg. The fertilized egg develops into a tadpole which has a tail and gills. The fertilized egg and tadpole stages are found in the water in the spring. The tadpole develops into an immature froglet, which is transformed into an adult frog by the process of metamorphosis. The tail is absorbed and the external gills are replaced by lungs. The adult frog lives on land and in the water.

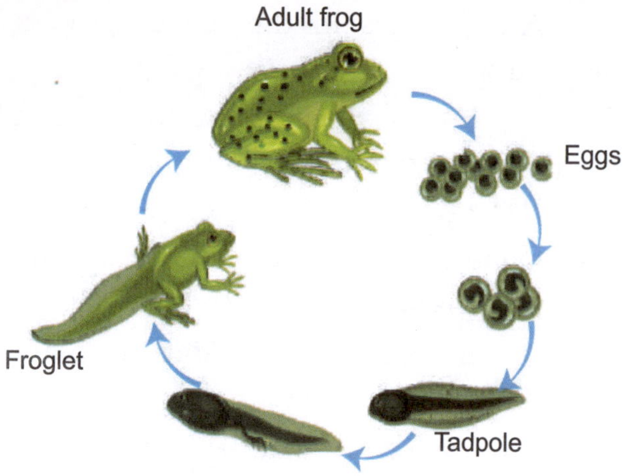

Fig. Different stages in the life cycle of a frog

Q 5. *Write short note on froglet.*

Ans. When the tadpole reaches the froglet stage, it is almost a full adult. At this point, the tadpole's gills have disappeared, and its lungs have enlarged. This means it is ready to leave the water and live on land. Once its tail disappears, it will become an adult frog.

Q 6. *Do frogs live in the water or on land?*

Ans. Frogs can live both on land and in water. They are called amphibians. Their respiratory organs are the lungs.

VI. OBJECTIVE TYPE QUESTIONS

1. *Match the following items given in Column A with that in Column B:*

Column A	Column B
(a) *Respiration*	(i) *grows upward*
(b) *Excretion*	(ii) *breathing in and out*
(c) *Shoot*	(iii) *Removal of wastes from body*
(d) *Pupa*	(iv) *movement in plants*
(e) *Spawn*	(v) *Changes into insect*
(f) *Opening of leaves*	(vi) *cluster of eggs in frog.*

2. *Fill in the blanks with appropriate words:*
   (a) *Living beings need .... for their growth and development.*
   (b) *The tiny................ inside a seeds develops into a plant.*
   (c) *The process of......... maintains the continuity of a kind of an animal.*
   (d) *The .... transforms into an adult mosquito.*
   (e) *All living beings respond to ....*
   (f) *Tiny pores called .... help plants to respire.*

3. *State whether the statements given below are True or False:*
   (i) *Anything that prompts living beings to respond is called stimulus.*
   (ii) *Growth is not a characteristic of living beings.*
   (iii) *Insectivorous plants are dependent on other plants for their nutrition.*
   (iv) *Opening of flowers is an example of movements in plants.*
   (v) *Mosquitoes breed in stagnant water.*

Multiple Choice Questions (MCQs)

Choose the correct option in the following questions

1. *Which of the following statement is incorrect?*
   (a) Cell is the structural unit of living things
   (b) Living and non-living things are made up of cells
   (c) Living and non-living things are made up of matter
   (d) Similar cells combine together to form tissues.

2. *Animals move*
   (a) to search their food
   (b) to search for shelter
   (c) to escape from their enemies
   (d) all of these

3. *Energy is released during the process of*
   (a) digestion (b) excretion
   (c) growth (d) respiration

4. *Which of the following is true for plants and animals?*
   (a) They make their own food
   (b) They need sunlight for energy
   (c) They respire to get energy
   (d) They move from one place to another

5. *Which of the following does not grow?*
   (a) Tree (b) eraser
   (c) baby (d) butterfly

6. *Which of the following is not a product of excretion?*
   (a) Carbon dioxide
   (b) energy
   (c) urine
   (d) sweat

7. *The germination of pea seeds requires one of these gases.*
   (a) nitrogen
   (b) oxygen
   (c) vapours of water
   (d) hydrogen

8. *Which is not a requirement for germination of a seed?*
   (a) favourable temperature
   (b) light
   (c) fertilizer
   (d) sufficient moisture

9. *The process of plants making their own food is called*
   (a) Germinate
   (b) Nutrients
   (c) Photosynthesis
   (d) Plant life

10. *Jagadish Chandra Bose was born in*
    (a) 1858
    (b) 1859
    (c) 1857
    (d) 1860

11. *The process in which some organisms change form in different stages of their life cycle is known as*
    (a) Life span
    (b) Germination
    (c) Metamorphosis
    (d) Reproduction

12. *An organism that is fully grown is called*
    (a) A pupa
    (b) A larva
    (c) An adult
    (d) A nymph

ACTIVITY 10.2 (*Page 188*)

- ***When a seed turns into a sprout, it is said to have germinated. Predict whether the seeds in each pot will germinate. Record your predictions for each pot kept under different conditions in Table.***

Ans.

Table: Effect of certain conditions on seed germination

Pot with bean seeds	Availability of			Seed germination		Possible reason for the observation
	Air	Sunlight	Water	Prediction	Observation	
A: In direct sunlight and without water	Yes	Yes	No	No	No seed germination	Water is necessary for the germination of seed
B: In direct sunlight and excess water	Yes	Yes	Yes (excess)	Yes	No proper seed germination	In presence of excess water, seeds can not germinate properly.
C: In complete dark and moist soil	Yes	No	Yes (limited)	Yes	Yes, seed can germinate	Light is not necessary for a seed to germinate. The majority of seeds grow most effectively in the dark
D: In direct sunlight and moist soil	Yes	Yes	Yes (limited)	Yes	Yes, seed can germinate.	Light is not necessary for seed to germinate. The majority of seeds grow most effectively in the dark

ANSWERS

1.

Column A		Column B	
(*a*)	*Respiration*	(*ii*)	*breathing in and out*
(*b*)	*Excretion*	(*iii*)	*Removal of wastes from body*
(*c*)	*Shoot*	(*i*)	*grows upward*
(*d*)	*Pupa*	(*v*)	*Changes into insect*
(*e*)	*Spawn*	(*vi*)	*cluster of eggs in frog*
(*f*)	*Opening of leaves*	(*iv*)	*movement in plants*

2. Fill in the blanks:
   (*a*) nutrition (food) (*b*) embryo (*c*) reproduction
   (*d*) pupa (*e*) stimuli (*f*) stomata
3. True or False:
   (*i*) True (*ii*) False (*iii*) False (*iv*) True (*v*) True

Multiple Choice Questions (MCQs)

1. (*b*) **2.** (*d*) **3.** (*d*) **4.** (*c*) **5.** (*b*) **6.** (*b*) **7.** (*b*) **8.** (*c*) **9.** (*c*) **10.** (*a*)
11. (*c*) **12.** (*c*)

VII. EXERCISE FOR PRACTICE

1. Name an animal which reproduces by eggs.
2. Which animal respires through gills?
3. The process of removing wastes from the body of living organisms is known as?
4. Name a plant which is produced from cuttings.
5. Give two examples of response to stimuli shown by animals.
6. How germination occurs in mung (bean) seeds?
7. Define stimulus. Give two examples of response to stimuli shown by plants.
8. Give characteristics of living organisms in detail.
9. Give differences between living and non-living things.
10. How excretion occurs in plants?
11. What is the need of excretion in animals?

NOTES

INTERESTING MIND MAP

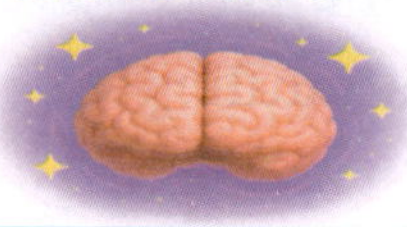

Nature's Treasures

1 Air

- It contains 78% nitrogen, 21% oxygen, and 1% argon, carbon dioxide and other gases.
- Moving air is called wind.
- Gentle blowing of wind is called breeze.
- Fast blowing of wind is called storm.

2 Water

- We use it for drinking, cooking, bathing, washing and cleaning.
- We use it for growing crops.
- We use it for industrial purposes.
- Rainwater harvesting helps to store water.

3 Energy from the Sun

- Sunlight helps plants prepare food.
- The sun provides heat and light to all the living beings on Earth.

4 Forests

- Forests provide food and shelter to many wild animals, birds and insects.

5 Soil, Rocks and Minerals

- Soil supports biodiversity.
- Rocks help construct houses, buildings, temples, roads, etc.
- Minerals help manufacture airplanes, cars, jewellery, cosmetics, and electrical and electronic equipment.

6 Fossil Fuels

- Petroleum, natural gas and coal are commonly called fossil fuels.

7 Natural Resources; Renewable and Non-renewable

- Resources made by nature are natural resources. E.g. sunlight.
- Renewable resources can be renewed easily. E.g. wind.
- Non-renewable resources cannot be easily renewed. E.g. petroleum.
- Human-made resources are created by human beings. E.g. electric bulbs.

8 Resources We Use

- We use many natural and human-made resources to meet our needs.

11

Nature's Treasures

I. POINTS TO REMEMBER

1. **Nature's Treasures**

   The **Nature's treasures** like **air, water, sunlight, forests, rocks, soil, minerals** and **fossil fuels** are required for our survival and make our life comfortable. These treasures of nature are known as Natural resources.

2. **Renewable or Inexhaustible Resources:** Resources like air, water, sunlight and forests get renewed, replenished or restored within a certain period of time. These are called **renewable resources** as **nature renews them**.

3. Increasing human population and their expanding needs have resulted into over-utilisation of natural resources on a much larger scale. Over the years, there is great pressure on forests due to increase in the demand of forest products.

4. We must use natural resources judiciously.

5. **Non-renewable or Exhaustible Resources**

   Non-Renewable resources are soil, rocks, minerals, fossil fuels (coal, petroleum and natural gas). These resources are not produced or replenished within a reasonable period of time. They are found in limited amounts and once used, they get exhausted. Fossil fuels take millions of years to form.

6. Air is a mixture of different gases.

7. Air contains nitrogen, oxygen, argon, carbon dioxide and other gases in small quantities.

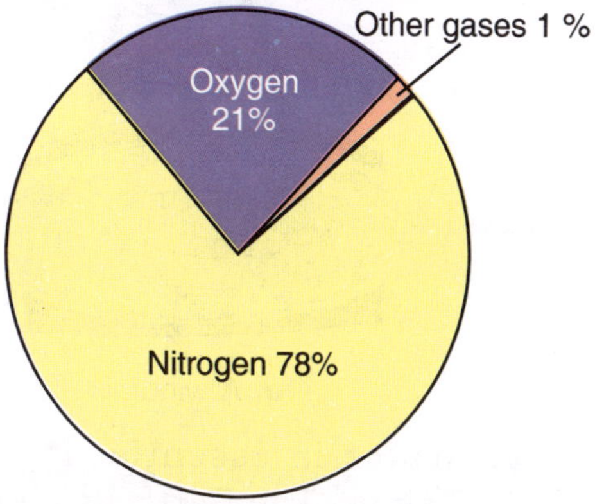

Fig. : Composition of air

8. Most of the living beings need oxygen rich air for their survival. We can live without eating food or drinking water for some days but we cannot live without air even for some time.

9. Air exerts force on objects that come in its way. This property of air is quite useful.

10. Moving air is called wind. It rotates the firki due to application of force.

Fig. Different types of firkis

11. A windmill farm is an area that has a large number of windmills which use the energy of the wind to generate electricity.

Fig. A windmill

12. Water is essential for all living beings. The Earth has life because water is present on this planet.

13. Rain is the main source of water.

14. Water covers about two-thirds of the Earth's surface.

15. Most of the water is found in oceans and seas. Only 0.7% of the total water on the Earth is available for use. This is the amount of water that we get from lakes, ponds and ground water through pumps, wells and tubewells.

16. Water that is fit for drinking purposes is called potable water. Water is very precious so we should not waste it.

17. Saline water of the oceans and seas is not fit for domestic, agriculture and industrial use.

18. Rainwater harvesting is one of the methods for conserving water.

Fig.: Rainwater Harvesting

19. The Sun is the main source of energy on the Earth.

20. We use heat and light from the Sun for various purposes.

21. Sunlight helps plants to prepare food by photosynthesis.

22. The solar panels capture the Sun's energy and produce electricity.

23. The heat of the sun causes evaporation of water which helps in **water cycle.**

24. Forests are large areas with dense growth of various types of plants, bushes etc. We call trees and bushes to be natural vegetation in a forest as they grow on their own.

25. Forests are the natural home for many wild animals, including birds and insects. Forest provide food and shelter to animals, insects and birds.

26. The large scale cutting down of the forest trees is called **deforestation**.

Large scale tree plantation is called **Afforestation**.

Reforestation should be encouraged on deforested area.

27. **Chipko movement** started in the early 1970s in Uttarakhand by tribal women.
28. Soil is the most important natural resources. Most plants grow in soil. The space between the soil particles not only provides sufficient air but also space for the roots to grow easily.
29. Plants and animals also become part of the soil as they decompose and decay.
30. The earth is made up of rocks and soil. Each rock is composed of different minerals which are naturally occurring substances in the earth.
31. Petroleum along with natural gas and coal are commonly called fossil fuels.
32. Natural gas is used for cooking and generating electricity.
33. Fossil fuels take millions of years to form. They are also found in limited quantities and once used they get exhausted. We should use them judiciously.
34. We should explore alternate sources of energy.
35. We must conserve our natural resources.

II. KEYWORDS

1. **Air :** We are surrounded by air, but we cannot see it. The air is a mixture of gases like nitrogen, oxygen, carbon dioxide and other gases in small quantities.
2. **Coal :** Coal is a combustible black or brownish-black sedimentary rock with a high amount of carbon.
3. **Forests:** A large area of land covered densely with trees and plants.
4. **Fossil fuels:** Fossil fuels are organic fuel resources found in the Earth's crust which have been formed in the past by compression of buried forests and other organic matter for millions of years e.g. coal, natural gas and petroleum.
5. **Natural Gas:** It is a fossil fuel, used for cooking and generating electricity. It is also used as a fuel for vehicles in the form of CNG (Compressed Natural Gas). It is cleaner than petrol and diesel.
6. **Human-made resources:** When human beings use natural materials to make useful things **for our convenience,** it is called **human-made resources**. For example, using naturally occurring wood to make furniture, doors, windows etc.
7. **Natural resources:** These are the essential resources that are found in the nature to sustain all life forms on the Earth. Common examples of natural resources include air, sunlight, water, soil, stone, plants, animals and fossil fuels.
8. **Non-renewable resources:** The resources which cannot be immediately replaced once they are depleted are called non-renewable resources. Examples of non-renewable resources include fossil fuels, such as coal, petroleum, natural gas and rare minerals.

9. **Petroleum:** Petroleum is a naturally occurring fossil fuel formed from the remains of microorganisms and plants buried deep beneath the Earth's surface.
10. **Renewable resources:** The resources which cannot be exhausted even after continuous utilisation are called renewable resources. Examples of renewable resources are the sun, air, water and forest.
11. **Rocks:** A rock is a solid collection of minerals from which important metals like aluminium, copper, iron, gold etc. are extracted.
12. **Soil :** It is a natural body comprised of solids (minerals and organic matter) liquid, and gases that occurs on the land surface.
13. **Sun:** The Sun is the luminous celestial star around which the Earth and other planets revolve. The Earth receives heat and light from the Sun. The Sun is the natural resource of energy and is composed mainly of hydrogen and helium.
14. **Water:** Water is essential for living beings and is used for daily activities like drinking, bathing, cooking, cleaning etc.

    Main source of water is rain. Water is a clear, odourless, tasteless and colourless liquid. Water covers about two-thirds of Earth's surface.
15. **Rainwater Harvesting:** It is a method to conserve water. In houses and buildings, the rainwater from roof goes into underground pits which is collected and stored to be used later on. It is an age old practice in India.

III. NCERT INTEXT QUESTIONS

Q. 1. ***What will happen if the Sun is not visible for a few days?*** ***(Page 216)***

1. We may have to depend on artificial lighting during day time also.
2. ______________
3. ______________

Ans.

2. With no sunlight, photosynthesis will not occur, that would make some of the plants weak but there are some larger trees that can survive for decades without sunlight.
3. There will be no natural light and heat so many natural phenomena like evaporation, transpiration, condensation etc. are affected.

Q. 2. ***What are the consequences of cutting a large forest area? Make a presentation or do a role play, or write a story or a poem that shows what could happen if we continue to cut down trees in our forests.*** ***(Page 217)***

Ans. The loss of trees and other vegetation can cause climate change, desertification, soil erosion, flooding, increased greenhouse gases in the atmosphere. Forests also provide food and shelter to many wild animals, birds and insect.

Presentation/Play/Story or Poem: Do it yourself.

IV. LET US ENHANCE OUR LEARNING (*Pages 227–229*)

Q. 1. ***Figure shows items related to natural resources. Match them with their jumbled up names. Make another table and write the names of these resources. Classify these resources as renewable or non-renewable.***

(See Table, Textbook page 227)

Ans.

Item	Jumbled up name	Name	Resources	Renewable or Non-renewable Resource
	ocrk →	Rock	Minerals	Non-renewable
	refost →	Forest	Forest	Renewable
	ndiw →	Wind	Air (Atmosphere)	Renewable
	atwre →	Water	River, Pond, Sea, Oceans, ground water	Renewable

Q. 2. ***State whether the following statements are True [T] or False [F]. If False, correct them.***

(*i*) Nature has all the resources to meet human needs. [ ]

(*ii*) Machines are a resource found in nature. [ ]

(*iii*) Natural gas is a non-renewable resource. [ ]

(*iv*) Air is a renewable resource. [ ]

Ans. (*i*) T (*ii*) F

Correct Statement: Machines are human–made resources.

(*iii*) T (*iv*) T

Q. 3. ***Fill in the blanks using the most appropriate option—***

(*i*) A fuel that is commonly used in two wheelers like scooters or bikes is.........

(*a*) Kerosene (*b*) Petrol

(*c*) Diesel (*d*) LPG

(*ii*) An example of a renewable resource is ....

(*a*) Coal

(*b*) Water

(*c*) Natural gas

(*d*) Petrol

Ans. (*i*) (*b*) Petrol

(*ii*) (*b*) Water

Q. 4. *Classify the following as renewable or non-renewable resources—coal, natural gas, forests and minerals.*

Ans.

Renewable	Non-renewable
–	Coal
–	Natural gas
Forests	–
–	Minerals

Q. 5. *Why do we say that petroleum is a non-renewable resource?*

Ans. Petroleum is said to be a non-renewable resource because it takes millions of years to form from the remains of microorganisms and plants that get buried deep inside the Earth. Once extracted and used, it cannot be replenished.

Q. 6. *It is difficult to regrow forests. Justify this statement.*

Ans. Regrowing forests is difficult because it takes many years for trees to mature. Additionally, the soil may become degraded, losing its nutrients and structure due to deforestation, making it less suitable for new plant growth. Human activities like development and agriculture can also interfere in reforestation efforts.

Q. 7. *Make a list of five daily activities in which you use natural resources. Suggest ways by which you can reduce their use.*

Ans.

S. No	Daily Activity	Natural Resource Used	Ways to Reduce use
1	Cooking	Natural gas	Use solar cookers
2	Drinking water	Water	Use a water-efficient taps
3.	Using paper	Trees (forests)	Use digital documents
4.	Using electricity	Coal, natural gas	Use energy-efficient appliances
5.	Driving a car	Petroleum	Use public transport or bicycles

Q. 8. *List four activities that are possible due to the presence of air.*

Ans. Four activities that are possible due to presence of air –

(*i*) Breathing

(*ii*) Generating electricity through wind turbines

(*iii*) Transportation through aeroplanes.

(*iv*) Flying kites

Q. 9. *How can you contribute towards enhancing the green cover of your locality? Make a list of actions to be taken.*

Ans. List of actions to be taken

(*i*) Encourage people to grow plants in their gardens.

(*ii*) Collaborate with local schools to create green initiatives.

(*iii*) Advocate for the protection of existing trees and green spaces.

(*iv*) Participate in community tree planting drives.

(v) Plant trees in local parks and open spaces.

Q. 10. ***In the given illustration, we see that food is being cooked. Answer the following questions—***

(*i*) What type of energy is being used for cooking?

(*ii*) Name one benefit and one drawback of using this type of energy for cooking.

Ans. (*i*) Solar Energy.

(*ii*) **Benefit:** Solar energy is a renewable and clean source of energy. Hence it is environment friendly.

Drawback: Dependence on Weather: Solar energy cannot be used during cloudy days or at night, which limits its reliability and convenience.

Q. 11. ***Cutting down trees on a large scale impacts the quality of the soil. Why do you think it is so?***

Ans. Without trees, the soil can be washed away by rain, leading to the loss of fertile topsoil. Fallen leaves from trees decompose and add organic matter to the soil, making it fertile. Cutting down trees affects the quality of soil because roots of trees help to bind the soil together thus preventing erosion.

Q. 12. ***Explain two ways in which human activities pollute the air. Propose one action which can help in reducing air pollution.***

Ans.

(*i*) Trees check the concentration of greenhouse gases by absorbing carbon dioxide. Deforestation reduces the number of trees, thus increasing the concentration of greenhouse gases.

(*ii*) Burning fossil fuels in vehicles and factories releases harmful pollutants like carbon monoxide and sulphur dioxide into the air.

Action to reduce air pollution: To decrease the number of fossil fuel-powered vehicles on the road encourage the use of public transport and electric vehicles.

Q. 13. ***A family uses solar panels to generate electricity, a gas stove to cook food and a windmill for pumping water from a well. What would happen if there were no sunlight for a week?***

Ans. If there is no sunlight for a week, the solar panels would not be able to generate electricity, leading the family to rely on alternate sources of power. Additionally, the growth of plants would be affected due to the lack of sunlight for photosynthesis.

Q. 14. ***Fill up the blanks using the following terms— (fossil fuels, forest, air, petroleum, coal, water and non-renewable resource)***

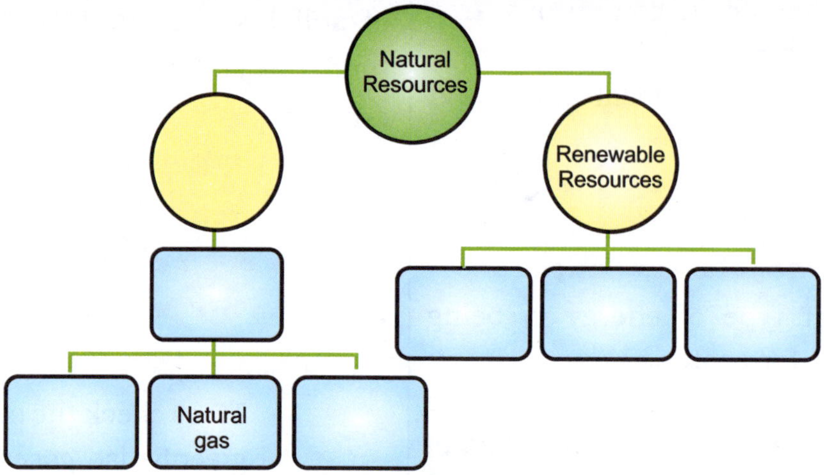

Ans.

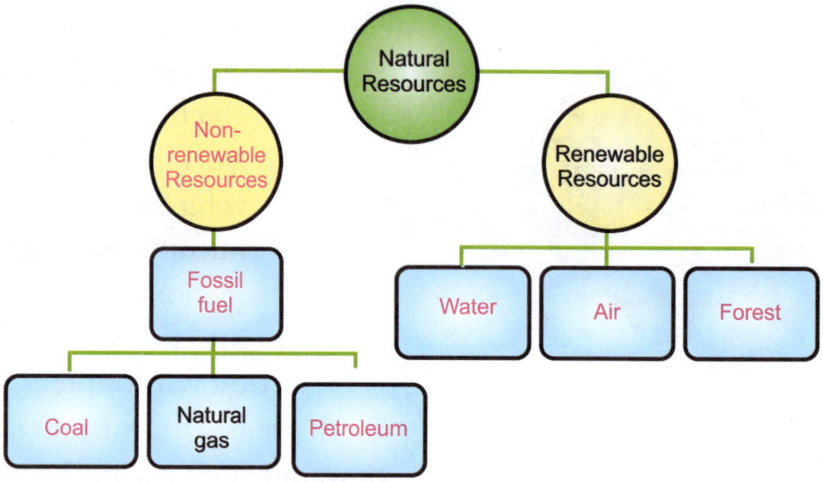

Q. 15. ***There is an increasing demand of trees to meet the requirements of industries and for housing. Therefore, trees are being felled. Is it justified? Discuss and prepare a brief report.***

Ans. Trees play an important role in maintaining **ecological balance** by providing oxygen, supporting wildlife, and preventing soil erosion. Large scale deforestation can lead to loss of biodiversity, climate change, and disruption of water cycles. Sustainable practices such as using alternative materials, implementing stricter regulations on tree felling, and promoting **reforestation** can help balance economic development with environmental conservation.

Q. 16. ***Propose a plan to use less water in your school. What steps would you take to make this plan happen and how would it help the environment?***

Ans.

Plan to Use Less Water

1. Use treated water for gardening purposes.
2. Implement a rainwater harvesting system.
3. Install water-efficient taps.

Steps to Implement the Plan

1. Monitor water usage regularly and set reduction targets.
2. Encourage student-led initiatives for water conservation.
3. Collaborate with local authorities and experts to install water-saving devices.

Environmental Benefits

1. Promotes sustainability and responsible water usage within the community.
2. Decreases the energy used in water treatment and distribution.

V. EXAM ORIENTED QUESTIONS

11.1 AIR

Q. 1. *What is wind?*

Ans. Moving air is called wind.

Q. 2. *Describe the composition of air.*

Ans. Air contains nitrogen (78%) and oxygen (21%). The remaining 1% (by volume) is shared by argon (0.34%), carbon dioxide (0.33%), other noble gases, oxides of nitrogen and sulphur *etc.*, in the decreasing order.

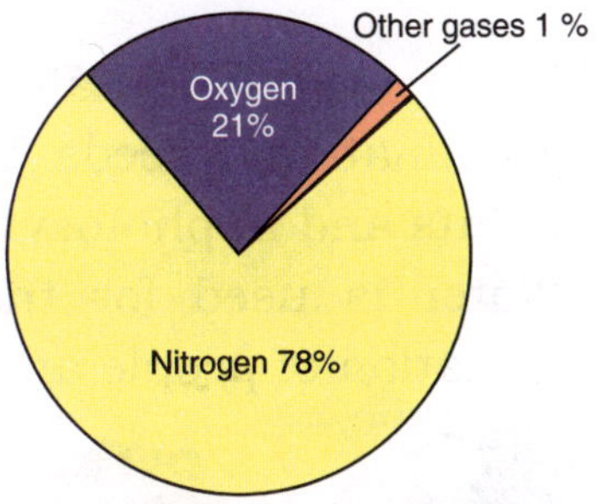

Fig. : The relative proportion of main gases present in air

Q. 3. *What will happen if the amount of oxygen is increased in the air?*

Ans. Air will become more combustible and many substances may undergo fast oxidation.

Q. 4. *Name the substances which are present in traces in air. What are these together called?*

Ans. Xenon (Xe), Krypton (Kr), Neon (Ne) and Helium (He) are present in traces in the air. These together form 0.02% of air and are called inert gases or noble gases.

Q. 5. *How will you prove that air is a mixture of several gases and not a compound?*

Ans. The following points prove that air is a mixture :

(*i*) The composition of air varies slightly from place to place.

(*ii*) Different components of air can be separated by physical processes.

(*iii*) Different components of air exhibit their characteristics, for example, O_2 in air supports combustion, CO_2 in air turns lime water milky.

Q. 6. *What are the properties of air?*

Ans.

(*i*) Air is present everywhere around us.

(*ii*) Air occupies space.

(*iii*) Air has no colour.

(*iv*) It is transparent.

Q. 7. What is atmosphere?

Ans. Our earth is surrounded by a thin layer of air. This layer is called atmosphere. It extends up to many kilometres above the surface of the earth.

Q. 8. *Why is atmosphere called the place where exchange of gases occurs in nature?*

Ans. We know that many gases are found in air. Some organisms live on land, some in water and some deep under the soil. They all need oxygen to respire. The land organisms take oxygen from the atmosphere. During respiration by living beings and burning of materials, carbon dioxide is produced along with some other gases. CO_2 is used by the plants during the process of photosynthesis and oxygen is released. All gases go into the atmosphere. Thus, atmosphere is a place in nature for gaseous exchange.

Q. 9. *The mountaineers carry oxygen cylinder with them while climbing high mountains. Why?*

Ans. The availability of oxygen decreases gradually as we go up in the atmosphere.

Q. 10. *Explain the following observations very briefly.*

(NCERT Exemplar)

(a) A firki does not rotate in a closed area.

(b) The arrow of weather cock points towards a particular direction at a particular moment.

(c) An empty glass in fact is not empty.

(d) Breathing through mouth may harm you.

Ans.

(a) Because of lack of air movement in closed area.

(b) It depends on the latest direction of the wind.

(c) It is filled with air.

(d) You may inhale dust or microorganisms present in air which may prove harmful.

Q. 11. *Name the gases present in air. Which one of them is most abundant?*

Ans. N_2, O_2, Ar (argon), CO_2, water vapour, neon (Ne), helium (He), krypton (Kr), xenon (Xe) are present in air. Nitrogen is most abundant.

11.2 WATER

Q. 1. *Write the sources of water on the earth.*

Ans. Oceans, Rivers, Springs, Tubewells, Rain water, etc.

Q. 2. *In which three forms, water exists on the earth?*

Ans. Water exists on the earth in all three physical forms : Ice, water and water vapour.

Q. 3. *Mention two main functions of water for living organisms.*

Ans.

(i) Water is essential for the germination of seeds, growth of plants and in photosynthesis.

(ii) Water is used for the transportation of people and goods.

Q. 4. *Why is ocean water not suitable for domestic use?*

Ans. Sea and ocean water contains large amounts of salts. It is due to these salts the ocean water is salty and cannot be used for drinking, washing and for irrigation purposes.

Q. 5. ***What is meant by conservation of water? Suggest three methods to conserve water.***

Ans. Careful and economical use of water and avoiding its wastage is called conservation of water.

(*i*) Use only the limited and required quantity of water.

(*ii*) To conserve water, we should plant more and more trees.

(*iii*) By collecting rainwater in tanks, ponds or by constructing check dams.

Q. 6. ***What is rainwater harvesting? Describe the method of rainwater harvesting.***

Ans. Rainwater harvesting is the collection of rainwater and storing it for future use. In this system rainwater is collected from the rooftops by means of pipes into storage tank for later use. Recycling water and water harvesting also help in saving water.

Methods of Rainwater Harvesting:

(*i*) **Rooftop rainwater harvesting:** In this system, the rainwater from the rooftop is collected in a storage tank, through pipes.

(*ii*) **Another method:** A big pit is dug near house for collecting rainwater. This pit is filled with different layers of bricks, coarse gravels and sand.

11.3 ENERGY FROM THE SUN

Q. 1. ***Name the main source of energy on Earth.***

Ans. The Sun.

Q. 2. ***What is photosynthesis?***

Ans. "The process, by which green plants make their own food from carbon dioxide (CO_2) and water (H_2O) in the presence of sunlight and green pigment (chlorophyll) is called Photosynthesis."

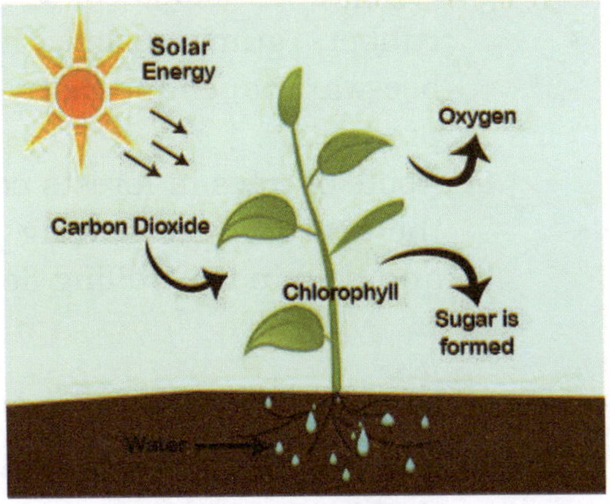

Fig. **Photosynthesis**

Q. 3. ***What is the ultimate source of energy for all living organisms?***

Ans. The Sun is the ultimate source of energy for all living organisms.

11.4 FORESTS

Q. 1. ***What are forests?***

Ans. Forests are large areas with dense growth of different types of plants (herbs, shrubs and trees). Forests are a natural home for many wild animals, including birds and insects. Forests provide food and shelter to them.

Q. 2. ***Why should we worry about the conditions and issues related to forests though they are far from us?***

Ans. We should worry about the conditions and issues related to forests even though they are far from us because forests play an important role for the sustenance of life on earth.

The importance of forests for us :

(*i*) Forests help in maintaining the ratio of oxygen and carbon dioxide in air.

(*ii*) Forests provide home to a wide variety of plants and animals.

(*iii*) Forests provide firewood, timber, medicines, fruits, rubber, gum, resins, honey, bee-wax, paper and many other products.

(*iv*) Roots of trees in forests control the speed of the flowing water and help in controlling floods.

Q. 3. ***Explain how animals living in the forest help it grow and regenerate.***

Ans. We can see seeds germinating in a decaying heap of animal droppings especially in rainy seasons and form seedling. These seedlings are the herbs and shrubs. The animals also disperse the seeds of certain plants and help the forest to grow and regenerate. The decaying animal dung and leaf litter also provides nutrients to the seedlings.

Q. 4. ***Name the movement started by common people to prevent the cutting of trees and thus, saving forests. When and where was it started?***

Ans. (*i*) **Chipko movement** started by local women.

(*ii*) It was started in early 1970s in **Uttarakhand** (previously part of Uttar Pradesh).

Q. 5. ***Explain Van-Mahotsav.***

Ans. Van-Mahotsav is a week-long event celebrated across the country during the month of July. It is a forest festival during which new plants and trees are planted and awareness about growing plants is raised.

Q. 6. ***Explain the role of forest in maintaining the balance between oxygen and carbon dioxide in the atmosphere.***

Ans. Plants release oxygen as a by product during the process of photosynthesis. This oxygen is inhaled by animals and plants for respiration. This respiration process releases carbon dioxide which is used again by plants during photosynthesis. In this way, use and consumption of oxygen and carbon dioxide goes on. Thus, forests (plants) maintain the balance of oxygen and carbon dioxide in the atmosphere.

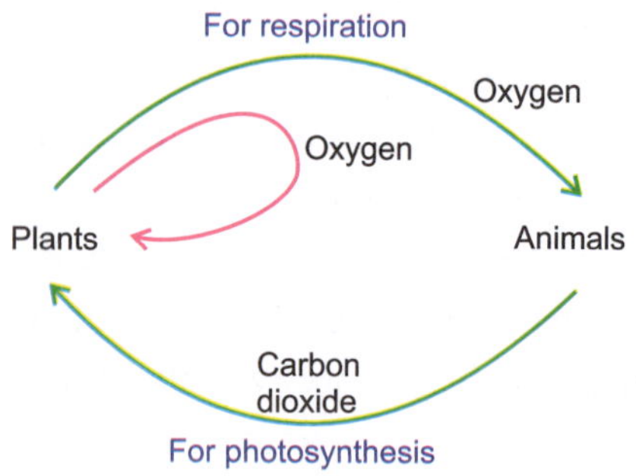

Fig. Balance of Oxygen and Carbon Dioxide

Q. 7. ***How does the forest floor look like?***

Ans. The forest floor looks dark-coloured and is covered with a layer of dead and decaying leaves, fruits, seeds, twigs and small herbs. The decaying matter is moist and warm.

Q. 8. ***What is the importance of dense bushes and tall grasses for animals living in the forest?***

Ans. The dense bushes and the tall grasses provide the food and shelter to the animals. They also protect them from predators living in the forest.

11.5 SOIL, ROCKS AND MINERALS

Q. 1. ***What is soil?***

Ans. Soil is made up of small pieces of broken rocks and decaying plants.

Q. 2. ***Why soil samples collected from different places have different colours?***

Ans. Soil samples collected from different places have different colours because they may contain different materials.

Q. 3. ***What are the natural agents of the soil?***

Ans. The earthworms are natural agents that help in turning and loosening the soil.

Q. 4. ***What is rock?***

Ans. Any natural mass of mineral matter that makes up the Earth's crust is called a rock.

11.6 FOSSIL FUELS

Q. 1. ***What is the full form of LPG?***

Ans. Liquefied petroleum gas.

Q. 2. ***Name the petroleum product which is commonly used for electric generators.***

Ans. Diesel is used as a fuel for electric generators.

Q. 3. ***What are fossil fuels? Name three fossil fuels.***

Ans. Petroleum, natural gas and coal are commonly called fossil fuels. They are formed from the remains of microorganisms and plants that got buried deep inside the earth, and were converted to petroleum, natural gas and coal. It takes millions of years for these fuels to form that is why they are called fossil fuels.

Q. 4. ***Name the petroleum product used to drive heavy vehicles.***

Ans. Diesel is used as a fuel for heavy motor vehicles and electric generators.

Q. 5. What is the full form of CNG?

Ans. Compressed Natural Gas.

11.7 NATURAL RESOURCES : RENEWABLE AND NON-RENEWABLE

Q. 1. ***What is a non-renewable or exhaustible resource?***

Ans. Natural resources that are limited in quantity are referred to as non-renewable resources. These resources cannot be regenerated in a small duration of time. These resources get exhausted once used so they are called non-renewable or exhaustible resources.

Q. 2. ***Which are the most commonly used renewable energy sources?***

Ans. Solar energy, wind energy, hydropower, tidal energy, and geothermal energy are some of the important examples of renewable energy.

Q. 3. What is meant by a renewable energy source?

Ans. The resources which get renewed or replenished within a reasonable period of time are called renewable resources. Air, water and forests are examples of renewable natural resources.

11.8 RESOURCES WE USE

Q. 1. ***What are the two types of natural resources?***

Ans. Renewable and non-renewable natural resources are the two types of natural resources.

Q. 2. ***List out four human-made resources you use in your home and four you used in your classroom.***

Ans. The list of four such resources which we use in our home are:

(*i*) Television (*ii*) Water
(*iii*) Furniture (*iv*) Utensils

The list of four resources that we use in our classroom are

(*i*) Book (*ii*) Chalk
(*iii*) Blackboard (*iv*) Water

VI. OBJECTIVE TYPE QUESTIONS

1. *Match the following items given in Column A with that in Column B:*

Column A		Column B	
(*a*)	Moving air	(*i*)	Water harvesting
(*b*)	Saving water	(*ii*)	Soil
(*c*)	Sunlight	(*iii*)	Breath
(*d*)	Disintegration	(*iv*)	Rock
(*e*)	Oxygen	(*v*)	Wind
(*f*)	Hand axes	(*vi*)	Source of energy

2. *Fill in the blanks with appropriate words:*
   (*a*) *Waste from homes and industries pollute ....*
   (*b*) *Windmills use the energy of winds to generate ....*
   (*c*) *......... is not fit for domestic, agriculture and industrial use.*
   (*d*) *Water is offered to the Sun early in the morning as an .... to the Sun.*
   (*e*) *Due to .... , the forest cover has been decreasing.*
   (*f*) *......... are natural agents that help in turning and loosening the soil?*
   (*g*) *Human beings have been using .... to make tools such as ....*
   (*h*) *Coal, wood and dung cakes were used as ....*
   (*i*) *When fossil fuels are burnt .... and .... are produced.*
   (*j*) *Water covers about .... of the Earth's surface.*

3. *State whether the statements given below are True or False:*
   (*i*) *Our body needs nitrogen to perform its functions.*
   (*ii*) *The air which surrounds the Earth is a mixture of gases.*
   (*iii*) *21 per cent part of air is occupied by oxygen.*
   (*iv*) *Saline water is fit for agriculture use.*
   (*v*) *We use heat and light from the moon for various purposes.*
   (*vi*) *In ancient times, India had a tradition of respecting, protecting and preserving forests.*
   (*vii*) *Petroleum is a fossil fuel.*

Multiple Choice Questions (MCQs)

Choose the correct option in the following questions

1. *Which of the following gas do we use in breathing?*
   (*a*) Carbon dioxide
   (*b*) Nitrogen
   (*c*) Oxygen
   (*d*) None of these.
2. *Wind is:*
   (*a*) air around us
   (*b*) rising hot air
   (*c*) air in motion
   (*d*) none of these.
3. *Which is not a property of air?*
   (*a*) It occupies space
   (*b*) It is transparent
   (*c*) It is a gas
   (*d*) It is a compound
4. *The main constituent of the air is:*
   (*a*) nitrogen (*b*) oxygen
   (*c*) carbon dioxide
   (*d*) hydrogen.
5. *Wind does not help in the movement of which of the following?*
   (*a*) Firki (*b*) Weather cock
   (*c*) Ceiling fan (*d*) Sailing yacht.

6. *Ground water is a*
(*a*) Renewable resource
(*b*) Non-renewable resource
(*c*) Exhaustible resource
(*d*) All of these

7. *The percentage of total drinking water available on earth is:*
(*a*) 0.3% (*b*) 15%
(*c*) 25% (*d*) 45%

8. *The process of collecting rainwater is called:*
(*a*) Rainwater collecting
(*b*) Rainwater recharging
(*c*) Rainwater harvesting
(*d*) Rainwater replenishing.

9. *The most impure water is:*
(*a*) rain water (*b*) river water
(*c*) sea water (*d*) none of these

10. *Which of the following is not a source of potable water?*
(*a*) Sea water (*b*) Well water
(*c*) River water (*d*) Rain water

11. *Out of these which source of energy is used in photosynthesis?*
(*a*) Coal (*b*) Petrol
(*c*) Wood (*d*) Sunlight

12. *Which of the following is a disadvantage of using solar power?*
(*a*) It is expensive to produce.
(*b*) It is not reliable in all weather conditions.
(*c*) It emits pollutants.
(*d*) It requires a large amount of land.

13. *Solar energy is harnessed using:*
(*a*) solar panels
(*b*) turbines
(*c*) dams
(*d*) geothermal wells.

14. *An example of fossil fuel is*
(*a*) paper
(*b*) wood
(*c*) plastic
(*d*) coal

15. *Which gas is produced, when coal is burnt in air?*
(*a*) Oxygen
(*b*) Hydrogen
(*c*) Carbon dioxide
(*d*) Nitrogen

16. *Full form of L.P.G is*
(*a*) Liquefied Petroleum Gas
(*b*) Liquid Petrol Gas
(*c*) Light Petroleum Gas
(*d*) None of the above.

17. *Which of the following is/are the use (s) of forests?*
(*a*) Provide food, shelter, water and medicines
(*b*) Prevent soil erosion
(*c*) Prevent flood
(*d*) All of the above

18. *Which of the following statements is incorrect?* (*NCERT Exemplar*)
(*a*) All living beings require air to breathe.
(*b*) We can feel air but we cannot see it.
(*c*) Moving air makes it possible to fly a kite.
(*d*) Air is present everywhere but not in soil.

19. *What is* ***not*** *true about moving air?* (*NCERT Exemplar*)
(*a*) It makes the windmill rotate.
(*b*) It helps in the movements of aeroplanes.
(*c*) Birds can fly due to presence of air.
(*d*) It has no role in water cycle.

ANSWERS

1.

Column A		Column B	
(a)	Moving air	(v)	Wind
(b)	Saving water	(i)	Water harvesting
(c)	Sunlight	(vi)	Source of energy
(d)	Disintegration	(ii)	Soil
(e)	Oxygen	(iii)	Breath
(f)	Hand axes	(iv)	Rock

2. Fill in the blanks:
   (a) Water resources
   (b) Electricity
   (c) Saline water
   (d) Expression of gratitude
   (e) Cutting of trees
   (f) Earthworms
   (g) Rocks, Hand axes
   (h) Fuels for cooking
   (i) Smoke and carbon dioxide gas
   (j) Two-thirds

3. True or False:
   (i) False (ii) True
   (iii) True (iv) False
   (v) False (vi) True
   (vii) True

Multiple Choice Questions (MCQs)

1. (c) 2. (c) 3. (d) 4. (a) 5. (c)
6. (a) 7. (a) 8. (c) 9. (c) 10. (a)
11. (d) 12. (b) 13. (a) 14. (d) 15. (c)
16. (a) 17. (d) 18. (d) 19. (d)

ACTIVITIES

ACTIVITY 11.3: Let us Find Out (Page 212)

Fill the Column II and Column III in following table.

Ans: Table: Wastage of water in your daily activities

Column I		Column II	Column III
Activity		How is water wasted?	Suggest ways to reduce wastage of water
1.	**Hand washing and face washing**	Taps are kept open with water running continuously cause wastage of water.	Turn the taps off immediately after washing hands and face or a mug is used for washing.
2.	**Washing clothes**	When small loads of clothes are washed in washing machines or by hand, water is wasted.	Wash full loads of clothes in washing machine or use buckets if washing of clothes is done with hand.
3.	**Washing utensils**	Using running water while rinsing utensils wastes a lot of water.	Use a bucket full of water while rinsing utensils.
4.	**Taking shower**	Bathing under shower for long duration cause excessive wastage of water.	Use a bucket of water for taking bath or use shower for short duration of time.
5.	**Cooking**	Washing vegetables and fruits under running water and cooking in excessive amount of water cause water wastage.	Wash vegetables and fruits in a container having water. Use proper amount of water to cook food.
6.	**Gardening**	Overwatering the plants cause a lot of wastage of water.	Using drip-irrigation reduces the wastage of water.
7.	**Brushing teeth or shaving**	A lot of water is wasted during shaving or brushing of teeth by keeping the tap open and water running.	Use a glass of water while brushing teeth, shaving or turn off the tap while brushing teeth. Open the tap only when water is required while brushing teeth or shaving.

***ACTIVITY 11.6:* Let us make a list of natural resources used (Page 225)**

Make a list of activities you do in your daily life and write down the natural resources that were used directly or indirectly for each activity. In Table, some items are already filled in. Using them as a guide, fill the remaining blank rows.

Ans.

Table: Natural Resources Used

Activity		Natural Resource
1.	Washing clothes	Water
2.	Making clay toys	Soil
3.	Collecting firewood	Wood
4.	Making kites	Bamboo
5.	Having breakfast	Water

VII. EXERCISE FOR PRACTICE

1. Are fossil fuels renewable?
2. State the reasons of over exploitation of forests.
3. What is the role of an individual in conservation of natural resources?
4. State one difference between renewable and non-renewable resources.
5. Define water harvesting.
6. What is the importance of water?
7. Write any three properties of air.
8. Write important uses of oxygen.
9. Write a note on good practices towards conserving forest.
10. Explain with example the Sun is the main source of energy on Earth.
11. What is Chipko Movement?
12. Write two uses of:
    (*i*) Rocks (*ii*) Minerals.
13. How are fossil fuels used in our daily life?

NOTES

1 Stars and Constellations

- Stars shine with their own light.
- The patterns of stars are called constellations. Eg. Orion, Canis Major, Taurus.

2 Night Sky Watching

- It helps us to see a large number of stars in cloudless night.

INTERESTING MIND MAP

Beyond Earth

4 The Milky Way Galaxy

- An extended faint band of light from near north to south across the sky is called the Milky Way Galaxy or Akasha Ganga.

5 The Universe

- The stars, galaxies, exoplanet, etc.

3 Our Solar System

- **The Sun:** The main source of energy on the earth being elevated to the status of a deity.
- **Planets:** Large nearly spherical objects revolving around the Sun.
- **Natural Satellites:** Objects revolving around planets.
- **The Moon:** The natural satellite of earth taking about 27 days to revolve once around the earth.
- **Asteroids:** Rocky and irregular shaped objects revolving around the Sun in paths lying between the paths of Mars and Jupiter.
- **Comets:** Objects of the outer regions of the Solar System having tail and made up of dust, gases, rocks and ice.

12

Beyond Earth

I. POINTS TO REMEMBER

1. **The Stars:** The Stars are much bigger than the Earth and some stars are bigger than the Sun also. **The Sun is also a star**. The stars have their own light which they emit. Stars appear to move from the East to the West. This is because our Earth rotates from the West to the East.
2. **Pole Star:** Pole star is the most shining star in the night sky. The pole star appears to be stationary. It is situated near the axis of rotation of the Earth and is thus helpful in finding direction.

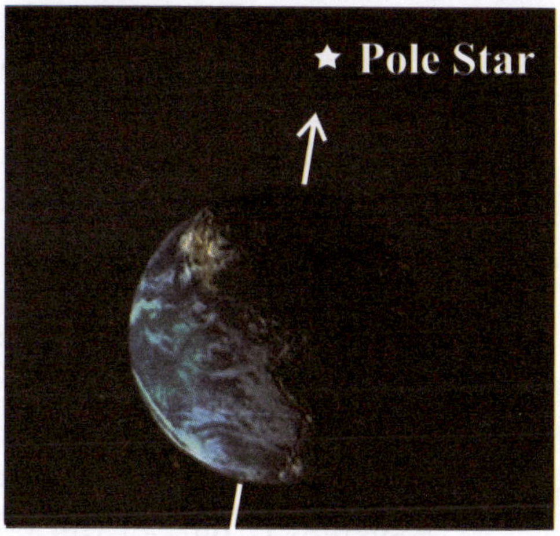

Fig. Pole Star

3. **Constellations:** The group of stars which appear to form some recognizable shape or pattern is known as **constellation**. These groups of stars or constellations are named after the objects which they seemed to resemble such as an animal, a human being. One of the most easily recognizable constellations is the **Big Dipper (Saptarishi)** (Sapta-seven, rishi-sages). It is a group of seven stars that forms a part of **Ursa Major** Constellation.

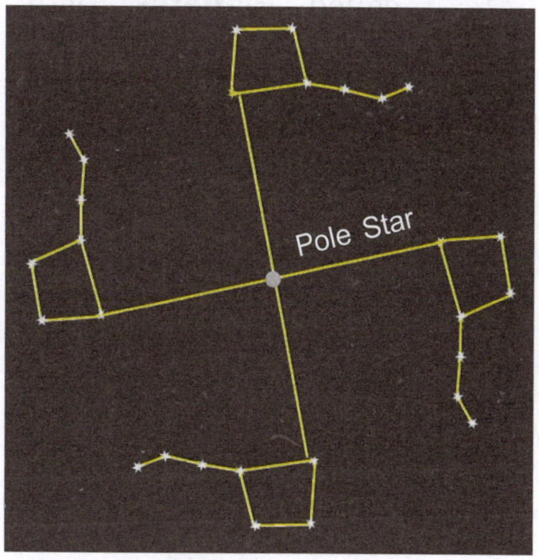

Fig. Ursa Major moves around the Pole star

- There are seven to eight bright stars, in which the middle three stars form the belt of the hunter. The four bright stars are arranged in quadrilateral shape.

- The constellation Canis Major contains a star called Sirius, which is the brightest star in the night sky.
- The constellation **Leo Major** has the shape of a lion.

4. **Solar System:** Our solar system consists of eight planets revolving around the Sun. It also consists of many other celestial bodies like asteroids, comets and meteors. The Sun is a star around which our Earth and all the planets along with their satellites revolve.

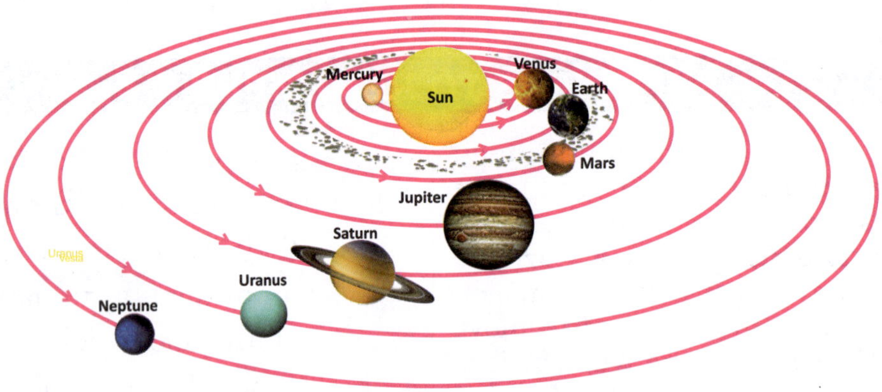

Fig. Solar System

5. **The Planets:** The celestial bodies that revolve around the Sun are called **Planets**. Eight planets revolve around the Sun in their fixed paths called orbits. These are **Mercury, Venus, Earth, Mars, Jupiter, Saturn, Uranus** and **Neptune** (as per ascending distance from the Sun).
6. **Inner Planets:** Four planets, **Mercury, Venus, Earth** and **Mars** are nearest to the Sun and are smaller in size. They have solid surfaces with rocks on them. They are called **Inner Planets**. They are also called **Terrestrial planets**.
7. **Four Outermost Planets:** **Jupiter, Saturn, Uranus** and **Neptune** are the outermost planets of the solar system. These are much larger in size than the Earth. These are mostly made of gases with ring-like structures made of dust and rocky material around them. They are also called **Jovian planets**.
8. **Dwarf Planets:** Smaller objects in the outer space including **Pluto**, are called **dwarf planets**.
9. **Satellite:** Objects that move around planets are called **satellites**. The planets thus can be called the satellites of the Sun.
10. **Moon:** The moon is a **natural satellite** of the Earth. It revolves around the Earth on its orbit. The moon moves around the earth in about 27 days.
11. **Milky Way Galaxy:** Our Solar System is part of the Milky Way Galaxy. It is also called **"Akaash Ganga"**. It has billions of stars like many other galaxies in the universe.

II. KEYWORDS

1. **Celestial bodies:** The Sun, the moon and all those objects shining in the night sky are called celestial bodies.
2. **Stars:** Stars are celestial objects that can produce their own light. They are extremely hot and very large.
3. **The Sun:** A huge star made up of fire and gases. It is present at the center of the solar system, and eight planets revolve around it.
4. **Pole Star:** It is one such star that appears to be stationary irrespective of the rotation of the Earth and is directly above the Earth's North pole in the sky.
5. **Moon:** It is a natural object which revolves around the Earth. The Moon is Earth's only natural satellite.
6. **Planet:** Celestial bodies that do not have their own heat and light and are lit by the light of the stars.
7. **Asteroid:** Irregular, spherical rocky bodies which also move around the Sun apart from the planets and satellites.
8. **Comet:** Objects with large tails made up of dust and ice that orbit the Sun.
9. **Constellation:** Groups of stars forming a particular pattern in the sky.
10. **Milky Way Galaxy:** Huge system of billions of stars, and clouds of dust and gases, which are seen as a beam of light across the sky of which our solar system is a part.
11. **Revolution:** The movement of an object around the Sun is called revolution.
12. **Satellite:** Objects that move around planets are commonly called satellites. They are smaller in size than planets.
13. **Solar System:** The Sun, eight planets, their moons (satellites) and some other celestial bodies known as asteroids and meteoroids form the solar system.
14. **International Astronomical Union (IAU):** It is an internationally recognized body with the mission to promote and safeguard the science of astronomy.

III. LET US ENHANCE OUR LEARNING *(Pages 249–251)*

Q. 1. ***Match the column:***

Column I		Column II	
(*i*)	Satellite of Earth	(*a*)	Orion
(*ii*)	Red planet	(*b*)	Venus
(*iii*)	Constellation	(*c*)	Mars
(*iv*)	Planet which is commonly called an evening star	(*d*)	Moon

Ans.

Column I		Column II	
(*i*)	Satellite of Earth	(*d*)	Moon
(*ii*)	Red planet	(*c*)	Mars
(*iii*)	Constellation	(*a*)	Orion
(*iv*)	Planet which is commonly called an evening star	(*b*)	Venus

Q. 2. ***(i) Solve the following riddle.***

My first alphabet is in MAN but not in CAN

My second alphabet is in ACE and also in FAN

My third alphabet is in RAT and not in CAT

My fourth alphabet is in SUN but not in FUN

I am a planet that moves around the Sun.

(ii) Make two similar riddles by yourself.

Ans. (*i*) **MARS**

(*ii*)

(*a*) My first alphabet is in VAN but not in PAN

My second alphabet is in EARTH and also in HEAVEN

My third alphabet is in ONE and not in TWO

My fourth alphabet is in SUN and also in FUN

My last alphabet is in STAR but not in RADAR

I am a planet that moves around the Sun.

Ans. VENUS

(*b*) My first alphabet is in EAT but not in BAT

My second alphabet is in FAT and also in SAT

My third alphabet is in RAT and not in MAT

My fourth alphabet is in TEN and also in NET

My fifth alphabet is in HAT but not in PAT.

I am a planet that moves round the Sun.

Ans. EARTH

Q. 3. ***Which of the following is not a member of our Solar System?***

(*i*) Sirius
(*ii*) Comets
(*iii*) Asteroids
(*iv*) Pluto

Ans. (*i*) Sirius

Q. 4. ***Which of the following is not a planet of the Sun?***

(*i*) Jupiter
(*ii*) Pluto
(*iii*) Neptune
(*iv*) Saturn

Ans. (*ii*) Pluto

Q. 5. ***Which is the brighter star, the Pole Star or Sirius?***

Ans. Sirius

Q. 6. ***An artist's representation of the Solar System is given in Figure. Is the order of the planets correct? If not, write the correct order in the boxes in the figure.***

Ans. The order of the planets in the figure is not correct. The correct order from the Sun is: Mercury, Venus, Earth, Mars, Jupiter, Saturn, Uranus and Neptune.

Q. 7. ***A portion of night sky with stars is shown in Figure. Look carefully and identify the groups of stars that form the patterns—the Big Dipper and the Little Dipper. Draw lines to connect the stars for these patterns and label them. Also, identify and label the Pole Star. You may refer to Fig. 12.4 for help.***

Ans.

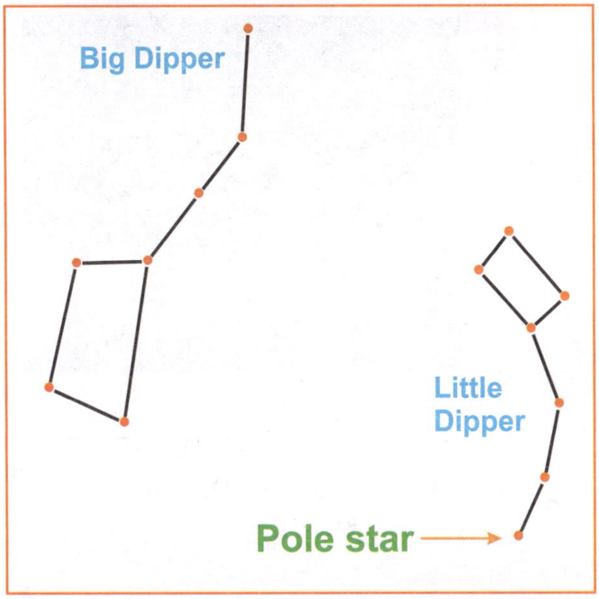

Q. 8. ***A portion of the night sky is shown in Figure. Draw lines to connect the stars for Orion and label the star Sirius. You may refer to Fig.***

Ans.

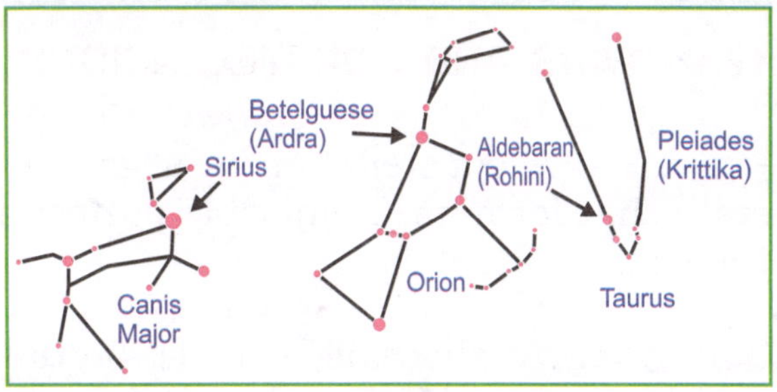

Q. 9. ***You can see stars fading away at dawn and appearing at dusk. During the day we do not see the stars. Explain why?***

Ans. During the day, the Sun's bright light outshines the stars, making them invisible to our eyes. The atmosphere scatters the sunlight, creating the blue sky and masking the faint light of the stars.

Q. 10. ***During a clear night, try to observe the Big Dipper 3–4 times at an interval of 2 to 3 hours. Also try to locate the Pole Star each time. Does the Big Dipper appear to move? Draw a rough sketch to illustrate this, mentioning the time in each case.***

Ans. The Big Dipper appears to move around the Pole Star due to the rotation of the Earth. Over a few hours, its position changes, making it seem as if it is rotating around the Pole Star.

Illustration: Do it yourself.

Q. 11. ***Think about the night sky and write a poem or a story on it.***

Ans. Do it yourself.

IV. EXAM ORIENTED QUESTIONS

12.1 STARS AND CONSTELLATIONS

Q. 1. *What is a constellation?*

Ans. A constellation is a group of stars that form a recognizable pattern in the sky.

Q. 2. *What is a shooting star?*

Ans. A shooting star is actually a meteor burning up in the Earth's atmosphere, causing a streak of light in the sky.

Q. 3. *Which is the closest star to the Earth?*

Ans. The Sun is the closest star to the Earth.

Q. 4. *Which star is nearest to us after the Sun?*

Ans. **Proxima Centauri** is the star nearest to us after the Sun.

Q. 5. *Which is the brightest star in the night sky?*

Ans. Sirius is the brightest star in the night sky.

Q. 6. *A star is ten light years away from the earth. Suppose it brightens up suddenly today. After how much time shall we see this change?* (*NCERT Exemplar*)

Ans. We will see the change seen after 10 years.

Q. 7. *Which device is used to observe faint stars which are not visible to the naked eye?*

Ans. Powerful telescopes are used to observe faint stars that are not visible to the naked eye.

Q. 8. *Which are the four main stars we know?*

Ans. Sun, Proxima Centauri, Alpha Centauri and Sirius.

Q. 9. *What is the distance between the Sun and the Earth?*

Ans. The distance of the Sun from the Earth is about 150 million km.

Q. 10. *What is Universe?*

Ans. The Universe is a large space consisting of celestial bodies like the stars, planets, galaxy, dust and gases.

Q. 11. *What causes stars to rise and set?*

Ans. This occurs due to Earth's rotation which is spinning around its own axis.

Q. 12. *Identify the following constellations:*

(*a*)

(*b*)

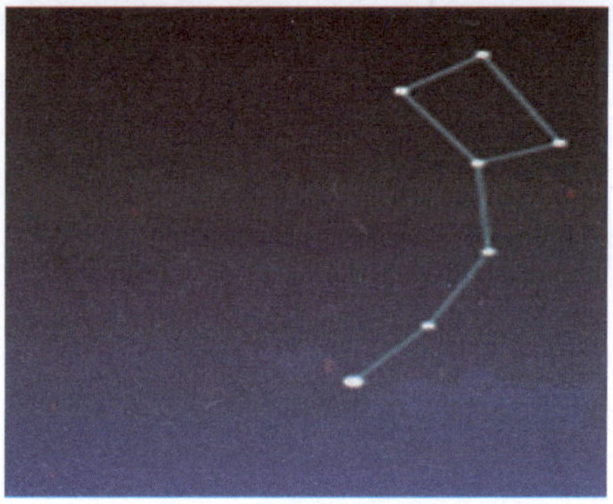

Ans.

(*a*) Ursa Major/Big Dipper

(*b*) Ursa Minor/Little Dipper

Q. 13. *What are the other names of Pole Star?*

Ans. Polaris/Dhruv Tara/ North Star/ Guiding Star are the other names of Pole Star.

Q. 14. *How do astronomers use constellations?*

Ans. Astronomers use constellations to identify and locate stars and other celestial objects in the night sky, aiding navigation and observation.

Q. 15. *Do stars emit light only during night?* (*NCERT Exemplar*)

Ans. No, they emit light all the time.

12.3 OUR SOLAR SYSTEM

Q. 1. *What is meant by the 'Solar System'?*

Ans. The sun, eight planets, satellites and some other celestial bodies known as asteroids and meteoroids form the solar system.

Q. 2. *How does a planet differ from a star?*

Ans.

S.No.	Planet	Star
1.	The celestial bodies which revolve around the Sun in certain orbit are called planets.	Stars are the celestial bodies which can emit heat and light continuously.
2.	Planets do not twinkle in the sky.	Stars twinkle in the sky.
3.	They do not have their own light.	They have their own light.
4.	They revolve around the sun.	They are fixed at a point.
5.	Planets are small as compared to stars.	They are very big in size.

Q. 3. *Why is the Earth called a unique planet?*

Ans. The earth is a unique solar system planet because:

(*a*) Conditions favourable to supporting life are only found on the Earth.

(*b*) The Earth is neither too hot nor too cold.

(*c*) There are water and air in it, which are very important for our survival.

Q. 4. *Why is the Earth called a blue planet?*

Ans. From the outer space, the earth appears blue because its three-fourths surface is covered by water. It is, therefore, called a *blue planet.*

Q. 5. *Why is the Sun important to our life?*

Ans. Sunlight is essential for plants to grow, which synthesise food and release oxygen for animals, including humans. The Sun is responsible for climate, seasons, weather, water cycle, winds—all of which are important for sustaining life on the Earth.

Q. 6. *What is revolution?*

Ans. The motion of the earth around the sun in its orbit is known as revolution.

Q. 7. *Which galaxy is our solar system part of?*

Ans. Our solar system is in the Milky Way Galaxy.

Q. 8. *Which planet is the hottest in our solar system?*

Ans. Venus is the hottest planet in our solar system.

Q. 9. *How many planets in the solar system are made of gases? Name them.*

Ans. Four planets are made of gases and they are also referred to as gas giants. They are Jupiter, Saturn, Uranus, and Neptune.

Q. 10. *Where do planets in the solar system orbit around?*

Ans. The planets orbit around the Sun.

Q. 11. *Why is Moon not considered a planet?*

Ans. The Moon isn't a planet because it orbits the Earth. It is a satellite.

Q. 12. *Which planet is known as the "Red Planet" and why?*

Ans. Mars is called the Red Planet because it appears red. This is because the surface of the Mars is reddish in colour.

Q. 13. ***Which planet is called "morning or evening star" and why?***

Ans. Venus is usually seen shining brightly at dawn and dusk, and is commonly called the **Morning Star** or the **Evening Star**, even though it is not a star.

Q. 14. ***What is a Dwarf Planet?***

Ans. A small sized celestial body that revolves independently around the sun is called the dwarf planet.

Q. 15. ***When is 'National Space Day' celebrated in India?***

Ans. 'National Space Day' is celebrated on August 23rd every year.

Q. 16. ***Why is Jupiter called the Stormy Planet?***

Ans. Jupiter revolves around itself with a great speed; hence Jupiter is called the Stormy planet.

Q. 17. ***What are artificial satellites used for?***

Ans. Artificial satellites are used for weather forecasting, long distance communication and remote sensing.

Q. 18. ***What is the other name of inner planets? Name them.***

Ans. Inner planets are also called **Terrestrial planets**. They are – Mercury, Venus, Earth and Mars.

Q. 19. ***What is the other name of outer planets? Name them.***

Ans. Outer planets are also called Jovian planets. They are- Jupiter, Saturn, Uranus and Neptune.

Q. 20. ***Why is Venus called the Twin Planet?***

Ans. Venus is considered as 'Earth's-twin' because its size and shape are very much similar to that of the earth.

Q. 21. ***Suppose the distance between the Earth and the Sun becomes half of its present distance. What is likely to happen to life?***

(NCERT Exemplar)

Ans. Life would cease. Radiation hitting the earth, including sunlight would increase by a factor of 4. Perhaps there would be a small area near the poles where some life could exist, but everywhere else there would be no life due to the four times radiation.

12.4 THE MILKY WAY GALAXY

Q. 1. ***What is a galaxy?***

Ans. A galaxy is a huge system of billions of stars, and clouds of dust and gases.

Q. 2. ***What is the shape of the Milky Way Galaxy?***

Ans. Our Milky Way Galaxy is a spiral galaxy having a whitish broad band. It looks like a spinning pinwheel when viewed from top or bottom.

Q. 3. ***What is the other name of Milky Way Galaxy?***

Ans. Milky Way galaxy is often known as "**Akaash Ganga**".

Q. 4. ***Why is our galaxy called Milky Way?***

Ans. Our galaxy is called the Milky Way because it appears as a **milky band of light in the sky** when we see it in a really dark area.

12.5 THE UNIVERSE

Q. 1. ***Define Universe.***

Ans. The Universe is a large space consisting of celestial bodies like the stars, planets, galaxy, dust and gases.

Q. 2. ***Which one of the following is arranged in order from biggest to smallest?***

(*a*) Galaxy, Universe, Solar System, Star, Planet
(*b*) Universe, Solar System, Galaxy, Planet, Star
(*c*) Solar System, Universe, Galaxy, Star, Planet
(*d*) Universe, Galaxy, Solar System, Star, Planet

Ans. (*d*)

Q. 3. ***What is the scientific study of universe called?***

Ans. The scientific study of universe is called Astronomy.

Q.4. ***What is the name of the successful mission by India which demonstrated end-to-end capability in safe landing and roving on the lunar surface?***

Ans. Chandrayaan-3 demonstrated end-to-end capability in safe landing and roving on the lunar surface.

Q. 5. ***What is the name of Chandrayaan-3 mission's lander and the rover?***

Ans. Chandrayaan-3 mission's lander is named **Vikram** and the rover **Pragyan**.

V. OBJECTIVE TYPE QUESTIONS

1. *Match the following items given in Column A with that in Column B:*

Column A		Column B	
(a)	*Biggest Planet*	(i)	*Venus*
(b)	*Coldest Planet*	(ii)	*Orion*
(c)	*Smallest Planet*	(iii)	*Uranus*
(d)	*Hottest Planet*	(iv)	*Mercury*
(e)	*Constellation*	(v)	*Halley*
(f)	*Comet*	(vi)	*Jupiter*

2. *Fill in the blanks with appropriate words:*

(a) *There are .... planets in our solar system.*

(b) *The .... is a star and it is in the center of the solar system.*

(c) *The inner planets have a .... surface.*

(d) *A large group of stars and other celestial bodies is called a ....*

(e) *Satellites are the celestial bodies that move around ....*

(f) *................ is called the windy planet because of the continuous strong winds that blow on it.*

(g) *The colour of stars changes according to their .... temperature.*

(h) *A/An .... is made of ice, dust and rocky material.*

(i) *A/An ....is made of metals and rocky material.*

(j) *A group of......... forming various patterns is called a ....*

(k) *A huge system of stars is called ....*

(l) *................ is the third nearest planet to the sun.*

(m) *Planets do not have their own .... and ....*

3. *State whether the statements given below are True or False:*

(i) *Pole star is a member of the solar system.*

(ii) *Uranus is the farthest planet in the solar system.*

(iii) *The Earth is our home planet.*

(iv) *The Sun is a satellite.*

(v) *The Moon has its own light; it does not reflect light from the Sun.*

(vi) *The Sun is a planet in our solar system.*

(vii) *The Earth is the only planet in our solar system that has liquid water on its surface..*

(viii) *The atmosphere on Mars is similar to that on Earth.*

(ix) *The Milky Way is the name of our solar system.*

4. *Give one word answer:*
   (*a*) Blue planet of the solar system.
   (*b*) Two planets between which Saturn lies.
   (*c*) Evening Star.
   (*d*) The galaxy which is our neighbour.
   (*e*) Planet with the largest number of satellites.
   (*f*) A celestial body that carries a tail along.
   (*g*) Stormy planet
   (*h*) Winds blow with extremely high speed on _________ .
   (*i*) A dwarf planet.
   (*j*) Nearest planet to Sun.
   (*k*) Second farthest planet from Sun.
   (*l*) Largest planet in our Solar System.
   (*m*) Planet having rings.
   (*n*) Farthest planet from Sun.
5. *Riddle Time: Solve the following riddles-*
   (*a*) Eight of us travel around the sun, you live on one. What am I?
   (*b*) I'm the planet that everyone calls "Red," But really my soil is rust-colored instead. Look up and you may spot me in the sky, I'm the orange-colored dot, way up high. Which planet am I?

Multiple Choice Questions (MCQs)

Choose the correct option in the following questions

1. ______________ *is the scientific study of the universe.*
   (*a*) Astronomy (*b*) Astrology
   (*c*) Science (*d*) Cosmology
2. *Which planet is called the stormy planet?*
   (*a*) Mercury (*b*) Jupiter
   (*c*) Mars (*d*) Venus
3. *The Sun is*
   (*a*) a star
   (*b*) a celestial body
   (*c*) the head of the solar system
   (*d*) all of these
4. *The term 'blue planet' indicate presence of*
   (*a*) land (*b*) water
   (*c*) oxygen (*d*) all of these
5. *The moon moves around the earth in about ______ days.*
   (*a*) 21 (*b*) 23
   (*c*) 27 (*d*) None
6. *Which of the following does* ***not*** *belong to the family of solar system?*
   (*a*) Planet (*b*) Galaxy
   (*c*) Meteors (*d*) Comet
7. *The Halley's Comet is seen after every*
   (*a*) 76 months (*b*) 76 years
   (*c*) 56 months (*d*) 56 years
8. *Ursa Major is a*
   (*a*) star
   (*b*) constellation
   (*c*) seen only with telescope
   (*d*) satellite
9. *Which planet has the largest number of satellites?*
   (*a*) Jupiter (*b*) Saturn
   (*c*) Mercury (*d*) Mars
10. *Which unit is used to measure astronomical distances?*
    (*a*) Leap year (*b*) Light year
    (*c*) Century (*d*) Sound year
11. *The stars forming a recognizable shape is called*
    (*a*) constellation (*b*) system
    (*c*) galaxy (*d*) asteroids
12. *Which star is nearest to Earth?*
    (*a*) Pole star (*b*) Cassiopeia
    (*c*) Orion (*d*) Sun
13. *What term is used for celestial bodies that revolve around the Sun in highly elliptical orbit?*
    (*a*) Comet (*b*) Meteors
    (*c*) Asteroids (*d*) Planets

14. *Which small objects revolve between the orbits of Mars and Jupiter?*

(*a*) Satellites (*b*) Comets
(*c*) Asteroids (*d*) Meteorites

15. *Which planet is called morning star or evening star?*

(*a*) Venus (*b*) Mars
(*c*) Jupiter (*d*) Mercury

16. *Orion is a*

(*a*) constellation (*b*) star
(*c*) planet (*d*) satellite

17. *Shooting stars are called*

(*a*) asteroids (*b*) galaxies
(*c*) meteors (*d*) andromeda

18. *The planet farthest from the Sun is*

(*a*) Uranus (*b*) Neptune
(*c*) Saturn (*d*) Mercury

ANSWERS

1. *Match item in Column A and Column B:*

Column A		Column B	
(a)	*Biggest Planet*	(*vi*)	*Jupiter*
(b)	*Coldest Planet*	(*iii*)	*Uranus*
(c)	*Smallest Planet*	(*iv*)	*Mercury*
(d)	*Hottest Planet*	(*i*)	*Venus*
(e)	*Constellation*	(*ii*)	*Orion*
(*f*)	*Comet*	(*v*)	*Halley*

2. Fill in the blanks:

(*a*) Eight (*b*) Sun (*c*) Rocky
(*d*) Galaxy (*e*) Planets (*f*) Neptune
(*g*) Surface (*h*) Comet (*i*) Asteroid
(*j*) Stars, constellation (*k*) Galaxy (*l*) Earth
(*m*) Heat, light

3. True or False:

(*i*) False (*ii*) False (*iii*) True (*iv*) False (*v*) False
(*vi*) False (*vii*) True (*viii*) False (*ix*) False

4. One word answer:

(*a*) Earth (*b*) Jupiter and Uranus (*c*) Venus
(*d*) Andromeda (*e*) Saturn (*f*) Comet
(*g*) Jupiter (*h*) Neptune (*i*) Pluto
(*j*) Mercury (*k*) Uranus (*l*) Jupiter
(*m*) Saturn (*n*) Neptune

5. Riddle Time:

(*a*) Planet (*b*) Mars

Multiple Choice Questions (MCQs)

1. (*a*) **2.** (*b*) **3.** (*d*) **4.** (*b*) **5.** (*c*) **6.** (*b*) **7.** (*b*) **8.** (*b*) **9.** (*b*) **10.** (*b*)
11. (*a*) **12.** (*d*) **13.** (*d*) **14.** (*c*) **15.** (*a*) **16.** (*a*) **17.** (*c*) **18.** (*b*)

VI. EXERCISE FOR PRACTICE

1. How much time does the earth take to complete one rotation and one revolution?
2. Which country became the first in the world to achieve a landing near the little explored Moon's South Pole?
3. How does an asteroid differ from a comet?
4. Name the two celestial bodies visible only in the night sky.
5. Draw sketches to show the relative positions of prominent stars in
   (a) Ursa Major (b) Orion
6. Look at the picture and identify whether it is a comet or asteroid.

(a)

(b)

7. To which galaxy does our solar system belong?
8. What is the mission of upcoming Chandrayaan-4?
9. Who are astronomers? Name a famous astronomer of ancient India.
10. Why we do not see Moon during the day?
11. Name any two constellations.
12. Explain about the closest and third closest planet to the Sun.
13. Why the earth has nights and days?
14. What is the reason of change in seasons?
15. What do you mean by star?
16. Name the star which remains fixed at the same place in the sky in the North.
17. What is the number of prominent stars in the Ursa Major?
18. What is solar system?
19. What are asteroids? Where are they located?
20. Name any two artificial satellites launched by our country.

NOTES

Golden® Sample Paper–I Class VI

Time: 2½ Hrs | **M.M.:** 80

General Instructions:

(i) This question paper contains 40 questions divided into four Sections A, B, C and D.
(ii) All questions are compulsory.
(iii) Section A comprises of 10 Multiple Choice Questions, 5 Fill in the Blanks Questions and 5 True / False Questions. Each question carries 1 mark.
(iv) Section B comprises of 8 questions of 2 marks each.
(v) Section C comprises of 8 questions of 3 marks each
(vi) Section D comprises of 4 questions of 5 marks each.

SECTION – A

(1 *Mark each*)

A. Tick (✓) the correct answer: **(1 × 10 = 10)**

1. The distance between Bengaluru and Mysuru is expressed in units of
   (*a*) decametre (*b*) metre (*c*) centimetre (*d*) kilometre
2. The place where living beings live is called their
   (*a*) Adaptation (*b*) Habitat (*c*) Habit (*d*) Movement
3. Which pair of these substances is likely to be attracted to a magnet?
   (*a*) Nail and Pencil (*b*) Eraser and Pencil
   (*c*) Nail and Safety pin (*d*) Plastic Ruler and Pencil
4. The pie chart shows the composition of air.

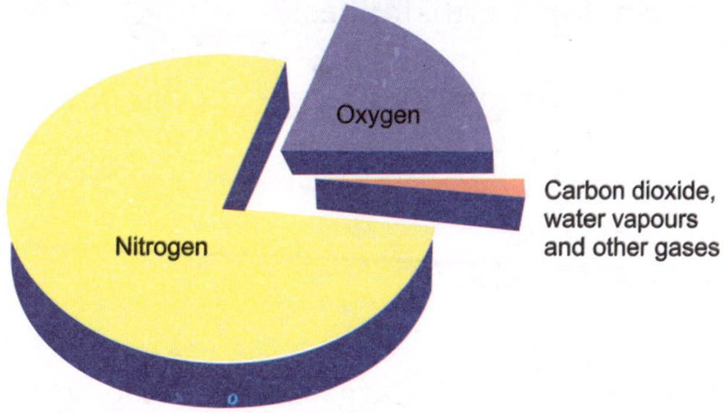

   Which is the most abundant component of air?
   (*a*) Oxygen (*b*) Nitrogen
   (*c*) Water vapours (*d*) Carbon dioxide

5. Plant cells synthesise their own food in the presence of sunlight. Which gas is used by the plants to synthesise their own food?
   (*a*) Oxygen (*b*) Nitrogen
   (*c*) Hydrogen (*d*) Carbon dioxide
6. A woman is suffering from goiter. Her diet is deficient in
   (*a*) Vitamin B_1 (*b*) Iron (*c*) Iodine (*d*) Calcium
7. Orion is a
   (*a*) constellation (*b*) star (*c*) planet (*d*) satellite
8. How are scientific experiments often conducted?
   (*a*) Alone (*b*) In large teams
   (*c*) By memorizing facts (*d*) Without asking questions
9. Which of the following materials is not soluble in water?
   (*a*) Sugar (*b*) Chalk powder (*c*) Salt (*d*) Vinegar
10. Which amongst the following methods would be most appropriate to separate grains from bundles of stalks?
    (*a*) Handpicking (*b*) Winnowing (*c*) Sieving (*d*) Threshing

B. Fill in the blanks: **(1 × 5 = 5)**

11. The device that measures temperature is called a ....
12. Falling of .... is called precipitation.
13. Mixture may be solid, liquid or ....
14. When fossil fuels are burnt .... and .... are produced.
15. There are .... planets in our solar system.

C. True / False: **(1 × 5 = 5)**

16. Herbs are usually short and sometimes do not have branches.
17. Food items like burgers and pizzas are a part of healthy diet.
18. There is a maximum attraction in middle of a bar magnet.
19. Clouds are the mixture of opaque gases.
20. Digital thermometers are safer than mercury thermometers because they do not contain toxic substances.

SECTION – B

(2 *Marks each*)

D. Short Answer Type Questions: **(2 × 8 = 16)**

21. What are insectivorous plants?
22. Define motion.
23. What is evaporation? State one large-scale use of the process of evaporation.
24. What is the difference between a shrub and a tree?
25. What makes the study of Science enjoyable?
26. Why do animals move from one place to other?

27. What is junk food?

28. What do you mean by magnetic field?

SECTION – C

(3 *Marks each*)

E. Short Answer Type Questions: (3 × 8 = 24)

29. What is a balanced diet? Write the components of balanced diet.

30. What is meant by transparent material, translucent materials and opaque materials?

31. What is photosynthesis? Why is it essential for plants?

32. Describe the differences between clinical and laboratory thermometers in terms of their use and range.

33. The seat of a two-wheeler parked on a sunny day has become very hot. How can you cool it down?

34. Name and describe briefly a method which can be helpful in separating a mixture of husk from grains. What is the principle of this method?

35. Explain the following observations very briefly.
   (*a*) A firki does not rotate in a closed area.
   (*b*) An empty glass in fact is not empty.
   (*c*) Breathing through mouth may harm you.

36. Identify the following constellations:

(*a*) 

(*b*) 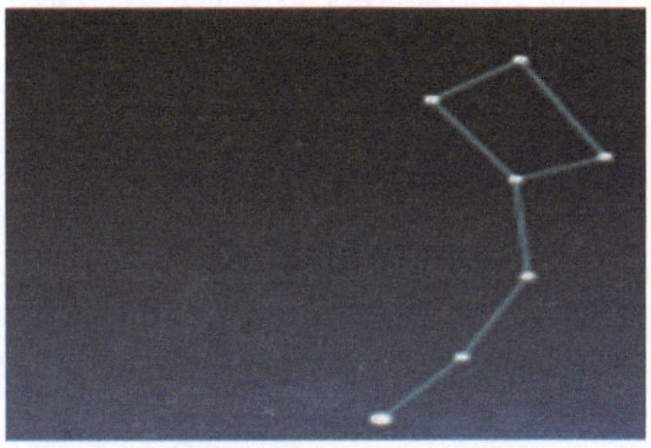

SECTION – D

(5 *Marks each*)

F. Long Answer Type Questions: (5 × 4 = 20)

37. What are transparent, translucent and opaque objects? Explain them giving suitable examples.

38. Distinguish between magnetic and non-magnetic materials. Give two examples for each of them.

39. Describe the process and precautions necessary for using a laboratory thermometer.

40. Why is there need for conserving water? Give two reasons.

Golden® Sample Paper–II
Class VI

Time: 2½ Hrs **M.M.:** 80

General Instructions:

(i) This question paper contains 40 questions divided into four Sections A, B, C and D.
(ii) All questions are compulsory.
(iii) Section A comprises of 10 Multiple Choice Questions, 5 Fill in the Blanks Questions and 5 True / False Questions. Each question carries 1 mark.
(iv) Section B comprises of 8 questions of 2 marks each.
(v) Section C comprises of 8 questions of 3 marks each
(vi) Section D comprises of 4 questions of 5 marks each.

SECTION – A

(1 *Mark each*)

A. Tick (✓) the correct answer: **(1 × 10 = 10)**

1. Nearly all the trains in winters run late because of a natural phenomenon known as

(a) smoke (b) fog (c) rain (d) cold

2. Like poles

(a) Repel (b) Merge (c) Dissolve (d) Attract

3. Four pieces of wooden sticks A, B, C and D are placed along the length of 30 cm long scale as shown in Fig. Which one of them is 3.4 cm in length?

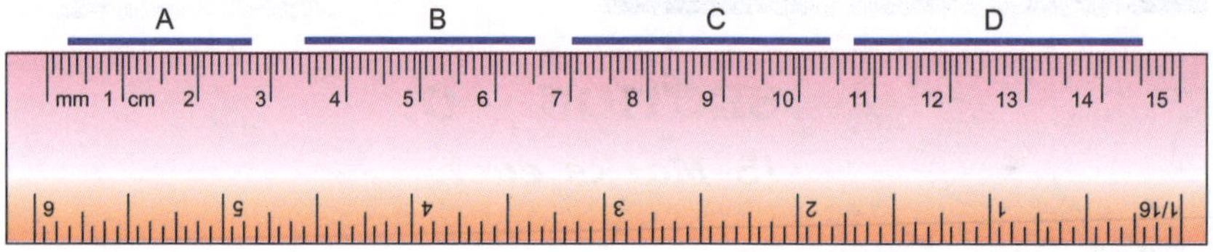

Fig.

(a) A (b) B (c) C (d) D

4. Which of the following gas we use in respiration?

(a) Carbon dioxide (b) Nitrogen
(c) Oxygen (d) None of these

5. Wind does not help in the movement of

(a) Firki (b) Weather cock
(c) Ceiling fan (d) Sailing yacht

6. The object that does not give out light on its own is the
   (*a*) star (*b*) lighted matchstick
   (*c*) light bulb (*d*) shining mirror
7. Which of the following helps a ship to move it in the right direction?
   (*a*) A thermometer (*b*) A speedometer
   (*c*) An anchor (*d*) A compass
8. The humans depend on plants for which one of the following?
   (*a*) food (*b*) fuel
   (*c*) oxygen (*d*) All of these
9. Sand from water is separated by
   (*a*) Sieving (*b*) Evaporation
   (*c*) Filtration (*d*) Sedimentation and decantation
10. Which of the following has fibrous root?
   (*a*) Wheat (*b*) Peas
   (*c*) Radish (*d*) Neem

B. Fill in the blanks: (1 × 5 = 5)

11. Our body contains .... water.
12. Sand is .... in water.
13. The attraction of a magnet is strongest at its ....
14. A falling stone exhibits .... motion.
15. The place where a plant or animal lives is called its ....

C. True / False: (1 × 5 = 5)

16. Roots hold the plant firmly in the soil.
17. Rocks are pure substances.
18. Length of a curved line cannot be measured with a metre scale directly.
19. A cylindrical magnet has only one pole.
20. Smoke is produced by the burning of fuels.

SECTION – B

(2 *Marks each*)

D. Short Answer Type Questions: (2 × 8 = 16)

21. What is Science?
22. What does your Sports teacher use to measure the length of the playground?
23. Suggest possible reasons explaining the appearance of water droplets of the outer surface of the glass tumbler containing lemonade.
24. The distance between Manu's home and his school is 3000 m. Express this distance in km.
25. Differentiate between: Temporary magnet and permanent magnet.
26. What is wind?
27. What is stem of a plant?
28. Write the importance of water for us.

SECTION – C

(3 *Marks each*)

E. Short Answer Type Questions: **(3 × 8 = 24)**

29. Few iron nails and screws got mixed with the wooden shavings while a carpenter was working with them. How can you help him in getting the nails and screws back from the scrap without wasting his time in searching with his hands?
30. Explain the life cycle of a frog.
31. Draw a neat and labelled diagram of a bar magnet.
32. Explain the following:
    (*i*) Circular motion (*ii*) Linear motion
33. What is a compass? How is a compass used to find directions?
34. What is atmosphere? Why is atmosphere essential for life on earth?
35. Explain how forests prevent floods.
36. Convert the following:
    (*i*) 55°C to °F (*ii*) 113°F to °C

SECTION – D

(5 *Marks each*)

F. Long Answer Type Questions: **(5 × 4 = 20)**

37. What are energy giving foods? Give five examples of energy giving foods.
38. Briefly describe the various types of habitats.
39. Explain the difference between taproots and fibrous roots with the help of diagrams.
40. Write the name of any four processes involved in water cycle and explain the process of water cycle.

❑❑❑